Industrial Competitiveness in East-Central Europe

Industrial Competitiveness in East-Central Europe

Edited by

Martin Myant

Reader in Economics, University of Paisley, UK

Edward Elgar
Cheltenham, UK • Northampton, MA, USA

Published by
Edward Elgar Publishing Limited
Glensanda House
Montpellier Parade
Cheltenham
Glos GL50 1UA
UK

Edward Elgar Publishing, Inc.
6 Market Street
Northampton
Massachusetts 01060
USA

A catalogue record for this book
is available from the British Library

Library of Congress Cataloguing in Publication Data

Industrial competitiveness in East-Central Europe / edited by Martin
    Myant.
        Includes index.
        1. Structural adjustment (Economic policy)—Europe, Eastern.
    2. Industrial policy—Europe, Eastern. 3. Industries—Europe,
    Eastern. 4. Competition, International. I. Myant, M.R. (Martin
    R.)
    HC244.I478   1999
    338.947—dc21   98–51382
                                                                   CIP

ISBN 1 84064 019 7

Printed and bound in Great Britain by
Biddles Ltd, Guildford and King's Lynn

Contents

Tables

Contributors

Martin Myant, Reader in Department of Accounting, Economics and Languages, University of Paisley, Scotland, UK.

Karel Zeman, Department of the Chief Economist, *Československá obchodní banka* (Czechoslovak Trade Bank), Prague, Czech Republic.

Věra Rodová, Department of the Chief Economist, *Československá obchodní banka* (Czechoslovak Trade Bank), Prague, Czech Republic

Zdeněk Souček, Director of Management Focus, International Consulting Group, Prague, Czech Republic.

Růžena Vintrová, Head of Economic-Analytical Laboratory, Czech Statistical Office, Prague, Czech Republic.

Petr Chvojka, Chief Economist, *Československá obchodní banka* (Czechoslovak Trade Bank), Prague, Czech Republic.

Karel Ujházy, Economist, Prague, Czech Republic.

Richard Outrata, Head of Department of International and Interregional Economics, Foreign Trade and Industrial Policy, Institute of Slovak and World Economics, Slovak Academy of Sciences, Bratislava, Slovak Republic.

Frank Fleischer, Research Fellow, German Institute for Economic Research, Berlin, Germany.

Kurt Hornschild, Head of Department of Industry and Technology, German Institute for Economic Research, Berlin, Germany.

Abbreviations

BMWi   Bundesministerium für Wirtschaft (German Ministry for the Economy).

CEEC   Central east European countries (Czech Republic, Slovakia, Hungary and Poland).

CEEC-5   Central east European five (as above plus Slovenia).

CMEA   Council for Mutual Economic Assistance.

DIW   Deutsches Institut für Wirtschaftsforschung (German Institute for Economic Research).

EBRD   European Bank for Reconstruction and Development.

EIU   Economist Intelligence Unit.

ERDI   Exchange Rate Deviation Index.

EU   European Union.

FAB   Forschungsagentur Berlin (Research Agency Berlin).

GDP   Gross Domestic Product

ILO   International Labour Organisation

IMF   International Monetary Fund

IMD   Institute for Management Development

NATO   North Atlantic Treaty Organisation

NIF   National Investment Fund

OECD   Organisation for Economic Cooperation and Development

PPP   Purchasing Power Parity

R&D   Research and Development

SITC   Standard International Trade Classification.

SME   Small and medium-sized enterprise.

ULC   Unit labour cost.

WEF   World Economic Forum.

WIIW   Wiener Institut für Internationale Wirtschaftsvergleiche (Vienna Institute for Comparative Economic Studies)

Preface

The contributions in this volume focus on the question of whether the economic transformations that have taken place in east-central Europe since 1989 are leading to the emergence of economies that can stand up to the competitive environment they will face within the European Union. Viewing competitiveness as the central issue means that the 'completion' of the transformation is not understood simply in terms of privatisation, liberalisation and macroeconomic stability. The key question is not whether the bare bones of a market system have been created, but whether foundations have been laid for sustainable growth and rising living standards.

This approach is in harmony with thinking in the EU and in the OECD where 'competitiveness policy' has gained considerable emphasis. Somewhat surprisingly, however, that concern seems to have been considered appropriate primarily in discussions of policy options for established market economies. It has played little role in advice to the countries of east-central Europe. Whenever difficulties or doubts arise in a country emerging from central planning, the emphasis switches back towards a standard and simple recipe based on completing privatisation as quickly as possible, avoiding state subsidies and pressing ahead with deregulatory measures. These may be essential ingredients for the development of a competitive economy, but they are not adequate alone and, if applied mechanically, can even have counter-productive consequences.

This point emerges in various different ways in the contributions to this volume. In Chapter 1 Martin Myant outlines the kinds of structural transformations that have been taking place and compares them with changes both in advanced market economies and in newly industrialising countries. This provides a basis for assessing the growth prospects of east-central Europe. There are differences between the individual countries, but the account points to serious gaps in the kinds of economic systems that have been created. There are no grounds on this basis for confidence that sustained and rapid growth will be possible across all the countries.

A more general assessment of the preconditions for a high level of competitiveness is provided in Chapter 2 in which Karel Zeman, Věra Rodová and Zdeněk Souček use and assess 'league tables' of country competitiveness. These point to some differences across east-central Europe, but also to some very consistent areas of weakness in the institutional frameworks required for an advanced market economy, in inputs that commonly come from governments and in the abilities of managements. A remarkable point to emerge is that some of the greatest strengths are to be found in features firmly established before 1989.

Růžena Vintrová covers macroeconomic themes in Chapter 3 and these support the conclusions of other chapters. Macroeconomic policies and conditions have varied between individual countries, but they have not created the ideal conditions for transformations into modern and competitive economies. Moreover, there could be dangers ahead from an attempt to apply the same criteria that are considered appropriate to more advanced market economies. Macroeconomic targets need to be based on a recognition of the countries' specificities and need to be in harmony with other aspects of policy, such as the need for higher levels of productive investment.

In Chapter 4 Petr Chvojka deals with the relationship between privatisation and restructuring and demonstrates that privatisation alone is not an adequate objective. The central aim of enterprise restructuring requires financial resources and the extent to which this is possible depends crucially on the form taken by privatisation. In some cases that form can create obstacles to restructuring while in others it can be the basis for future success.

In Chapter 5 Karel Ujházy and Karel Zeman provide an analysis of investment in east-central Europe. This helps explain the apparent paradox of high investment rates in two countries, the Czech Republic and Slovakia, that do not seem to be reflected in higher growth rates than in Poland and Hungary where investment rates are substantially lower. The differences are largely explained by differing levels of investment in infrastructure, electricity generation and environmental projects. These may prove an essential basis for growth in the future, but the immediate implication is that much of the structure of investment retains striking similarities to that of the pre-1989 period. There is therefore a sense in which investment appears as a passive factor in structural terms, reinforcing a sectoral distribution inherited from the past rather than leading the push towards more modern sectors.

Richard Outrata covers the transformation in Slovakia in Chapter 6. In a number of respects the country appears to have performed rather well, but it relies very much on economic strengths inherited from the past. Its governments have a strong verbal commitment to policies promoting industrial development, but much of this has remained at the level of generalisations and declarations. Rather surprisingly, Slovakia is behind the Czech Republic in the implementation of some specific measures in this area despite the boasts of former Czech governments that they were successfully shunning thoughts of industrial policy and of intervention in the free market.

In Chapter 7 Martin Myant analyses restructuring in Czech enterprises confirming and amplifying the constraints noted in other chapters.

Managements have suffered from lack of finance and from limited experience in a market environment. They have, however, been very active in seeking out strategies for survival, and in some cases even for substantial growth, that enable them to cope at least to some extent with these constraints.

In Chapter 8 Frank Fleischer and Kurt Hornschild outline the stage reached by the east German transformation. This clearly is not an example to follow and can even be seen as a warning against an over-hasty dash to join western Europe. Nevertheless, there are some very different lessons from eastern Germany as government bodies have gone some way to recognising the need for specific policies to ensure the survival of a research base in industry without which future growth may be impossible.

The research for these contributions was financed by the European Commission's Phare ACE 1995 Programme. The contributors met at two workshops. The first, held in Vienna in May 1997, led to the publication of preliminary results and conclusions in English in *Ekonomický časopis*, the journal of the Institute of World and Slovak Economics of the Slovak Academy of Sciences. The second workshop, held in Prague in November 1997, led to a substantial development of the contributions. Following substantial discussion and revisions, they are now published in this volume. Apart from the contributors commenting on each other's contributions, further helpful criticisms and suggestions were made by Mike Danson of the University of Paisley.

1. The Tigers of Tomorrow? Structural Change and Economic Growth in East-Central Europe

Martin Myant

This chapter is intended to present a general overview and assessment of the post-1989 transformation of the four east-central European economies in terms of structural change. This provides an essential background for the chapters that discuss themes relating to macroeconomic policies and privatisation, as a serious judgement on the appropriateness of those policies must depend on an analysis of how far they have led to the emergence of technologically-advanced and modern economies. The structural transformations are therefore compared with those that have taken place in market economies including particularly the so-called Asian 'tigers' which have achieved outstanding growth rates over recent decades. Serious economic difficulties in the later 1990s are a further warning against taking any particular country or group of countries as a model to be followed precisely. Nevertheless, they cannot detract from the extent of economic transformations that took place in the period when the countries of east-central Europe were stagnating under central planning and then struggling with problems of creating modern market economies.

Differences are very clear, raising doubts about the growth potential of the east-central European countries, referred to throughout as CEECs, and pointing towards a possible critique of the strategies that have been adopted in east-central Europe. A discussion of the implications of modern economic growth theory and comparisons with the growth paths of rapidly advancing market economies suggests some consistent weaknesses, although there are differences of degree between the individual countries. The achievement of rapid economic growth would seem to require far greater attention to the development of the institutional framework associated with a modern market economy – a theme that is taken up again in the concluding chapter – and that in turn depends on a more active role for government.

1

A FALTERING RECOVERY

The figures in Table 1.1 show the transformation process in four east-central European countries in terms of changes in GDP levels. The very deep 'transformation recession' of the early years of the decade was caused to a certain extent by the effects of liberalisation and the shifting structure of domestic demand, to a certain extent by restrictive macroeconomic and monetary policies and to a certain extent by the collapse of trading relations between the members of the former CMEA trading bloc. The relative importance of these factors is difficult to estimate, but the decline in output in Poland in 1990, before the other countries, reflected its earlier moves towards price and trade liberalisation and the adoption of sharply restrictive policies: the continuing decline in 1991 was to a much greater extent due to a drop in exports to the former Soviet Union. The effects were combined in the former Czechoslovakia in 1991, probably in roughly equal measure. In Hungary restrictive policies were applied more gradually: the fall in domestic demand was already under way in 1990 and intensified in 1991 when it combined with the loss of export markets. The reduction in trade with the former CMEA countries, for reasons explained later, had less of an impact in this case than in the former Czechoslovakia (Myant, 1993, Kornai, 1995, Chapter 7, EIU, 1997, p.14).

Table 1.1 Annual percentage growth rates in GDP in east-central Europe, 1990–1997

	1990	1991	1992	1993	1994	1995	1996	1997
Poland	−10.2	−7.0	2.6	3.8	5.0	7.0	6.1	6.9
Hungary	−3.5	−11.9	−3.0	−0.8	2.9	1.1	1.3	3.0
Czech Republic	−1.2	−11.5	−3.3	0.6	2.7	5.9	4.1	1.0
Slovakia	−2.4	−14.5	−7.0	−4.1	4.9	6.8	6.6	6.5

Source: Statistical office publications of respective countries.

The assumption among policy makers was that the successful creation of the basics of a market economy would lead to rapid recovery from a brief recession. A period of sustained growth was expected to follow. The figures show how far this has been achieved. Hungary has faltered and generally appears to have been growing more slowly than the others. The Czech Republic saw decline giving way only to a minimal recovery in 1993. The economy was held back by the negative effects of the break-up of the Czechoslovak federation at the beginning of that year. Growth then appeared to be accelerating, but then slowed down markedly.

Slovakia suffered from the break with the Czech Republic, with a sharp drop continuing into 1993, but has subsequently done somewhat better. The nearest to an unequivocal success appears to be Poland.

These are certainly not startling growth rates when compared with the annual figures approaching 9 per cent sustained over long periods by the fastest growing newly industrialised countries. South Korea had reached a per capita GDP level at current exchange rates more than 50 per cent above that of Czechoslovakia and 135 per cent above that of Poland in 1989. By 1997 South Korea's per capita GDP was twice that of the Czech Republic, again comparing by current exchange rates.

Current per capita GDP levels in CEECs are also low by western European standards. When measured by purchasing power parity, as discussed in detail in Chapter 3, they ranged in 1996 from 59.3 to 31.5 per cent of the EU average for the highest, the Czech Republic, and the lowest, Poland. When measured by current exchange rates the relative levels fall to 30 per cent for the Czech Republic and to 21 per cent for Poland. Assuming that the exchange rate will tend to converge towards the purchasing power parity level, so that the latter is the most relevant figure for the long term, a 5 per cent growth rate in CEECs alongside 2.5 per cent growth rate in the EU would enable the former to catch up in between a further 30 and 50 years. A recalculation of relative GDP levels, using a slightly different methodology covered in Chapter 3, can point to a slightly more optimistic picture. Nevertheless, the general conclusion remains unchanged. The figures in the table above give no grounds for assuming that CEECs can significantly close the gap with the average EU level in the foreseeable future. It would appear as likely, at least for some, that the gap might even widen. Grounds for this fear emerge not only from past GDP growth rates but from the evidence on the nature of structural change in the following section.

STRUCTURAL CHANGE

Structural change itself is a relatively vague and flexible concept and is followed here through the overlapping themes of changes in the broad sectoral structure of the economies, in the organisational structure of economic activities, in the branch structure of industry and in the commodity structure and orientation of exports. There can be no doubting a sharp break from the past, but there are also elements of continuity which explain many of the differences between the individual countries. Comparisons with some very different market economies help to show both how far the CEECs have been undergoing a similar transformation and where they stand in relation to other market economies.

This points to some conclusions that should be deeply worrying to policy makers. Despite some clear similarities, there are important aspects of the structural transformations in the CEECs that seem to be taking the economies backwards towards activities more usually associated with less advanced economies. The significance and extent of this is revealed from a step-by-step account of the different aspects of structural change.

Table 1.2 shows the changes in broad sectoral structure with similar falls in employment in industry and construction and increases in employment in services in the Czech Republic, Slovakia and Poland. The change has been substantially smaller in Hungary and is not very different in that case from the shift that took place over the same time period in the UK or South Korea.

Table 1.2 Broad sectoral structure of east-central European and selected market economies by percentages in total employment

		Agriculture	Industry and construction	Services
Poland	1989	27.3	36.3	36.5
	1996	22.1	31.7	46.2
Czech Republic	1989	11.9	47.1	41.0
	1996	6.3	42.0	51.7
Slovakia	1989	13.8	44.5	41.7
	1996	9.1	39.9	51.0
Hungary	1989	11.4	35.6	53.0
	1996	8.4	33.0	58.6
South Korea	1989	17.9	35.4	46.7
	1996	11.6	32.5	55.9
United Kingdom	1989	2.2	32.7	65.1
	1996	2.0	27.4	70.6

Note: 1990 and not 1989 for South Korea.

Source: Calculated from OECD, 1997, and figures from the Statistical Office of the Slovak Republic.

These declining shares of agriculture and industry and construction, alongside a growing share for service sector activities in both employment and GDP, have been familiar features of advanced market economies in recent decades. Explanations include rapid advances in productivity in the first two sectors, pointing to a sharper fall in employment than output share, the organisational separation of service from productive activities, the growth in demand for personal services relative to goods as incomes rise and a destruction of manufacturing industry in the face of international competition. This last element was practically inevitable in advanced market economies for branches of industry that require only relatively unskilled labour, but 'deindustrialisation' could also affect more advanced branches. This has aroused fears, especially for a period in the UK, of a more general loss of competitiveness for manufacturing as a whole (cf Rowthorn and Wells, 1987 and OECD, 1990).

Experience in the CEECs exhibits some similarities to changes in advanced market economies, but also some very important differences. The broad sectoral shifts are again the result of a number of distinct processes. The growth in the service sector partly reflected its poor development under central planning, suggesting a delayed satisfaction of a 'latent' demand. Particularly in so far as it was associated with the growth in new small businesses in trade and personal services, this was a direct benefit of the relaxation of laws restricting private enterprise. Service sector growth also partly reflected organisational changes, with service activities separated from manufacturing, and the need for business services in a market economy. The decline in agricultural employment is most marked in the Czech Republic, where the sector was hit hard by falling domestic demand in 1991, but neither the extent of the decline nor the final figure reached appear remarkable when set against experience in growing market economies. The decline in employment in industry and construction was, unlike cases in growing market economies, typically not the result of improving productivity. The analogy is much closer with the 'deindustrialisation' stemming from a failure of exports alongside import penetration leading to a drop in demand for much of the product range, as discussed below.

The changes in organisational forms followed primarily from the sub-division of larger state-owned enterprises, usually associated with privatisation, and the emergence of new, small private companies. The rise in self-employment varies widely across the group of countries partly because of its importance in agriculture and partly because of its importance in other activities before 1989. There are also differences between countries stemming from the different legal frameworks and this makes precise comparisons difficult. Nevertheless, the general trends are clear. According to the countries' official statistics, the self-employed had by 1996 increased from effectively zero to 11.8 per cent of the labour force in the Czech Republic and to 6.0 per cent in Slovakia with a minimal proportion working in agriculture. In Hungary the numbers classified as running their own individual businesses grew from 4.5 per cent in 1989 to 12.4 per cent of the labour force in 1996 (cf Kornai, 1997, p.161). In Poland the self-employed were 25.7 per cent of the working population in 1989 rising to 35.1 per cent in 1995. When agriculture is excluded, the numbers rose from 4.9 per cent of the labour force in 1989 to 15.3 per cent in 1995.

Table 1.3 Structure of production by branches of industry in east-central Europe, percentage of total, 1989 and 1995

	Czechoslovakia			Poland		Hungary	
	1989	Czech Republic, 1996	Slovakia, 1995	1989	1995	1985	1994
Extractive industries	4.5	6.7	2.4	5.0	7.8	2.3	1.5
Electricity, gas and water	4.6	7.5	10.9	2.9	9.7	9.9	12.3
Manufacturing	91.0	85.8	86.6	92.1	82.5	87.8	86.2
Food, drink, tobacco	15.1	17.5	13.6	23.5	22.8	20.9	24.4
Light industry	7.6	5.3	5.1	12.2	5.7	8.3	5.2
Wood, paper and print	5.2	5.9	7.3	5.6	10.0	3.6	5.5
Chemicals, rubber, glass, ceramics	19.3	15.2	23.4	13.0	18.5	22.5	22.4
Metallurgy	11.8	11.0	17.3	10.1	6.4	11.8	10.0
Metal working and engineering	16.5	10.1	6.6	12.9	5.6	18.9	17.2
Electrical goods and electronics	5.6	3.7	4.2	5.4	4.6		
Transport equipment	8.3	10.4	7.0	7.0	8.6		
Other manufacturing	1.6	2.9	2.0	1.8	0.8	1.8	1.4

Note: Polish figures are not fully comparable with the 1989 figure showing only electricity while other utilities appear with other manufacturing. Electrical goods and electronics and transport equipment are included within Metal working and engineering in Hungary.
Source: Statistical office publications of the respective countries, using ISIC classification.

Within the manufacturing sector the extent and direction of changes in the importance of different branches varies slightly between countries, albeit with some clear common features. Table 1.3 shows the changes in the four CEECs. In 1989 the structures in the two parts of the Czechoslovak federation were fairly similar, although the Czech Republic had a stronger representation than Slovakia in extractive industries, metallurgy and engineering. Slovakia was better represented in chemicals and electronics. The post-1989 period has seen a shift towards basic and extractive industries and away from light industry, engineering and electronics.

Slovakia shows a particularly strong bias towards chemicals and metallurgy. The growth in the share for transport equipment in the Czech Republic is the clearest sign, albeit rather a small one, of a movement towards a structure more characteristic of advanced market economies.

In Poland the shift towards extractive industries is even clearer and, again, transport equipment has shown some increase while other branches of engineering have suffered a sharp decline. Hungary appears to have enjoyed much greater stability. Its extractive industries were already in decline before 1989 and the same trend has continued. Light industry has shown only a small drop while the weight of the engineering branches, after a dip at the start of the decade, has returned roughly to its pre-1989 level of importance. Thus, as in other aspects of the transformation, Hungary has experienced a far less dramatic break from established trends.

TRADE REORIENTATION

The key factor behind the change in the branch structure of industry is the changing structure of foreign trade, and particularly of exports. Here the common feature across all four countries has been a rapid reorientation of exports towards the advanced market economies and, in particular, towards the EU. There are differences between individual CEECs both in the extent of change and in the structure emerging at the end of the process. These stem partly from past history but may also reflect the effects of more recent policy choices. Thus both Poland and Hungary were already more strongly oriented towards the western European market before 1989. Exports to advanced market economies accounted for 43 per cent of Poland's total exports in 1989 rising to 72 per cent in 1996 while the European CMEA countries' share fell from 37 per cent to 21 per cent over the same period. For Hungary the share of exports to European market economies grew from 35.6 per cent of the total in 1989 to 64.4 per cent in 1995. For the former Czechoslovakia the rise in the advanced market economies' share was from 31 per cent in 1989 to 66 per cent for the Czech Republic in 1995 (77 per cent if exports to Slovakia are excluded) and to 41 per cent for Slovakia (63 per cent if exports to the Czech Republic are excluded).

This geographical reorientation has been accompanied by a shift in the product structure of exports, as shown in Table 1.4. The staple exports between CMEA countries included a high proportion of finished products, such as machinery and consumer durables. As product types these are technologically quite sophisticated and are associated with exports from more advanced countries but, within the protected CMEA environment, their quality was low and they stood little chance in more competitive markets. Thus with the shift in export orientation came a shift towards the export of primary products and semi-manufactures as the kinds of products that could most easily find a foothold in competitive markets. The export of complete, finished products, such as machinery, has suffered a sharp decline. A remarkable feature has been the importance of light industry exports, despite a declining share in industrial output. This point is taken up later.

Table 1.4 Exports by industrial origin, per cent of total value, CEECs

	Poland		Czechoslovakia		Czech Republic	Slovakia
	1989	1995	1989	1994	1994	1994
Agriculture	5.9	3.3	0.8	3.4	3.5	2.9
Mining, quarrying	9.9	7.8	2.2	3.4	4.7	1.1
Manufacturing	81.3	88.7	97.0	96.4	91.8	96.0
Food, drink, tobacco	6.5	7.8	2.1	5.1	5.5	4.0
Textiles, garments, leather, footwear	5.6	14.1	9.5	10.0	9.2	10.5
Wood and wood products	1.1	3.6	1.1	3.6	3.7	3.1
Paper and print	0.6	2.8	1.4	3.5	2.3	5.1
Chemicals, rubber	9.1	11.2	8.1	17.5	14.2	21.3
Products from non-metal minerals	1.1	2.8	2.9	5.6	6.4	4.0
Basic metals	9.9	12.3	7.0	14.9	11.2	19.5
Metal manufacture	39.8	32.9	63.7	32.4	33.6	28.1
Other manufacturing	10.4	1.2	1.3	3.7	5.6	0.5

Source: UN, 1995.

The figures in Table 1.5 help to put this into context. The UK, an advanced market economy, shows very little change in export structure in the years after 1989. The Asian 'tigers', however, have undergone substantial shifts away from textiles, which are generally associated with competition through low wages, and towards metal manufacture. There are differences between them, with for example Hong Kong remaining more dependent on the textile sector, but the structural change in CEECs appears to be in the reverse direction. Metal manufacture exports have either fallen significantly or, in the case of the former Czechoslovakia, suffered a massive decline. Compensating growth may come from light industry, although it seems more typically to be from chemicals and basic metals, the highly capital- and energy-intensive sectors that grew up under central planning.

Table 1.5 Exports by industrial origin, per cent of total value, selected market economies

	United Kingdom		South Korea		Singapore		Hong Kong	
	1989	1995	1989	1995	1989	1995	1989	1995
Agriculture	2.0	1.5	2.9	1.4	4.7	2.1	2.3	1.1
Mining, quarrying	7.2	6.8	0.2	0.1	0.4	0.3	1.5	0.9
Manufacturing	90.8	91.7	96.9	98.5	94.9	97.6	96.2	98.0
Food, drink, tobacco	5.6	6.3	1.4	1.2	3.9	2.7	2.8	2.5
Textiles, garments, leather, footwear	4.9	4.7	30.9	16.8	5.1	2.7	34.1	26.6
Wood and wood products	0.2	0.2	0.3	0.1	1.5	0.3	0.4	0.5
Paper and print	2.5	2.9	0.7	1.1	1.2	1.1	1.5	1.7
Chemicals, rubber	17.7	18.0	7.5	12.4	23.4	14.0	8.6	11.7
Products from non-metal minerals	1.3	1.3	1.3	0.6	0.4	0.5	0.8	1.0
Basic metals	5.5	4.9	6.8	5.4	3.0	2.4	1.6	2.5
Metal manufacture	48.0	50.3	43.9	58.9	54.1	70.3	35.7	41.3
Other manufacturing	5.1	3.1	4.1	1.9	2.4	3.6	10.7	10.2

Source: as Table 1.4.

The differences in end result include the very strong emphasis in Slovakia on the export of basic metals, chemicals and paper products, which is consistent with the changing branch structure of industry. These, as discussed in Chapter 6, come from a very small number of strongly export-oriented firms that are crucial to the country's trade performance. In the Czech Republic the trend has been similar to that in Slovakia, but with not so strong a bias towards these basic materials and the retention of more metal manufacture. In Poland's case the same trend is tempered by a stronger emphasis on mining and quarrying, reflecting raw material endowments, and on the textile sector. In all of these cases the heritage of the past is extremely important in defining the exact structure that is emerging. The process, however, has been a very similar one of using whatever base exists to find products that can be exported.

Precisely comparable figures are not available for Hungary, but a slightly different method of classification of product groups suggests a somewhat more stable structure with a strong emphasis on exports from agriculture, minimal change in the share of the broad groupings of raw and basic materials, which remain generally below the level of other CEECs, and a smaller drop in the share for machinery and transport equipment which, by 1995, had risen again to surpass the levels of other CEECs. This is in line with other evidence both of a less dramatic structural change in Hungary and of a possibly more solid base for future growth.

TRADE AND INDUSTRIAL RESTRUCTURING

These common features and differences across CEECs make it possible to bring together the various dimensions of structural change. The importance of foreign trade varies between the countries. Figures from the respective statistical offices show that over the 1993–5 period exports were equivalent to 63 per cent of GDP in Slovakia, 53 per cent in the Czech Republic, 30 per cent in Hungary and 23 per cent in Poland (Nachtigal, 1997). Poland has also done better at protecting its own domestic market leading to a recovery from the depths of recession that is much more evenly spread. All main branches of industry as recorded in Poland's Statistical Yearbooks increased their real output between 1990 and 1996 and only a few sub-branches, such as a number of specific types of machinery that had previously been exported, suffered a near total collapse in output.

In Hungary output growth was altogether weaker and recovery has varied across industrial branches. The restrictive package of March 1995 was followed by renewed decline for textiles, chemicals and some other branches. The most consistent growth has come from engineering which fits with the argument that Hungary has been experiencing export-led growth around technologically more advanced sectors, although the overall growth has been held back by the restrictions on domestic consumption (cf Kornai, 1997).

In the Czech Republic more sub-branches were exposed to the collapse of demand from the former CMEA, as there had been a greater dependence on that market beforehand. The resumption of growth was most impressive in transport equipment. Following a 28.5 per cent fall in output in Czechoslovakia as a whole in 1991 and continuing decline to a low point in 1994, output expanded to 11 per cent above the 1991 level in 1997. A number of branches continued with very sharp further falls in output with light industry unable to counter progressive import penetration after the sudden loss of export markets. The Czech textile and garment industries, following a 36.3 per cent drop in Czechoslovakia in 1991, showed a further 32.4 per cent decline by 1997. Leather and footwear, 35.5 per cent down in 1991, fell by a further 47.6 per cent to 1997.

In Slovakia there was disaster for the armaments industry that had previously supplied Warsaw Pact and Third World countries. Light industry has also faced continuing difficulties: much of it too had grown up around exports to the East. Recovery could come around transport equipment, growing rapidly after 1994 thanks to inward investment by Volkswagen, and from the basic industries built up under central planning.

STRUCTURAL REGRESSION

The view that different branches of manufacturing are associated with growth at different levels of economic development is well established in the development economics literature (Chenery, Robinson & Syrquin, 1986). Detailed studies of the sectoral structure of CEEC exports confirm a move towards those sectors associated with the lowest or the 'middle' levels of development (Myant *et al.*, 1996, Outrata, 1997). An investigation of revealed comparative advantage in trade with the EU (Landesmann, 1996) showed a strong specialisation towards exports from the most labour- and energy-intensive sectors alongside a weak representation from the most capital-, R&D- and skill-intensive sectors. Particularly the need for a high input from skilled labour seemed to be a severe disadvantage across all the countries. There was, however, some sign of a structural shift in the case of Hungary with the underrepresentation for R&D-intensive sectors clearly declining, although still below the level of their share in all imports into the EU. There is no sign of a similar improvement in the other countries, although figures for the Czech Republic and Slovakia are only available from 1993.

Trends across broad sectors do not reveal the complete picture. A related but slightly different approach conceptualises development into a number of stages depending on the driving force for establishing and improving international competitiveness, without assuming a precise link between specific sectors and the stage of development, although there certainly are general relationships. Thus Porter (1990) uses a model of a factor-driven stage for gaining competitive advantage, meaning the exploitation of raw material endowments or a cheap labour force, followed by an investment-driven and subsequently an innovation-driven stage. Light industry typically uses relatively unskilled labour and the activity can often move to seek out the cheapest labour available. However, experience in some advanced market economies, particularly Italy, demonstrates that the industry can also prosper by being highly innovative, emphasising quality and adapting rapidly to changes in demand (Best, 1990). This may involve varying degrees of contracting out to lower wage countries, but a significant part of the value-added remains in the richer country.

It is therefore necessary to look inside sectors rather than just believing the figures for sectors in aggregate and this can be done by using comparisons of the kilogram price of exports into the EU. A high kilogram price is an approximate indicator of a higher product quality, or of a greater input from skilled labour. This method gave a clear indication of the low quality of manufacturing exports from CEECs before 1989 (Myant, 1989a and 1989b). It could give a deceptive impression as the indicator does not show the costs of production or of imported components. With the CEECs becoming more closely integrated with the western European economies, an increase in the kilogram price could be achieved by exporting complete products that have only been assembled by relatively unskilled labour out of expensive imported components. An improvement, particularly if small and if restricted to products that could fit into this category, should therefore be treated with caution. Nevertheless, the results of one substantial comparative study (Landesmann & Burgstaller, 1997), including a sample of engineering and light industry branches, indicate a transformation towards the export of products requiring a lower level of technology and skill, albeit with some indications of a possible move up the quality scale in the most recent years.

The 'bad' signs are a bias towards exporting products with lower kilogram prices and an especially poor representation among those with the very highest values. The four countries of east-central Europe appear to be doing significantly better than the former Soviet Union, but are behind the Asian 'tiger' economies, the poorer EU members and, at least in terms of export product quality, not doing much better than India or China. The 'good' signs are a tendency towards quality improvement. The price per kilogram of the selected group of engineering industry exports into the EU was 50 per cent of the average figure for intra-EU trade for Hungary in 1988, rising to 74 per cent in 1994. The figure for Poland's exports increased over the same period from 40 per cent to 53 per cent while those for the Czech Republic and Slovakia were 61 per cent and 51 per cent respectively in 1994 compared with 46 per cent for Czechoslovakia in 1988. There was a similar narrowing of a somewhat smaller gap for the light industry branches of textiles, garments and footwear. There was no similar improvement from countries of the former Soviet Union.

These improvements in the quality indicator were accompanied by increases in market share, although the levels remained very low. Thus the four countries together increased their share of imports in the selection of engineering branches from 0.34 per cent to 1.07 per cent and their share of imports in the sectors of light industry from 0.97 per cent to 1.52 per cent. They remained well behind the four Asian tigers whose import share in the engineering branches grew from 4.7 per cent in 1988 to 5.9 per cent in 1994 while falling from 12.4 per cent in light industry to 6.2 per cent over the same period. They were, however, well above the level of developing countries, such as India, for the engineering branches.

Choosing a different sample of sectors might reveal a slightly different outcome and a different ordering of success among the countries of east-central Europe. Thus the passenger car sector was excluded and that is more important in the Czech Republic than in the other countries. Nevertheless, the general picture is consistent with that already presented. The economies of east-central Europe have undergone a very substantial transformation, but the switch in trade orientation towards the EU has been accompanied by a shift for the economies as a whole towards exporting simpler products and maintaining their competitive position on the basis of low wages. This did not lead to the elimination of all activities associated with higher wage levels and there are some signs of a shift back towards a higher quality level, although its strength and meaning require further investigation.

A LIMITED GROWTH POTENTIAL

Taken as a whole, this evidence on the nature of the structural changes in CEEC economies gives good grounds for doubting their potential for sustained growth. That is dependent on a further process of structural change towards the rapidly growing sectors and products that characterise advanced economies. There are signs of this, but they are weak. The real depth of the economies' weaknesses was masked by growth rates out of the depths of the transformation recession that partly reflected one-off processes, the effects of which have gradually faded, leading towards slowdown and possible stagnation. This general point is clearest for the Czech Republic and the least applicable to Hungary and Poland where change had been taking place more gradually over a longer period (Myant, 1996).

The former Czechoslovakia saw the most sudden and sweeping transformation, and recovery from the depths of depression can be linked to a number of identifiable elements. The first, already under way before the economy had reached its low point in late 1991, was the growth in new small businesses largely in the service sector. The demand was effectively already present, as this sector had been underdeveloped under central planning. There was no threat from imports for these kinds of activities, but the number of new businesses formed soon flattened off. This was associated with a shift in sectoral structure from industry towards services, but not towards the services for businesses that have become a source of substantial invisible exports in the UK and other advanced market economies.

The second was the shift in exports towards the EU using already existing technology and equipment. Thus the exports of raw materials and semi-manufactures, such as steel, required minimal adaptation from enterprises. They simply had to find new markets for products that had previously been used domestically or traded within the CMEA. This was most pronounced in Slovakia. Many firms in light industry and engineering could produce under contract from western European firms. This process was already under way for light industry before 1989 in the cases of Poland and Hungary and took off rapidly in the Czech Republic in 1991. It was somewhat slower in Slovakia.

These processes of transferring to export on the basis of existing technology soon begin to encounter limits. The export of basic materials into western Europe was held in check by protectionist measures and accusations of dumping, although there is still continuing growth for some products. Contract work in light industry is not particularly profitable and cannot support high wages. CEECs have some advantages over more distant manufacturing locations as they can deliver more quickly and adapt more immediately to changes in demand. There is, however, competition between them and with other locations around the Mediterranean that make this a poor basis for long-term growth. There is more potential for the engineering industry but, without substantial technological advance, it is not a basis for rapid growth.

The third source of recovery from depression was a growth in exports based on new investment from multinational companies. In every CEEC there has been strong recovery in the motor industry and in some cases also in electronics and electrical goods. The potential would appear to be greatest in Hungary, with the highest per capita level of inward direct investment, but the overall levels, as indicated in Chapter 4, are low by the standards of countries at comparable levels of development.

Although there clearly is a basis for growth from inward investment, its extent has not been sufficient to cover for the structural weaknesses in the CEEC economies. The clearest demonstration of this is the tendency towards balance of payments current account difficulties, pointing to an inability to earn enough from exports to maintain the income levels to which the population aspires. Growth in consumption has been both a major stimulus to GDP growth and a cause of the growth in imports which has in all countries usually been above the level of the growth in exports. The result has been balance of payments current account deficits reaching 9.4 per cent of GDP in Hungary in 1994, 10.2 per cent in Slovakia, 7.6 per cent in the Czech Republic and, as originally calculated, 6.3 per cent in Poland, all in 1996. These are high levels by international standards and are generally considered unsustainable over more than a couple of years.

The responses have varied between countries. Both Slovakia and Poland accepted from early on the need for currency devaluations and for measures to restrict imports. Poland altered the methodology for calculating the current account by shifting various transactions from the capital account, probably coming closer to reflecting the true situation. It thereby achieved a dramatic improvement in its figures. Hungary introduced a package of policy measures in March 1995 to pre-empt the possibility of a major crisis. This included steady currency devaluation, cuts in public spending and wage restraint. The deficit was reduced to 3.8 per cent of GDP by 1996, but at the expense of a reduction in the GDP growth rate to 0.8 per cent. There was also a shift in privatisation policy to attract inward investment and this, apart from immediately boosting the capital account, may have contributed to a basis for future growth.

The Czech government introduced a similar emergency package in two stages in April and May 1997, following criticism and pressure from the IMF but, with privatisation largely complete, could not imitate the steps attracting inward investment. The result, as in Hungary, was a slowdown in economic growth which had previously been heavily weighted towards expanding domestic consumption. It should, however, be noted that Czech growth was not particularly rapid even in the months before the austerity packages were introduced. As could be expected in so open an economy, growth had been reduced by the growing import penetration and the poor performance of exports.

The Czech Republic may provide the clearest case of an attempt at free-market purity reaching its limits, meaning in this case a steadfast refusal to take steps to limit imports albeit alongside a determination to maintain a stable exchange rate. More generally, however, there must be doubts about the ability of other countries to achieve or sustain high rates of growth on the basis of the current policy frameworks. The later sections of this chapter therefore work towards the basis for an alternative policy approach around a discussion of international experience. The next section strengthens the conclusion that macroeconomic stabilisation plus the free market is not an adequate basis for growth by considering effects elsewhere in the world and by a discussion of how far it is supported by empirical studies of economic growth.

STABILITY AND GROWTH

The belief in the primacy of the price mechanism, the benefits of privatisation and the importance of restricting the rate of inflation have been at the core of advice given by the IMF to numerous countries facing difficulties and are also firmly embedded in the current economic orthodoxy. The transformation strategies in Poland and the former Czechoslovakia in the crucial period early in the decade were based on the IMF's prescription for countries facing severe external and internal imbalances and the IMF again influenced austerity packages in Hungary in 1995 and, even more clearly, in the Czech Republic in 1997.

The IMF, of course, is primarily concerned with handling problems of external disequilibrium rather than ensuring long-term growth. Nevertheless, both in its general statements and in the analyses it publishes of individual countries, the IMF leaves little doubt of a belief that application of its policy recommendations will lead towards 'the path of higher, sustainable growth' (eg Nsouli *et al.*, 1995, p.53). Its advice, including that to CEECs, has ignored other factors that might affect longer-term growth, such as R&D, innovation policies or the importance of education. All economies are reduced to a few standardised macroeconomic variables.

Despite this prevailing orthodoxy, the evidence that the price mechanism, the free market, macroeconomic stabilisation and private ownership are the whole key to success is rather weak. IMF sponsored studies, including one comparing a sample of eight developing countries, confirm that 'no country shifted to a distinctly more rapid pace of growth' after the application of its stabilisation package (Goldsbrough *et al.*, 1996, p.5). Those countries that had been growing rapidly beforehand continued to do so, while those that had been relatively stagnant continued to experience slow growth after stabilisation. Larger comparative studies, including one of 36 low-income countries, suggest that differences in education and health standards may overwhelm the effects of policies advocated by the IMF (IMF, 1997, pp.25–6).

There are also theoretical grounds for doubting the strength of the standard IMF message. Many academic studies and basic economics textbooks give apparently solid reasons for expecting clear links between the macroeconomic stability and economic growth performance. Thus high rates of inflation, or unanticipated increases in the inflation rate, could reasonably be expected to contribute to an atmosphere of uncertainty in which private-sector investment would be discouraged. However, as indicated in Chapter 3, even IMF studies do not show a particularly strong relationship between inflation rates and growth, although very high levels of the former do appear to be related to low levels of the latter. Moreover, plenty of other factors could have an even greater influence on business confidence, such as the institutional and legal framework, or the specific policies pursued by governments.

This point can gain support from studies on economic growth based on the neo-classical tradition. Thus it was clear as soon as serious empirical studies started to appear that increases in the inputs of the basic factors, labour and capital, explained very little of observed economic growth. The bulk was left to a 'residual' that could be reduced with the inclusion of more inputs, such as the contribution of a more educated labour force. There is still always a gap between growth in measurable inputs and growth in measurable outputs which, in the classic empirical study, was attributed to vague notions of 'advances in knowledge' or reductions in the lag in their application (Denison, 1967).

Highlighting the importance of education and advancing knowledge could point to an important role for governments. These are areas that have typically been dependent on public sector inputs and convincing arguments can be made out for market failure. This would at least seem to be an important caveat to the fashionable insistence on 'small government' as the necessary basis for growth. It also points to very serious areas of weakness in CEECs which are not advanced in world terms in education or science (see below, Chapter 2).

There is, however, a major theoretical weakness with work developed from the neo-classical framework which makes it very difficult to pin down what role government should try to play. The implicit assumption is that the contributions of the different factors can be treated as if operating completely independently of each other and can therefore be added together by simple arithmetic. It is, however, intuitively self-evident that they interact. Thus, for example, the adoption of new technology could be expected to be greatly helped by a higher level of education for the workforce. The two could even be inseparable, in the sense that one could be ineffective without the other.

This same criticism applies to the 'new', 'endogenous' growth theories that try to link technical progress to investment and to include human capital as an input to technical progress (eg Romer, 1990). Education and knowledge are still presented as if they influenced growth in a very direct and separable way. This understates and oversimplifies the ways in which they can influence economic performance and may thereby also oversimplify the possible role of governments. Thus, apart from a direct impact on formal R&D, education can contribute to making workforces more flexible and responsive to new ideas and possibly more willing to seek out minor innovations. This could in turn be influenced by, or even dependent on, an institutional environment that encourages good industrial relations, a factor that could again be influenced by governments. Thus the government's contribution need not only be in providing measurable inputs. It may have a crucial role in en-suring a balance between them and in creating the basis for their interaction.

Nevertheless, modern growth theory has encouraged a range of empirical studies that feed directly into the studies of comparative competitiveness discussed in Chapter 2. Barro (1997), using data from over 80 countries, reported a fairly narrow range of only 11 variables that could explain approximately half of the variation in growth rates between countries. There seemed to be particularly clear relationships between male schooling, with one extra year increasing growth rates by 1.2 percentage points, and a rule of law index, with the gap between the worst and best figures accounting for an increase in growth rates by four percentage points.

Barro's results also confirm how difficult it is to find any independent, ultimate source of economic growth. Thus a high rate of investment is clearly an important factor, with the fast-growing Asian tiger economies experiencing exceptionally high levels, but is itself closely related to education and the rule of law. It therefore finds no place as an independent explanatory variable. The result is perhaps not surprising as the benefits of new investment may depend on having a skilled and adaptable workforce. Investment would also have little point without legal protection.

Results also point to the dangers of over-emphasising the most easily measur-able variables. Thus Barro's studies rather confirm the doubts over the IMF's ten-dency to place such strong emphasis on inflation. The relevant data are easily available and can be studied across 132 countries for the most recent years. At inflation rates below 20 per cent per annum, 'the relation between growth and in-flation is not statistically significant' (Barro, 1997, p.95). There is no sign of a relationship in the other direction, but any negative relationship between inflation and growth at low levels of inflation is so weak as to be barely detectable in the face of other much stronger determinants. There certainly is not a relationship strong enough to justify making this the central policy objective overriding other possible contributors to growth.

Barro also finds evidence to support the view that 'big government' is bad for growth. The relationship is not particularly important with a 7 percentage point cut in the government's share of GDP required for a one percentage point increase in growth. Moreover, rather surprisingly, government spending has been defined to exclude outlays that are likely to improve productivity, such as education, and also to exclude defence spending. It would therefore seem very dangerous to treat this too simply as a policy prescription. It is at best a warning against certain kinds of government spending rather than government spending in general.

PATHS AND STAGES OF GROWTH

Thus the results of studies based on neo-classical growth theory can point to a role for government beyond that envisaged by free market enthusiasts, but they do not show how the different factors contributing to growth interact and this limits their value for drawing policy conclusions. For that it is necessary to depart from the implicit assumption that all growth paths are essentially similar, depending on the contributions of similar factors that can be expected to have similar effects in all cases. In reality, different countries can follow significantly different, but none-theless equally successful, growth paths. The role of different contributory factors may be substantially different and that applies particularly to the role of govern-ment. There also are major differences in the nature of growth depending on the level the economy has reached or, to use the typology adopted by Porter, its stage of competitiveness. Thus at the earliest, factor-driven stage there may be a require-ment for no more than a degree of stability, a basic economic infrastructure and a functioning legal system that can give security for investors. That was largely enough in the early stages of growth in the most advanced Asian tiger economies and has been the key to dynamism based on inward investment in light industry in those that have followed, such as Thailand (cf Dixon, 1996, and Warr & Nidhiprabha, 1996).

Porter, however, makes clear that relatively few countries progress beyond this into the investment-driven phase. This transition does not follow automatically from the presence of a functioning market system. Porter's account fits broadly with Japan's experience in which the government played an active role in protecting new industries, in encouraging firms to develop coherent strategies, in identifying sectors and products with the greatest growth potential and in helping ensure finance was available. It did not direct economic activities, but it did provide 'paternalistic guidance' (Tsuru, 1993, p.79) to the firms that were the key actors in the growth process.

There are debates over the role of the government in post-war Japanese growth, with doubters concentrating on examples where advice was ignored. This, however, cannot detract from the evidence that the general direction of economic development was in line with thinking that emerged jointly between big firms and government (Wade, 1990, pp.328–31, Best, 1990). Moreover, experience else-where confirms the importance of government decisions in the initiation of the investment-driven stage. Thus the emergence from scratch in the post-war world of a steel industry, the archetypal representative of the investment-intensive indus-tries, seems explicable only in terms of decisions by governments. It simply does not emerge out of a market system alone.

Porter's innovation-driven stage depends on a rather different role from government. Again, however, the development of an autonomous capacity for innovation is not a natural result of a free market and price mechanism. International comparative studies of innovation suggest that it emerges 'through the operation of a complex set of institutions' (Nelson, 1996, p.4), including government, the education system, university research establishments and private companies (cf *Commercialisation Enquiry*, 1996). The government cannot direct the process 'from above', but its role is extremely important in creating a range of necessary preconditions for the development of innovative industries, particularly as those sectors most associated with innovation have very high requirements for the most skilled labour. Thus UK Census of Production figures show a ratio of professionals – meaning roughly those with higher education – to the total labour force of 1.6 per cent for leather goods, including footwear, but of 18 per cent for data-processing equipment.

The behaviour of firms themselves is crucial and there is a strong body of opinion that puts the success of economies at this level down primarily to the presence of successful firms, although the factors influencing their success are far from clear. To some extent the local institutional environment clearly is important, again as a precondition. However, it interacts with the behaviour of firms in a way that cannot simply reflect the operation of a relatively small number of measurable economic variables, not least because the performance of individual firms within a single country varies very widely. Nevertheless, cross-country studies do point to some possible generalisations.

Comparative studies of UK innovative behaviour have pointed to weaknesses in the technical training of managers and poor organisation of R&D, leading to a failure to take advantage of new technological possibilities, a lack of attention to innovation as a competitive weapon and poor training and hence relative inflexibility of the labour force (eg Mason and van Ark, 1996, Pavitt, 1980). A more general element may be the firm's time horizon. A short time horizon, blamed frequently on reliance on a financial yardstick and a need to ensure steady financial returns (eg OECD, 1986, p.42–3), is often seen as discouraging the taking of risks without which innovation is impossible. This, however, does not embody all aspects of the problem. A firm could have a long time horizon and still make serious strategic errors, generally lack imagination or have little interest in using technological innovation as a part of its strategy.

Nevertheless, the available comparative studies on innovation in advanced market economies leave rather a bleak impression on the prospects for CEECs to move towards the innovation-driven stage. At the start of the transformation process, the enterprises inherited from central planning were poorly prepared for this. They lacked experience of strategic thinking and had little need in the past for long-term plans of their own. Various elements of the transformation process have hampered the development of strategic thinking, as indicated in following chapters. Where privatisation has led to clear control by 'outsiders' it is often accompanied by concentration on short-term financial considerations.

Nevertheless, to reemphasise the point, even those managements not under threat from outside, and with access to sources of finance, are quite capable of making strategic decisions that will not lead them to innovation and technological advance. They can instead be strongly tempted into building their own diversified empires including prestige activities such as buying football clubs – as is the case for the Košice steel producer in Slovakia – or failing enterprises with famous brand names from the past, as has been tried by the Škoda–Plzeň heavy engineering combine in the Czech Republic. The extent to which this can be seen as a result of faulty transformation strategies is taken up for the Czech Republic in Chapter 7. As the next section indicates, experience in other countries shows that development into the 'innovation-driven' stage has been possible, although it depends on governments pursuing the policies appropriate for the country concerned.

FOLLOWING THE TIGERS?

The best known recent economic 'miracles' have been in East Asia, but their experiences have played very little role in thinking behind policy making in CEECs. South Korea has even been presented as a case of success for the market and from following price signals, although those who put such arguments in general terms also, in the course of a more complete account, reveal an 'awareness that it is not the whole truth' (Michell, 1988, p.5). IMF involvement has concentrated simply on standard 'adjustment' concerns and sees nothing more (eg Aghelvi and Márquez-Ruarte, 1985). The alternative view has been put many times (eg Amsden, 1989), but its advocates often seem to be on the defensive, battling against an ideological block around the insistence that success simply has to be attributed to following market signals. The empirical evidence points clearly to a very consistent pattern of state involvement which was crucial in determining the country's growth, including the sectoral structure and the emergence of big firms.

The crucial point was the stage when the potential for a low-wage economy appeared to be in danger of exhausting itself. In terms of Porter's framework, governments recognised the limited further potential for the factor-driven stage. From 1973, the South Korean government adopted a very clear and conscious strategy of developing heavy and chemical industries. There is documentable evidence of a decision to follow the Japanese example in taking the most modern techniques available (Enos & Park, 1988, p.228). There is no serious question that this was crucially important in setting South Korea's development path. Indeed, the export pattern that emerged was remarkably similar to that of Japan, despite a substantially lower income level (Petri, 1988, pp.53–8). It can be argued that mistakes were made along the way, but it is not plausible to maintain that all the positive elements of South Korean growth could have been achieved without the government's role.

The Korean development strategy included the development of a steel industry, based on the systematic acquisition and assimilation of technology and overseen by the government. For the engineering industry the government set targets and gave help to those firms that involved themselves in its strategy. Far from prices and market signals determining this transformation, the evidence is clear that the state had to push and cajole firms into participating in the development strategy (Rhee, 1994). It used its control over financial flows – banks were state-owned until the early 1980s and closely linked to the government in the following years – to direct investment into chosen activities and it held back imports that could threaten the newly-developing industries. The degree of protectionism increased during the 1970s and became high relative to other developing countries (Wade, 1990, p.308).

The government even pursued the conscious aim of copying, albeit not exactly, the Japanese structure of large combines. This was done through various forms of state patronage enabling the growth of a few small companies into the chaebol. Five of these large combines already accounted for 20 per cent of manufacturing assets by 1985 (Lee, 1997, pp.18–28). Several have become firmly established in the Fortune 500 list of all companies. In 1997 Daewoo, with 265,000 employees, took eighteenth place while Hyundai and Samsung were just outside the top 100. Needless to say, no firm from east-central Europe has figured in the list at all.

The beginnings of a transition to the 'innovation-driven' phase, with the development by Korean industry of its own products, were associated with a less directive role for government. It moved more towards the Japanese model of 'paternalistic guidance'. The basis, however, had been laid with the creation of the broad industrial structure through the 1970s and, above all, with the emergence of large companies that could challenge established brand names with modern products. Thus, for example, the electronics sector grew up in line with government objectives through the 1970s based around the gradual mastering of the manufacture of more sophisticated components. It was the government that took steps to ensure the development of a research base both by establishing its own institutes and by giving incentives and encouragement to firms to link up with government initiatives and to start up their own research. Gradually, the big private companies have undertaken more of the work themselves (Bloom, 1992, pp.54–6). The government's overall share in total R&D spending had fallen from 90 per cent in 1965 to well under 30 per cent by the early 1990s (Bloom, 1992, p.14).

It should be added that the government has also consistently encouraged the development of the necessary highly-skilled labour force to such an extent that South Korean growth has even be described as 'education-led'. The numbers in higher education increased from 0.6 per cent of the population in 1970 to 4.2 per cent in 1992. The equivalent increase in the UK was from 1.1 per cent to 2.5 per cent while the CEECs saw only small increases, for example from 0.9 per cent to 1.1 per cent in Czechoslovakia.

South Korea, however, illustrates only one possible development path. Amid the fascination with the relative success of tiger economies and the hopes in CEECs that their example can be followed, it is often not noticed how diverse their experiences have been. Taiwan followed a slightly different path, although its government too had a clear orientation towards encouraging sophisticated products with the fastest growing demand. There was, however, no analogous process of large firm creation. Hong Kong differed even more markedly and appears to have skipped the investment-driven and possibly also the innovation-driven phases, at least as usually understood. Its manufacturing base has remained tied to export-oriented low-wage activities carried on largely in small firms which lack their own brand names and manufacture to contracts from outside. Nevertheless, an important change was forced, as in South Korea, by the appearance of a labour shortage and with it rising wage levels. The change, however, was towards becoming a service, distribution and contracting base for manufacturing work undertaken elsewhere in Asia and particularly on mainland China.

Hong Kong's manufacturing employment was actually declining by the 1980s. By 1991 it is estimated that three times as many industrial workers may have been employed by Hong Kong firms on the mainland as on Hong Kong itself (Yu, 1997, p.84). The colony had become a centre for outward investment on a scale that is remarkably high even for a developed economy. Unfortunately, official figures have not been reported and only estimates are available, but they suggest, for example, a total of $21.9 bn over the 1986–9 period (OECD, 1993, p.47). With this went an adamant insistence that there need be no thoughts of an interventionist approach in economic development: the philosophy was very firmly 'that business-men normally know what they are doing, and that civil servants should keep out of their way as much as possible' (Wong, 1993, p.87). This gives a slightly mis-leading impression as the Hong Kong authorities were pushed by South Korean and Taiwanese successes into active support for technological advance in the electronics industry (Wade, 1990, p.333). Nevertheless, the strong emphasis on financial services required less of a directive role than in the other countries.

By way of contrast Singapore appears as a country that depended to an extra-ordinary extent on inward investment. The government, facing the same problem of an exhaustion of the potential of the cheap-labour road, took a definite decision to encourage skill- and R&D-intensive industries (van Liemt, 1988, pp.32–3). This required an active strategy and the government set clear objectives, incidentally indicating that it had 'no ideological commitment to free enterprise as such' (Huff, 1994, p.339). Foreign companies became almost completely dominant, accounting for 86 per cent of manufacturing exports by 1990 (ibid, p.320) with US-owned electronics and electrical goods manufacturers the most important. Domestically-owned firms remained small and of much less economic significance. The Singapore government also set the conscious aim of becoming a service centre for neighbouring countries in south east Asia and that required ensuring the necessary legal and macroeconomic environments and an excellent transport and communications infrastructure. Again, the government set the objectives and took the lead where the private sector was unable or unwilling to undertake the work.

CONCLUSION

The growth potential for CEECs should be enormous. They are close to advanced market economies in Europe and a number of them are likely in the near future to become EU members. They already have reasonably advanced and diversified economic structures that place them above the level of developing countries. Nevertheless, the evidence from recent economic performance is rather patchy and comparison of their structural transformations with the experience of both developed market economies and newly industrialised countries does not encourage confidence. A basis has been created for some economic growth, but not for rapid enough growth to close the gap with the advanced economies of western Europe.

The point can be amplified around Porter's framework of stages of competitiveness. The lowest, factor-driven stage is of limited relevance to CEECs. They are not rich in raw materials and they cannot compete by low wages alone with the simplest products as wage levels are already well above those of many Third World countries. The current importance of light industry exports appears anomalous and the potential and problems of these branches are investigated for the case of the Czech Republic in Chapter 7. The conclusion is that the structure and financial strength of firms emerging out of privatisation gives little chance either of competing by low wages alone or of creating a modern and innovative light industry.

Nor is there any potential for taking this phase to a higher level by following the example of Hong Kong. There have been efforts to benefit from contracting out work to countries of the former Soviet Union, but the business environment there is very risky and CEEC firms have no particular advantages over those from developed market economies. Indeed, their smaller size and financial weakness makes it very difficult to launch even relatively modest business ventures to the East.

Porter's investment-driven stage, the basis for government-led growth in South Korea and for much of Japanese growth in the 1950s, is also of limited relevance for the long term, despite a shift towards precisely these kind of industries. Growth in demand is not particularly rapid, major EU producers do not welcome lower-wage competition and have sought means to protect their own markets, production is environmentally harmful, the CEECs are not rich in the relevant raw materials and there is a strong potential threat from lower-cost producers in the former Soviet Union. It has made sense to produce and export raw materials and basic metals, taking advantage of the results of investment undertaken under central planning, but it would not make sense to devote substantial further investment to these kinds of activities. All serious policy studies have pointed to the case for reducing the weight for these sectors while modernising a core that may be able to compete successfully.

Rapid growth therefore ultimately depends on a presence in the most rapidly growing product groups associated with Porter's 'innovation-driven' stage. Here the contrast with newly industrialised countries is the most dramatic. Structural change in the CEECs has involved a shift away from such activities. To a certain extent this is a deceptive impression as the decline has been in the production of low-quality goods in sectors associated with high technology. Moreover, there are exceptions, with some development particularly in the motor vehicle industry around inward investment by powerful multinational companies and signs of an improvement in technological level particularly in parts of Hungarian industry. Nevertheless, there is a clear contrast with Asian 'tiger' economies in which conscious strategies were pursued to create favourable conditions for technological advance.

The weakness of the base for the innovation-driven stage can be illustrated around two key elements of the necessary institutional framework. The first is the absence of big firms that could establish brand names and compete on a world scale. The assumption in the early years after 1989 was that central planning had left 'giants' that enjoyed monopoly positions in their domestic markets. It would be more realistic to view the enterprises in the region as small by international standards and to emphasise their minimal experience of modern management and business methods. Indeed, in terms of their potential for independent innovative activity, they are more like small or medium-sized enterprises than multinational companies. Privatisation was, if anything, associated with fragmentation and the biggest domestically-owned manufacturing firms left by 1994, measured by turnover, were the East Slovak steel producer of Košice, with 25,800 employees, followed by two somewhat smaller Polish steel makers.

As already indicated, the absence of one's own firms need not be a barrier to reaching a high technological level. Inward investment by multinational companies can be at least a partial substitute. It is, however, only under quite exceptionally favourable conditions that a country can base its whole development around this. In general, inward direct investment by the world's leading firms in more than basic assembly work is most likely where there is already a strong infrastructure, including education, transport and communications, language abilities, and an established industrial structure. In other words, it often appears as a complement rather than a substitute for development in which domestic firms play a prominent role. East-central Europe, despite its wage levels below western European levels, has not proven to be particularly attractive. Czech governments up to 1998 even resisted pressure to create a system of incentives analogous to countries of western Europe which were condemned as an unnecessary intervention in the free market.

The second element of the necessary institutional framework, which can affect the potential both for domestic firm development and for inward investment, is the science and education base. This is strongly influenced by governments. Research across the region has declined in terms of numbers of employees and its share of GDP. The Czech Republic, for example, devoted 1.2 per cent of GDP to research and development in 1994 compared with an OECD average of 2.2 per cent and a figure of 2.9 per cent for Japan. Higher education was well behind the levels of advanced countries and Asian tiger economies in 1989. Despite subsequent growth, the overall levels are still relatively backward. Thus the science and education bases do not correspond to the innovation-driven stage of growth.

This is the core of the argument uniting the following chapters. The transformation strategies pursued in CEECs vary slightly between individual cases, as becomes clearer from the discussions of the macroeconomic environments and privatisation policies, but the outcomes remain essentially similar. Centrally-planned economies have been converted into market economies, but the exclusive concentration on creating free markets and converting state into private property, alongside a fear of anything that could be criticised as an interventionist approach, has led to an underestimation of the importance of other forms of government activity that are normal in both advanced and rapidly growing market economies.

REFERENCES

Aghelvi, B. and J. Márquez-Ruarte (1985), *A Case of Successful Adjustment: Korea's Experience During 1980–84*, IMF, Washington, D.C., Occasional Paper, No.39.

Amsden, A. (1989), *Asia's Next Giant: South Korea and Late Industrialization*, Oxford: Oxford University Press.

Barro, R.J. (1997), *Determinants of Economic Growth: A Cross-Country Empirical Study*, Cambridge, Massachusetts: The MIT Press.

Best, M. (1990), *The New Competition: Institutions of Industrial Restructuring*, Cambridge: Polity Press.

Bloom, M. (1992), *Technological Change in the Korean Electronics Industry*, Paris: OECD.

Chenery, H., S. Robinson and M. Syrquin (1986), *Industrialization and Growth: A Comparative Study*, Washington D.C.: The World Bank.

Commercialisation Enquiry: Final Research Report (1996), Glasgow and Edinburgh: Scottish Enterprise and The Royal Society of Edinburgh.

Denison, E.F. (1967), *Why Growth Rates Differ*, Washington, D.C.: The Brookings Institution.

Dixon, C. (1996), 'Thailand's rapid economic growth: Causes, sustainability and lessons', in M. Parnwell (ed.), *Uneven Development in Thailand*, Aldershot: Avebury.

EIU (Economist Intelligence Unit) (1997), *Country Profile Czech Republic*.

Enos, J.L. and W.-H. Park (1988), *The Adoption and Diffusion of Imported Technology: The Case of Korea*, London: Croom Helm.

Goldsbrough, D., *et al.* (1996), *Reinvigorating Growth in Developing Countries: Lessons from Adjustment Policies in Eight Economies*, Washington, D.C.: IMF.

Huff, W.G. (1994), *The Economic Growth of Singapore*, Cambridge: Cambridge University Press.

IMF (1997), *The ESAF at Ten Years: Economic Adjustment and Reform in Low-Income Countries*, Washington, D.C., IMF Occasional Paper No.156.

Kornai, J. (1995), *Highway and Byways: Studies on Reform and Post-Communist Transition*, Cambridge, Massachusetts: The MIT Press.

Kornai, J. (1997), *Struggle and Hope*, Cheltenham, UK and Lyme, US: Edward Elgar.

Landesmann, M. (1996), *Emerging Patterns of European Industrial Specialization: Implication for Labour Market Dynamics in Eastern and Western Europe*, Vienna Institute for Comparative Economic Studies, Research Report No.230.

Landesmann, M. and J. Burgstaller (1997), *Vertical Product Differentiation in EU Markets: the Relative Position of Eastern European Producers*, Vienna Institute for Comparative Economic Studies, Research Report No.234a and 234b.

Lee, Y.-H. (1997), *The State, Society and Big Business in South Korea*, London: Routledge.

Mason, G. and B. van Ark (1996), 'Productivity, machinery and skills in engineering: An Anglo-Dutch comparison', in D.G. Mayes (ed.) (1996), *Sources of Productivity Growth*, Cambridge: Cambridge University Press.

Michell, A.R. (1988), *From a Developing to a Newly Industrialised Country: The Republic of Korea 1961–82*, Geneva: International Labour Office.

Myant, M. (1989a), *The Czechoslovak Economy 1948–1988: The Battle for Economic Reform*, Cambridge: Cambridge University Press.

Myant, M. (1989b), 'Poland – the permanent crisis?', in R. Clarke (ed.), *Poland: The Economy in the 1980s*, Harlow: Longman.

Myant, M. (1993), *Transforming Socialist Economies: The Case of Poland and Czechoslovakia*, Aldershot, UK and Brookfield, US: Edward Elgar.

Myant, M. (1996), 'Towards a policy framework in east-central Europe', in M. Had (ed.), *Economic Policy Framework in CEECs for the Process of Moving towards the European Union*, Prague: The Foundation for the Study of International Relations.

Myant, M., F. Fleischer, K. Hornschild, R. Vintrová, K. Zeman and Z. Souček (1996), *Successful Transformations? The Creation of Market Economies in Eastern Germany and the Czech Republic*, Cheltenham, UK and Brookfield, US: Edward Elgar.

Nachtigal, V. (1997), 'Česká ekonomika v Evropě 1. poloviny 90. let', *Politická ekonomie*, **45**, pp.631–655.

Nelson, R.R. (1996), *The Sources of Economic Growth*, Cambridge, Massachusetts: Harvard University Press.

Nsouli, S., *et al.* (1995), *Resilience and Growth Through Sustained Adjustment: The Moroccan Experience*, IMF Occasional Paper No.117.

OECD (1986), *Productivity in Industry: Prospects and Policies*, Paris.

OECD (1990), *Economies in Transition*, Paris.

OECD (1993), *Foreign Direct Investment Relations between the OECD and the Dynamic Asian Economies: The Bangkok Workshop*, Paris.

OECD (1997), *Labour Force Statistics*, Paris.

Outrata, R. (1997), 'Structural changes and competitiveness in Slovak industry', *Ekonomický časopis*, **45**, 480–499.

Pavitt, K. (ed.) (1980), *Technical Innovation and British Economic Performance*, London: Macmillan.

Petri, P. (1988), 'Korea's export niche: Origins and prospects', in D.M. Leipziger (ed.), *Korea: Transition to Maturity*, Oxford: Pergamon Press Inc.

Porter, M. (1990), *The Competitive Advantage of Nations*, London: Macmillan.

Rhee, J.-C. (1994), *The State and Industry in South Korea*, London: Routledge.

Romer, P. (1990), 'Endogenous technological change', *Journal of Political Economy*, **98**, 71–102.

Rowthorn, R. and J. Wells (1987), *Deindustrialization and Foreign Trade*, Cambridge: Cambridge University Press.

Tsuru, S. (1993), *Japan's Capitalism: Creative Defeat and Beyond*, Cambridge: Cambridge University Press.

UN (United Nations) (1995), *International Trade Statistics Yearbook*, New York.

Van Liemt, G. (1988), *Bridging the Gap: Four Newly Industrialising Countries and the Changing International Division of Labour*, Geneva: International Labour Office.

Wade, R. (1990), *Governing the Market: Economic Theory and the Role of Government in East Asia Industrialization*, Princeton: Princeton University Press.

Warr, P.G. and B. Nidhiprabha (1996*), Thailand's Macroeconomic Miracle: Stable Adjustment and Sustained Growth*, Washington, D.C.: The World Bank.

Wong, W. (1993), 'Foreign direct investment: The Hong Kong experience', in OECD, 1993.

Yu, Tony F. (1997), *Entrepreneurship and Economic Development in Hong Kong*, London: Routledge.

2. Competitiveness in East-Central Europe

Karel Zeman, Věra Rodová and Zdeněk Souček

This contribution is built around an assessment of the most accessible multi-dimensional studies of competitiveness which have in turn been developed from modern theories of economic growth discussed in Chapter 1. These studies are used as a basis for identifying weaknesses in the position of four countries of east-central Europe, the Czech Republic, Slovakia, Hungary and Poland, by means of a comparison with countries of the European Union. Slightly different methodologies are used by two different bodies. The first to use the multi-dimensional approach was Klaus Schwab in 1980 under the auspices of the World Economic Forum in Geneva. *The Global Competitiveness Report*, issued every year, evaluated 53 countries in 1997 by their performance in various indicators of competitiveness (WEF, 1996a, and WEF, 1997). They were selected as 'the dominant players in the global economy' and accounted for well over 90 per cent of world output, of world exports and of total foreign direct investment.

This has been followed by an annual publication from the International Institute for Management Development, the IMD, of Lausanne in Switzerland. Annual competitiveness reports were produced in cooperation with the WEF's *Global Competitiveness Report* between 1989 and 1995. In 1996 and 1997 IMD published *The World Competitiveness Yearbook* which covers 46 countries, selected, as in the WEF study, as key players in world terms. These also tend to be the countries for which data are easily available. They are, however, by no means all advanced, or rapidly advancing, countries including, apart from OECD members and Asian tigers, such countries as India, China, Russia, and Brazil. The two bodies still follow essentially very similar methodologies, ascribing a rating to each of the countries included from a weighted average of an enormous number of indicators. In the IMD's case, 244 indicators have been grouped into eight factors: domestic economy, internationalisation, government, finance, infrastructure, management, science and technology and people (IMD, 1996, and IMD, 1997).

Different approaches have been favoured by the OECD and the EU which generally avoid such precise attempts to construct 'league tables'. Nevertheless, the European Commission has made general assessments of the likely ability of countries of east-central Europe to withstand the competitive pressures associated with full EU membership. There are dangers in taking these 'league tables' too literally, but they nevertheless are helpful in highlighting key weaknesses in particular countries and hence in facilitating an assessment of the transformation in CEECs. Thus the overall score may be of questionable value, depending on a somewhat arbitrary weighting of different factors, but the very low scores in certain indicators, such as those relating to the quality of management, point at the very least to an agenda for further research.

A further section in this chapter therefore attempts to show in more detail the meaning of the low level of Czech management. This emerges as a key weakness across east-central Europe and as one that is not obviously susceptible to simple policy prescriptions. At the same time, however, it must be considered – alongside changes in the institutional and financial framework discussed in Chapter 4 – to be among the most crucial for achieving a general improvement in economic performance.

THE MEANING OF COMPETITIVENESS

Competitiveness is not a simple concept. It can at the most straightforward level be defined as 'the ability of a country or company to, proportionally, generate more wealth than its competitors in world markets' (WEF & IMD, 1995), or as a nation's capacity to achieve economic growth (WEF, 1996a). However, such narrow definitions are not unambiguous. Success in competing internationally can be achieved on the basis of low wages or heavy social or environmental costs which need not represent an increase in general social welfare. Many definitions, particularly those related to policy formulation, therefore try to exclude these possibilities by broadening the objective beyond a narrow interpretation of economic performance. Thus the OECD (1995) describes competitiveness policy as supporting the ability of companies, industries, regions or supra-national regions to generate and sustain high factor income and factor employment levels.

The EU has followed a similar line, clearly relating its notion of competitiveness to policy objectives such as the creation of employment and raising living standards. Thus it includes several elements in a broad definition. An economy is said to be competitive if its productivity increases at a rate similar to or higher than that of its major trading partners with a comparable level of development, if it maintains external equilibrium in the context of an open free-market economy and if it realises a high level of employment (EC, 1997).

The growing complexity of definitions of competitiveness has been accompanied by a recognition of the complexity of the factors that may influence it. Emphasis has shifted away from static notions of comparative advantage, based traditionally on factor endowments, towards the notion of 'competitive' advantages which 'are based on more qualitative factors and can thus be influenced, to a large degree, by corporate strategies and by public policies' (EC, 1994, p.71).

Competitiveness, then, depends on variables that can themselves be varied, such as government policies and the institutional framework. It is an intrinsically dynamic and multi-dimensional concept in which by no means all the key factors are well understood. That applies particularly to those in the social and political fields.

A very wide range of policy areas could be important here and there is plenty of scope for disagreement over the relative importance of different factors. Thus the necessary preconditions for competitiveness have been presented by the World Economic Forum (WEF, 1996b) under three broad headings. The first is the abundance of productive inputs, such as capital, labour, infrastructure and technology. The second is an optimal mix of economic policies such as low taxes, little interference and free trade. The third is the existence of sound market institutions, such as the rule of law and the protection of property rights.

It is easy to present a theoretical basis for giving these priority and a number of empirical studies point in the same direction. However, it is very clear from empirical studies that no single factor has great explanatory power on its own. This can justify, while indicating possible reservations to, the somewhat eclectic approach required for the formulation of 'league tables' of competitiveness. The measures used include a mixture of indicators of 'performance', some derived from survey responses from over 2,000 managers active in the country concerned and some from published statistical sources. Both methodologies also contain a number of indicators of past performance, in the sense of results achieved in growth, productivity or export success, alongside a number of indicators of 'potential', such as educational standards or resources devoted to science. All of these indicators are believed to contribute to the potential for future economic growth, although the links between 'potential' and 'performance' indicators are by no means precisely defined. Similarly, the appropriate relative weights for the indicators must be open to debate.

THE POSITION OF EAST-CENTRAL EUROPE

The position of the selected CEECs in the Competitiveness Scoreboard over the 1994–7 period can be introduced with some standard macro-economic performance indicators. These place the CEECs firmly towards the bottom of the league.

Table 2.1 Levels of GDP per employed person in selected CEECs, as per cent of the EU average

	1995	1996
Czech Republic	46	47
Slovakia	41	44
Hungary	36	36
Poland	31	32
Austria	106	105
Germany	103	104
Ireland	106	108
Portugal	63	63

Note: Figures are derived from GDP in current prices compared at purchasing power parities.
Sources: *WIIW Monthly Report* 1997, No.3, and *OECD, Main Economic Indicators*, 1997, No.9.

Table 2.1 indicates the extent of the gap in levels of GDP per employed person compared on the basis of purchasing power parities. CEECs could reasonably wish to compare themselves with other central European countries, hence the inclusion of Germany and Austria, and with small member states of the EU that were until recently somewhat below the average per capita GDP level, such as Portugal and Ireland. However, even the best case, the Czech Republic, was still way behind Portugal and reached only 47 per cent of the EU average. Other countries were substantially lower, with Poland on only 32 per cent of the average.

Tables 2.2 and 2.3 show a variety of possible measures of competitiveness performance. The rate of labour productivity growth is significant as an indicator both of the dynamism of an economy and of the likelihood of narrowing the gap with the current 15 European Union members in the near future. The figures point to a possible acceleration, but it is neither definite enough nor substantial enough to give any real confidence. The experience of other smaller EU countries that started with productivity levels below the EU average, the examples here being Portugal and Ireland, suggests no grounds for assuming particularly rapid growth in the near future. It is therefore reasonable to assume a continuation of a substantial productivity gap for some time to come.

Table 2.2 Macroeconomic competitiveness indicators in selected CEECs and EU countries, labour productivity and unit labour costs

	1994	1995	1996	1997	1998
GDP in constant prices per employed person, per cent per annum					
Czech Republic	1.9	3.0	3.5	1.3	3.3
Slovakia	6.8	4.5	6.1	5.4	5.0
Hungary	5.1	3.5	1.6	2.5	3.0
Poland	6.9	6.0	5.1	3.6	3.3
Austria	2.8	2.2	1.3	1.7	1.9
Germany	3.6	0.2	2.6	3.1	2.4
Ireland	4.2	5.6	4.4	4.0	3.7
Portugal	1.7	3.3	2.4	2.5	2.4
All EU	3.2	1.9	1.5	1.9	1.9
Unit labour costs in the business sector, per cent per annum					
Czech Republic	16.8	17.0	12.1	10.3	9.2
Slovakia		6.2	10.1	8.5	10.5
Hungary	11.7	14.0	17.6	17.2	15.5
Poland	25.7	24.4	20.2	15.4	11.8
Austria	–0.3	1.5	0.9	0.3	0.3
Germany	–0.4	0.9	–0.3	–0.9	–0.1
Ireland	–1.5	–3.6	–0.1	–0.5	0.4
Portugal	5.4	3.0	2.6	0.8	0.6
All EU	–0.3	1.4	1.8	1.3	1.3

Sources: *European Economy* 1997, No.5, *OECD, Economic Outlook*, 1997, No.61, *WIIW Monthly Report*, 1997, No.9.

The figures for unit labour costs, measured in local currencies, show a more rapid growth than that of labour productivity. As discussed in detail in Chapter 3, this still leaves the absolute level low in comparison with the EU.

This remains the most obvious competitive advantage for the CEECs. However, as the figures indicate, it is under some degree of threat, in so far as labour cost increases are not balanced by devaluation.

Table 2.3 Macroeconomic competitiveness indicators in selected CEECs and EU countries, employment rates and unemployment rates

	1994	1995	1996	1997	1998
Ratio of employment to population of working age, per cent					
Czech Republic	84.1	83.8	84.1	83.9	83.9
Slovakia					
Hungary	59.7	58.3	58.0	57.7	57.7
Poland	73.6	72.3	71.5	71.5	71.7
Austria	67.8	67.1	66.6	66.2	66.0
Germany	69.7	69.1	68.8	68.6	68.5
Ireland	62.7	62.6	63.5	64.3	65.2
Portugal	67.8	67.4	67.7	67.5	67.4
EU-15	66.3	66.2	66.2	66.2	66.4
Unemployment rates, per cent, commonly used definitions					
Czech Republic	3.2	3.0	3.1	4.2	5.4
Slovakia	14.8	13.1	12.8	12.2	11.6
Hungary	10.8	10.3	10.6	10.5	10.4
Poland	14.4	13.3	12.4	11.7	11.1
Austria	5.9	5.9	6.2	6.4	6.2
Germany	9.6	9.4	10.3	11.1	10.9
Ireland	14.7	12.1	11.3	10.8	10.5
Portugal	6.9	7.2	7.3	7.1	7.0
EU-15	11.6	11.2	11.3	11.2	10.8

Sources: As Table 2.2.

The employment rates are surprisingly variable with that in the Czech Republic consistently high by EU, and CEEC, standards. Hungary, on the other hand, has a substantially lower figure. Part of the explanation comes with the unemployment figures which show the very low level for the Czech Republic. The significance of this for competitiveness is two-fold. On the one hand, a low level of unemployment is seen within the EU as a key objective of competitiveness policy. In addition, it could be taken as an indication of economic success in terms of a high level of output.

There is, however, a question mark over that with the suspicion that the high level of employment may actually reflect a low level of restructuring within enterprises. This is taken up in subsequent contributions and especially in Chapter 7. For present purposes, three key points are important. The first is that some closures of, or substantial labour reductions in, a number of loss-making enterprises might seem logical, but the numbers affected in the major, well-publicised cases are now rather small. The second is that this does not explain the substantial differences among CEECs: the case for enterprise rationalisation is not obviously stronger in the Czech Republic than elsewhere.

Table 2.4 External performance of selected CEECs and EU members

	1994	1995	1996	1997
Export performance				
Czech Republic	–5.4	–3.5	–2.9	–5.7
Slovakia				
Hungary	13.2	–9.0	3.6	3.3
Poland	11.9	8.6	2.4	5.3
Austria	0.9	2.0	–0.6	–0.5
Germany	0.2	–5.6	0.7	1.1
Ireland	5.0	12.9	4.2	2.8
Portugal	3.0	2.3	4.1	2.5
All EU	1.0	–0.9	–0.1	–0.1
Current account, per cent of GDP				
Czech Republic	–0.2	–2.7	–8.0	–7.0
Slovakia	4.7	3.7	–10.1	–9.9
Hungary	–9.7	–5.5	–3.9	–4.0
Poland	–1.8	–1.9	–6.3	–8.2
Austria	–0.9	–2.0	–1.8	–1.7
Germany	–1.0	–1.0	–0.6	0.1
Ireland	2.7	2.4	1.2	0.9
Portugal	–1.7	–0.3	–0.4	–0.2
All EU	0.3	0.7	1.0	1.4

Note: Export performance is measured as the annual percentage change in the ratio of export volume growth to total world export market volume growth.
Sources: As Table 2.2.

The third is that there would be scope for reductions in employment in many enterprises. This, however, need not be obvious to managements, many of whom believe themselves to be experiencing a serious labour shortage. The reductions could only take place as part of a more comprehensive restructuring process, involving improvements in the technological and organisational levels. This point is touched on later in this contribution.

There is less scope for debate over the implications of Table 2.4. The low level of Czech unemployment has not been supported by a high level of export performance. The average growth rate of exports has been lower than that of the development of export markets, as measured by the growth in world trade. Moreover, it has been accompanied by persistent current account deficits. Perhaps the most striking point is the trend towards deterioration, especially in the Czech Republic.

The comparison with the EU as a whole is clearly unfavourable, but the difference from Portugal and Ireland is even greater. If there were a genuine gain in the CEECs' competitiveness relative to the EU, they could be expected to show at least the sort of favourable trends in export performance exhibited by the smaller, rapidly growing EU members. Their failure to do so is fully consistent with growing balance of payment deficits stemming largely from growing imports of consumer rather than investment goods, or at least than investment goods that can contribute to export potential within a reasonable time period.

RESULTS OF MULTI-DIMENSIONAL ANALYSES

The analyses based on a variety of indicators of competitiveness 'potential' point to a broadly similar general conclusion. As Table 2.5 indicates, the CEECs were well towards the bottom of the league of 46 countries and behind all those in the EU apart from Greece. Portugal, however, also records a poor score. Comparisons across the 1994–7 period could point to some tendency towards improvement, but it is not dramatic and, in the case of Poland, amounts to little more than a slight movement away from almost the very bottom.

Table 2.6 gives slightly different results from the World Economic Forum's study. The competitiveness index is based on the weighted average derived from 155 indicators of potential for medium-term growth. The selection was influenced by economic growth literature and regressions against past growth performance, but inevitably retained a strong element of arbitrariness. In general, a lesser weighting was given to assessments from the executive survey, but this was considered the main source for information on the quality of infrastructure and technology and the only source for information on management quality and civil institutions. The second column in Table 2.6 therefore gives an indication of how far these kinds of factors were judged positively. There is, of course, the reservation that survey data is inevitably subjective and information may be further questioned in view of the relatively small number of respondents with any genuine knowledge of the smaller countries under consideration.

Table 2.5 Overall competitiveness rating trends in selected countries

	1994	1995	1996	1997
Czech Republic	39	39	34	35
Hungary	41	41	39	36
Poland	45	45	43	43
Austria	11	11	16	20
Germany	6	6	10	14
Ireland	21	22	22	15
Portugal	30	32	36	32

Source: IMD, 1996 and 1997.

Table 2.6 Alternative competitiveness ratings of selected countries in 1997

	Competi-tiveness index	Competitiveness rating from executive survey	Market Growth Index	Potential Growth Index, 1996
Czech Republic	32	31	42	35
Slovakia	35	46	46	
Hungary	46	41	48	45
Poland	50	36	36	37
Austria	27	32	34	31
Germany	25	4	11	40
Ireland	16	33	41	23
Portugal	30	45	39	42

Source: WEF, 1997.

The third column is an indicator of the likely contribution of the country concerned to further economic growth and is therefore biased by country size. The Growth Index ranks medium-term growth prospects by incorporating past performance with the competitiveness index. Thus Poland is helped by its rapid recent growth while the other CEECs are pulled down by their slower recoveries from the transformation depression. In general, the results are similar to those shown by the WEF, although the variations in rankings are a warning against taking them too precisely. The IMD's indication of a possible improvement across the region is slightly surprising in view of the relative weighting of 'processes' and 'assets', with the latter suggesting a greater improvement.

All the three CEECs quoted here have a better competitiveness rating position measured from past accumulated assets, measured by 31 criteria, than from processes, measured by 118 criteria. Assets of a country represent its natural factor endowments, such as land, raw materials and labour, and the results of past investment. In the case of the CEECs they are partly a heritage from the centrally-planned period, which ended at the end of the 1980s, and partly the result of transformation during the 1990–97 period. Investment in many branches has been low since 1990 so that, at least in many sectors, much of the current capital stock is inherited from the past.

The assets contribute to economic performance by processes which are results of decisions taken by the government, firms and households. The method of classification chosen includes indicators such as current GDP, inflation or spending on R&D among 'processes'. There is scope for questioning exactly what should be included here, but those indicators subject to current decisions, albeit ones that may be strongly influenced by the heritage from the past, are generally listed as 'processes'.

The argument is that processes play a key role in the efficient utilisation of the inherited assets and in determining how far that heritage from the past can contribute to economic competitiveness. The implication of these comparisons is that the CEECs are particularly weak not in the possession of assets but in their utilisation. This is noteworthy as transformation strategies have concentrated, in theory at least, on creating the institutional environment based on private ownership and the application of sound financial rules within which assets could be used most efficiently.

The IMD analysis (IMD, 1996, p.27) assesses the weight of assets in determining relative competitiveness at over 60 per cent in all three CEECs. The remaining 40 per cent is attributed to processes. The influence of inherited assets is even larger in the Czech Republic and Hungary. As Table 2.7 indicates, this is an area in which they have surpassed Portugal in the league table, although in terms of processes they remain some way behind. At the other extreme are the smaller newly industrialised countries with Singapore recording a weighting of 42 per cent for assets and 58 per cent for processes.

The picture is fairly similar for measures of 'internationalisation processes', as shown in Table 2.8. These contain two broad elements, attractiveness and aggressiveness, although the same indicator can find a place under both headings. Attractiveness, measured by 120 criteria, relates both to potential inward investment and to cooperation with indigenous firms. Among the indicators used are cultural openness, labour costs and fiscal policies. The CEECs appear to have improved their ranking somewhat, suggesting some success in creating an inviting domestic environment. However, they still remain well behind the EU.

Table 2.7 Competitiveness ratings by assets and processes in selected countries

	1994	1995	1996
Assets			
Czech Republic	33	33	29
Hungary	32	34	31
Poland	43	44	40
Austria	18	18	18
Germany	3	10	17
Ireland	24	24	24
Portugal	29	30	36
Processes			
Czech Republic	41	40	38
Hungary	42	43	42
Poland	45	44	43
Austria	10	10	14
Germany	6	6	9
Ireland	17	18	16
Portugal	34	35	36

Source: IMD, 1996.

This is fully consistent with measures of foreign direct investment as a per cent of GDP. Figures for 1996 show the highest share in Hungary with 4.5 per cent, followed by the Czech Republic on 2.3 per cent, by Poland on 2.1 per cent and finally by Slovakia on 0.9 per cent. This is roughly in line with their rankings in the league table.

The second broad element of internationalisation, 'aggressiveness', refers to the willingness of indigenous firms to invest abroad or to seek cooperation with companies in other countries and is measured by 102 criteria. This too has improved in all the CEECs, but the level remains low. The Czech Republic does slightly better than the others, a result which appears plausible as it does have a number of prominent firms with a long record of international experience.

Table 2.8 Competitiveness rating trends by internationalisation processes

	1994	1995	1996	1997
Attractiveness				
Czech Republic	37	35	33	34
Hungary	35	34	32	29
Poland	43	43	38	41
Austria	9	9	11	16
Germany	7	7	10	13
Ireland	20	22	20	15
Portugal	27	29	29	30
Aggressiveness				
Czech Republic	37	39	34	34
Hungary	43	43	40	36
Poland	45	44	42	43
Austria	12	15	18	21
Germany	6	7	9	14
Ireland	21	22	20	11
Portugal	36	36	39	38

Source: IMD, 1996 and 1997.

Tables 2.9 to 2.16 show a variety of further indicators of competitiveness potential, derived from the IMD's study. Accepting the overall low position of the CEECs and the possible trend towards some improvement, the performances of individual CEECs are slightly different. Table 2.9 shows the results for the 'domestic economy', which is largely a survey of standard macro-economic indicators, such as GDP, investment, savings and the cost of living. All the CEECs suffer from their relatively low GDP levels and from the poor recent growth performance associated with the 'transformation depression'. These results are therefore of limited significance as predictors of likely future performance.

Table 2.9 Competitiveness rating trends, domestic economy

	1994	1995	1996	1997
Czech Republic	43	43	34	36
Hungary	40	41	43	44
Poland	44	40	40	39
Austria	24	20	24	27
Germany	12	12	19	26
Ireland	19	17	16	5
Portugal	35	36	42	40

Source: As Table 2.8.

Table 2.10 Competitiveness rating trends, internationalisation

	1994	1995	1996	1997
Czech Republic	32	32	34	24
Hungary	34	37	30	21
Poland	45	45	42	44
Austria	13	16	20	18
Germany	10	9	9	7
Ireland	12	10	10	12
Portugal	24	26	32	15

Source: As Table 2.8.

The 'successes' appear to be internationalisation and human resources and labour market flexibility, as shown in Tables 2.10 and 2.11. The former is strongly influenced by the high degree of economic openness, with the improvement largely due to a somewhat better record in attracting inward investment. The relatively low score for CEECs as a whole stems from balance of trade and balance of payments results and, in fact, from the poor incentives for inward investment. Hungary does slightly better than the Czech Republic on incentives to inward investment while Poland, with poor results in attracting inward investment and a greater emphasis on protectionist measures, has remained near the bottom of the table. It is an open question whether policies towards foreign trade have not been too open in the Czech Republic, contributing to the balance of payments difficulties. Greater protectionism may be a significant contributory factor to the more broadly-based economic growth experienced in Poland, as suggested in Chapter 1.

Table 2.11 Competitiveness rating trends, human resources and labour market flexibility

	1994	1995	1996	1997
Czech Republic	30	28	28	24
Hungary	32	32	33	29
Poland	35	35	30	35
Austria	8	8	5	9
Germany	10	16	12	19
Ireland	20	23	24	20
Portugal	26	29	32	32

Source: As Table 2.8.

The human resources and labour market flexibility indicators give good results for the Czech Republic partly because of low unemployment and partly because of a positive assessment of 'attitudes and values'. It is, however, poorly rated for skilled labour and enrolment in higher education, a somewhat negative element of the heritage from the past touched on in Chapter 1. A remarkable point is that all the CEECs score well for long years of compulsory education and for the high participation of women in the labour force, two factors that very clearly are part of the positive heritage from before 1989.

Table 2.12 Competitiveness rating trends, infrastructure

	1994	1995	1996	1997
Czech Republic	41	40	35	29
Hungary	33	32	24	23
Poland	45	46	45	36
Austria	12	12	13	14
Germany	7	10	12	7
Ireland	22	22	21	22
Portugal	32	37	39	35

Source: As Table 2.8.

The infrastructure including transport, energy and the environment, evaluated by 28 criteria, also appears as an area of relative success. The comparison is shown in Table 2.12. Both Hungary and the Czech Republic score well for their road and rail networks and come out ahead of Portugal in their overall scores. Hungary is even close to the level of Ireland. Poland is some way behind, with a substantially worse transport infrastructure, and all the CEECs score badly on the use of computers and modern communications methods, although recent investment in telecommunications is helping the Czech Republic, and even more clearly Hungary, to move up the table. This, then, is an area in which the heritage of the past is important, but post-1989 investment is also beginning to play a role.

As Table 2.13 indicates, the CEECs have also recorded a slight improvement in the operation of financial markets, measured by 17 criteria, although it is still very low by EU standards and Poland has actually shown a deterioration. The elements included here include indicators of the macro-economic framework, such as short-term interest rates, alongside indicators of the success in creating a sound institutional framework.

Table 2.13 Competitiveness rating trends, finance

	1994	1995	1996	1997
Czech Republic	37	39	33	35
Hungary	43	43	43	38
Poland	44	42	44	45
Austria	10	12	14	21
Germany	6	7	8	9
Ireland	19	22	23	20
Portugal	34	28	29	27

Source: As Table 2.8.

Financial markets do appear as one of the keys to a successful market economy. The CEECs appear backward in the creation of the necessary institutional framework, despite the existence of an adequate material foundation. Indeed, all appear poor on the legal and regulatory framework for the capital market. Poland is assessed somewhat more negatively, although it is unclear why and this may reflect a weakness of the survey method. The Czech Republic is the only one criticised for weak controls on insider trading, but the finance category does not appear as a particular weakness. It is an open question whether perceptions of the Czech Republic will have remained even as favourable as suggested by these figures after a series of financial scandals in 1997 and in view of the widespread phenomenon of 'tunnelling' discussed in Chapter 7.

Three other areas point to more consistent disappointments. Table 2.14 shows the assessment of the governments' performance in supporting the competitiveness of CEECs. This, measured by 34 criteria, is very low in all three countries. In the case of the Czech Republic it is deteriorating and in Poland it is almost at the very bottom. Only in Hungary is there an improvement, and then only by three places. In all three CEECs the rating position is substantially lower than that of all the EU member states used in the comparison.

The reasons behind the low assessment generally reflect the assumption that 'small government' is best, but vary somewhat between the countries. The Czech Republic actually does well for minimising budget deficits, but does badly on justice, security and the legal framework. Hungary does slightly better with the 'political system' helping, while Poland is very bad on taxes, the lack of decentralisation and bureaucracy. There is scope for questioning the assumptions behind these results. As already indicated in Chapter 1, the view that 'small' government is always best needs to be treated with some caution. The size of the state budget may be less important than the effectiveness with which it is used and how much is devoted to activities likely to contribute to future competitiveness, such as education.

Table 2.14 Competitiveness rating trends, government

	1994	1995	1996	1997
Czech Republic	36	36	34	41
Hungary	42	42	40	39
Poland	45	44	43	45
Austria	26	22	27	26
Germany	10	13	19	25
Ireland	24	27	23	12
Portugal	25	29	32	30

Source: As Table 2.8.

Table 2.15 Competitiveness rating trends, science and technology

	1994	1995	1996	1997
Czech Republic	35	44	43	44
Hungary	36	39	36	28
Poland	39	38	37	42
Austria	15	13	11	19
Germany	3	3	3	3
Ireland	21	21	14	7
Portugal	44	41	35	43

Source: As Table 2.8.

Table 2.16 Competitiveness rating trends, management

	1994	1995	1996	1997
Czech Republic	42	42	39	42
Hungary	43	43	38	40
Poland	44	40	37	44
Austria	10	10	17	21
Germany	17	17	20	25
Ireland	22	24	21	12
Portugal	36	34	41	43

Source: As Table 2.8.

Results are also poor in indicators of the level of science and technology, measured by 17 criteria. These are shown in Table 2.15. All the CEECs score very poorly on financial resources. Hungary does better than the others thanks to what is considered to be a high level of science education and of qualified engineers. In the case of the Czech Republic and Poland there has been a further deterioration. This is very dangerous for the future long-term economic growth in these countries, because science research and technological development are potentially an important driving force for long-term productivity and economic growth and for strengthening competitiveness. It is fully consistent with other contributions which point to CEEC enterprises being forced by their weaknesses in modern technology to compete in less lucrative lower-tech branches and products.

Perhaps the only consistently clearer weakness across the CEECs is the quality of management shown in Table 2.16. This is measured by 25 criteria. These include such factors as customer orientation, the time needed to launch a new product, the level of social responsibility of managers, the sense of entrepreneurship and innovation, labour costs, the relations between management and employees, the number of industrial disputes, strategic orientation and quality control. The overall picture is one of deterioration, although that is also true of Portugal. The Czech Republic scores well only on the indicator for the number of industrial disputes. Poland scores well on entrepreneurship. Remarkably, all score well on remuneration for managers, but that is not matched by a positive view of 'competent senior managers'. Corporate performance appears as one of the most important bottlenecks for CEEC enterprise competitiveness. The next section therefore pursues this in more detail for the case of the Czech Republic, thereby pointing towards themes taken up in the concluding chapter on the areas in which policy interventions could be desirable.

CZECH MANAGEMENT STRATEGIES

Czech management performance has been influenced by three groups of constraints. The first stems from the heritage of central planning. This brought its specific working methods but, above all, meant that there was no need for many branches of sophisticated modern management practice, such as marketing and financial control. The past also brought ideas about labour discipline and the assumption that wages could be expected irrespective of the results of the enterprise. Elements of this have been continued both in people's minds and in post-1989 labour legislation. This heritage therefore meant that managements were confronted with the need to make very substantial, and possibly often courageous, changes to past practices.

The second group of constraints follows from the nature of the transformation process for the economy as a whole. The tight financial regime, at the same time as the loss of traditional eastern markets, meant that many enterprises were burdened with heavy debts at precisely the time when they should have been trying to restructure. It could therefore be seen as something of a success that most enterprises work, the market is supplied with basic products and services, exports have been reorientated to the West and social harmony has been maintained within enterprises while many have achieved substantial reorganisation and reduction in labour forces.

The third stems from the ability and experience of managers themselves. This could also be seen as a result of the past but, unlike the stock of physical assets built up over decades, it is an area in which changes could come relatively quickly and cheaply, given the right conditions. Managements need to see themselves facing a battle for survival, but a battle in which success could bring substantial rewards. There is still a tendency to retreat into the view that 'we are not in the war', meaning that it is impossible to compete at a world level but possible to survive with many practices largely unchanged. The extent and nature of the changes required mean that the environment in which they operate has a strong influence, from which it follows that government policies can play an important role.

Ultimately, however, the core of the problem is the need for a more active approach from enterprise managements and this is an area of very clear weakness. The point can be illustrated around the key task of the formulation and realisation of a corporate strategy. This is both a necessity for enterprise success and an activity the discussion of which can highlight other areas of weakness.

The first question is whether the enterprise has its own strategy at all, or not. Even seven years after the social and economic changes of 1989, many managements of significant Czech enterprises have not taken this step in any systematic way, using arguments along the lines of 'a strategy cannot be prepared due to lack of time', 'the time is so uncertain that it is impossible to prepare any strategy' or 'we have the strategy in our heads'.

Even the existence of a corporate strategy is, of course, no guarantee of its appropriateness or adequacy. A number of further questions arise as to how far it represents a genuine attempt at offensive behaviour, in the sense of actively trying to change the enterprise's situation, how far it embodies flexibility, and whether the aim is to achieve the best possible economic results and high-quality products. There are important questions over whether the strategy aims to penetrate new markets, is responsive to customer needs, is based on the latest scientific knowledge and, finally, whether it can be implemented within a reasonable time scale.

A strategy can be offensive in two directions, externally and internally. There have been some steps towards an externally offensive strategy from some Czech firms, but there have also been pressures in the opposite direction. The liquidation of commercial sections of embassies and the fragmentation of some former foreign trade companies probably made it harder for many Czech firms to take advantage of new possibilities abroad. Some, including the heavy engineering combine Škoda–Plzeň, the Škoda car manufacturer now majority owned by Volkswagen, the Prague engineering combine ČKD and the manufacturer of industrial ventilation equipment ZVVZ of Milevsko, are making a serious effort to expand into world markets. They have found new customers, for example in the Far East and Latin America, and have begun to win back markets in the former Soviet Union. This, then, is an area of improvement showing potential for overcoming the weaknesses of the past. At least the big firms that have survived from the past and have found markets for their traditional, or somewhat improved, products can look forward to a future.

The position is far less impressive for internally offensive behaviour. Managements have shown little enthusiasm for a systematic attack on costs, the introduction of new products, and measures to raise labour productivity. Where they perceive a labour shortage they have responded by recruiting rather than by looking for vigorous internal reorganisation to achieve better use of labour resources. There are objective causes for these weaknesses, as outlined above, but the initiative in making changes must eventually come from managements. So far, due partly to a lack of will and partly to an underestimation of the significance of this side of the transformation, they have not shown the courage to reorganise internal operations along the lines of a modern enterprise. They can survive with small adaptations to existing production programmes, but they cannot appear as serious competitors on the world stage.

An appropriate strategy, apart from being offensive, must be based on a thorough understanding of the factors likely to influence the company's position and that can only be derived from a systematic study of worldwide trends in technology and markets. This is rare. The closure of research and development activities in many enterprises, although they were not particularly effective even before 1989, is both a reflection of the underestimation of the need for a systematically forward looking approach and a factor that makes its development in the future more difficult. Thus Czech enterprises were weak in modern computer-controlled design and manufacturing methods before 1989 and have in many cases reduced their ability to make up the gap. There are some exceptions. Some firms have come together to create their own common research institutes. These could be examples for other forward-looking companies to follow, but do not as yet represent the general situation.

As a result of this and other weaknesses, managements are left with very little genuinely deep knowledge of trends in technology or market demand and often formulate forecasts as little more than extrapolations of past trends. An inevitable result is also a frequent failure to allow flexibility into the strategy in the form of possible alternative scenarios. Such rigidity must carry further risks, as any definite prediction of future development is almost impossible, no matter how impressive the methodology used.

This links back to the weaknesses in internal restructuring. The formulation and presentation of a flexible strategy in several compatible variants can itself be part of the process of preparing employees for the realities of the modern world economy. They too need to be flexible and adaptable, and that is easier to accept if there is a more general awareness of the complexities and unpredictabilities of the company's position.

Such a change in orientation ultimately depends on actions of managements, but that does not mean that a government can wash its hands of all responsibility. Improvements in management practice can be encouraged by a range of supportive measures. The financial constraints, imposed partly by the nature of the transformation process, are themselves extremely important, as discussed in Chapter 4. Enterprises have been hampered, among other factors, by a weak pro-export policy of the state, by the unsatisfactory state of the banking system, by an unequal position towards foreign firms, by the poor functioning of the courts and by low labour discipline which partly reflects the low rate of unemployment. They could also be helped more directly by measures that support the formulation of an appropriate strategy and the development of appropriate technology.

Depending on how managements react, and on how far governments take steps to create a favourable environment for their restructuring, it is possible to visualise two extreme scenarios. In the first, the Czech economy will achieve rapid economic growth and achieve a harmonious integration into the EU as an advanced country. Under the second, the failure of enterprise restructuring will leave the Czech Republic to the fate of a 'banana republic', a reservoir of cheap labour and a convenient location for ecologically undesirable production.

It is already clear that the second scenario, in undiluted form, is extremely unlikely. There already are some Czech firms, albeit particularly those under foreign ownership, that are capable of playing a role on the international stage. Nevertheless, in the absence of policies of government support, with the full liberalisation of imports, with continuing neglect of the domestic research base and with a failure to improve the functioning of the legal system, success may remain confined to a small number of larger enterprises. Smaller firms, and those without strong international links already, will find it very difficult to prosper in such a hostile environment.

A more supportive environment, possibly even including some temporary protective measures for Czech manufacturers, could bring better results. The key need is to help firms recreate a network of foreign representation, rebuild or build from scratch a strong research potential and help them acquire genuine expert knowledge on world trends and strategic options. With the right environmental preconditions, a significant body of firms could hope to compete at a high level within the EU.

An 'excessively' supportive environment, including general protection against imports and financial support to all enterprises, could be expected to bring negative results. The primary need is for managements to undergo a very substantial change in thinking and activities and a soft environment would do nothing to encourage that. The aim of government policies should be to create conditions in which that change is made possible, but also seen by managements as necessary.

CONCLUSION

The conclusion from this argument differs slightly from that of the European Commission in its *Agenda 2000* documents on the capacity of CEECs to withstand competitive pressure and market forces within the EU. It is generally optimistic about the countries' prospects and sees weaknesses largely in the failure to complete the transformation in the sense of privatisation and institution building. It does not emphasise the possible need for a stronger emphasis on policies specifically aimed at improving competitiveness and corporate performance.

Thus for the Czech Republic it is predicted that a continuation of past efforts at industrial restructuring, albeit with some reinforcement in the case of heavy industry, should ensure that there are no major problems of integration into the single market. For Slovakia there may be a need for more diversification away from its current heavy emphasis on heavy industry. Hungarian industry, following a somewhat more vigorous restructuring than that of other countries, is felt likely to face no serious problems. Poland is assumed to need substantial restructuring in largely state-owned heavy industries.

These assessments assume, but do not strongly emphasise, accompanying improvements in the education and research infrastructures. The stress, however, is on continuation of past policies. This chapter points towards a less confident conclusion. The CEECs face a very difficult task in overcoming their past weaknesses and that may require a substantially more active role for governments, oriented towards encouraging a more active approach from managements.

REFERENCES

EC (European Commission) (1994), *Growth, Competitiveness, Employment: The Challenges and Ways Forward Into the 21st Century*, White Paper.

EC (European Commission) (1997), *1997 Annual Economic Report, Growth, Employment and Convergence on the Road to EMU*, Brussels.

IMD (International Institute for Management Development) (1996), *The World Competitiveness Yearbook 1996*, Lausanne.

IMD (International Institute for Management Development) (1997), *The World Competitiveness Yearbook 1997*, Lausanne.

OECD (1995) *Competitiveness Policy: A New Agenda?*, Paris.

WEF (World Economic Forum) (1996a), *The Global Competitiveness Report 1996, Executive Summary*, Geneva.

WEF (World Economic Forum) (1996b), *World Link*, WEF, July / August.

WEF (World Economic Forum) (1997), *The Global Competitiveness Report 1997, Executive Summary*, Geneva.

WEF & IMD (1995), *The World Competitiveness Report 1995*, Geneva and Lausanne.

3. The Macroeconomics of Structural Transformation

Růžena Vintrová

Much of the discussion of macroeconomic issues relating to the accession of countries of east-central Europe to the European Union has been based on the implicit assumption that they can be judged by the same criteria as the advanced countries of western Europe. Analyses of the process of convergence frequently follow the Maastricht criteria, focusing on fiscal and monetary aspects, while key characteristics of the real economy tend to be ignored. The Maastricht criteria were set as conditions for involvement in the European Monetary Union and relate to countries which are already at similar economic levels. They pose great difficulties for the less developed EU countries, where their mechanical application could have even less fortunate consequences. The central argument here is that the order of priority for standard objectives of economic policy – economic growth and employment, the inflation rate, balancing external payments and the state budget – need not be the same for a country during transformation as for the long-established market economies of western Europe. Indeed, rigid application of the same criteria may threaten the prospects for economic growth and for macroeconomic stability itself.

Moreover, evaluations of development in the CEECs often assume away initial differences in economic level, labour productivity, unit labour costs, as well as comparative price levels. These macroeconomic characteristics showed wide divergences from the start with important implications for economic policy, particularly in the priority order of economic objectives, even among five central European countries that started at fairly similar levels of development. The risks that can follow from ignoring these differences between individual countries, and between them and the most advanced countries of western Europe, should be clear from the example of eastern Germany: large-scale industry collapsed with re-unification, destroyed by west German competition before it could adapt to new conditions, leading to high unemployment and an enormous financial burden for the western part of the country.

Table 3.1 Macroeconomic indicators of the CEEC-5 in the transformation period

	Czech Republic	Hungary	Poland	Slovakia	Slo-venia
GDP (real, in %)					
Index 1996/90	97.5	89.1	117.4	92.2	112.8
Rate of growth average 1991–6	−0.4	−1.9	2.7	−1.3	3.3
Rate of growth 1996	3.9	1.3	6.1	6.6	3.1
Rate of growth 1997	1.0	4.4	6.9	6.5	3.8
Rate of inflation					
1993–6 annual average	12.2	23.3	28.8	13.1	18.6
1997	8.5	18.3	14.9	6.1	8.4
Rate of unemployment					
1993–6 annual average	3.6	9.6	13.4	12.3	7.9
1997	4.7	8.1	11.2	11.6	7.0
Investment to GDP ratio					
1993–6 annual average	30.0	19.5	16.4	30.3	20.0
1997	30.7	22.4	21.2	38.6	
National savings rate					
1995	30.2	18.3	22.5	30.6	23.1
1996	27.9	23.1	19.2	28.2	23.4
Balance of current account					
% of GDP 1995	−2.7	−5.6	4.5	2.2	−0.1
1996	−7.6	−3.7	−1.0	−10.2	0.2
$ bn 1995	−1.4	−2.5	5.5	0.4	−0.0
1996	−4.3	−1.7	−1.4	−1.9	0.0
Foreign debt					
$ bn 1996	20.4	27.6	40.6	7.8	4.0
% of GDP	37.2	66.7	32.2	43.3	22.2
% of exports	69.6	170.7	129.6	74.6	40.8
Imports/aggregate supply					
1996	37.7	28.7	21.6	41.2	35.6

Notes: GDP figures for Slovenia show the four-year results for 1993-1996. Inflation is measured by the average annual change in the consumer price index. Unemployment figures are percentages, following the ILO methodology. Investment ratios show gross fixed capital formation as a percentage of GDP. Savings rates show gross national savings as a percentage of GDP. Current account balances are measured as percentages of GDP. Aggregate supply shows GDP plus imports.
Source: *Statistical Bulletin CESTAT*, 1997, 1998 and author's calculations.

This chapter therefore compares the principal macroeconomic characteristics of the Czech Republic, Hungary, Poland, Slovakia and Slovenia, the five central

European Five that make up the Central European Free Trade Area (CEFTA) with the exception of the late joiner Romania. They will be referred to below as the CEEC-5.

Their macroeconomic performance is shown in broad outline in Table 3.1. By the end of 1996 GDP had passed its 1990 level only in Poland, but there was some tendency across the group for an acceleration in growth rates. There was also a general trend towards a reduction in inflation levels. All were still high by western European standards, albeit with the Slovak figure closest to what might be considered acceptable elsewhere. Unemployment levels were lowest in the Czech Republic, but none have been outside the ranges experienced in recent years in parts of western Europe. The investment and savings ratios show re-markably large divergences: these have often been misinterpreted and are there-fore discussed in some detail both in this chapter and in Chapter 5. The indicators of the countries' external positions point to a tendency towards deficits which are very pronounced in some of the countries. Foreign debt also remains high in Poland and Hungary. The final row confirms the variations in the degree of de-pendence on foreign trade, with Poland, as indicated in Chapter 1, much more self-sufficient than the others.

An analysis of these macroeconomic factors can be deepened by a comparison with the existing European Union members, referred to as the EU-15, thanks to the harmonisation of statistical methodology with EU countries and to the European Comparison Programmes, referred to as ECP. These are prepared by the OECD and Eurostat, the EU's statistical agency, every three years with the latest one for which full results were available in 1998 relating to 1993 (UN, 1997). Comparisons of GDPs and other macroeconomic indicators by current exchange rates give misleading results which partly reflect widely varying price levels. These studies therefore use purchasing power parities (PPPs), calculated for a representative basket of goods and services.

With their help, it is possible to be more precise about the risks, such as un-desirable price shocks, that may be expected with accession to the EU. The con-clusion is that harmonisation of familiar macroeconomic indicators cannot be separated from harmonisation of real economic levels and therefore should not be seen as a rapid process that will follow the same course in every country.

INFLATION, RESTRUCTURING AND GROWTH

In the long run rapid economic growth based on economic restructuring and a low rate of inflation are two interlinked economic goals that can be assumed to be in harmony: low inflation has a beneficial effect on the stability of economic growth. In the short- and medium-term, however, an excessively fierce disinflation may be very costly in its impact on economic growth. Thus the relationship between these two goals may vary at stages of a country's development.

There is therefore no easy answer to the question of the optimal combination of the rate of economic growth and the extent of disinflation in transition countries. A policy of minimum inflation, such as the one supported by the economically most developed countries of the world, does not match the needs of the CEEC-5: it could stifle the necessary restructuring of production and lead only to economic stagnation. A better model and inspiration would seem to be the experience of rapidly-growing, 'young' market economies which have developed their own targets for suppressing inflation while maintaining rapid economic growth. Even that, particularly in view of more recent problems in the Far East, cannot be taken as a precise model.

The experiences of countries that once found themselves in similar conditions to those of today's Central European transition economies are discussed in the IMF's empirical analysis *The Rise and Fall of Inflation* (IMF, 1996) which recaps the experience of more than a hundred countries over the last 30 years. It clearly shows that countries with a high inflation rate recorded substantially lower, and sometimes even negative growth, while countries with a low inflation rate enjoyed a much more favourable growth performance.

This conclusion holds not only for hyperinflation but also for per annum inflation rates substantially above the 10 per cent range. Below that level, however, the relationship is much less clear. Various wage and price rigidities become important particularly at low, single-digit inflation rates and these greatly increase the costs of disinflation. Thus the low downward elasticity of nominal wages means that adjustments in wage relationships can be made relatively easily under conditions of mild inflation. The necessary growth rate in nominal wages can be estimated at 2–3 per cent a year for developed market economies, but it could be much higher in the case of rapidly developing or changing economies.

The IMF's analysis also showed that the costs of disinflation, in terms of the loss of economic growth, differ substantially for different inflation levels and between countries at different levels of economic maturity. For young, rapidly-developing economies, the ceiling of disproportionately high costs of disinflation seems to be higher than that for developed economies. Over the 30-year period under investigation, a number of developing market economies managed to maintain high economic growth rates between 5 per cent and 10 per cent over a long period alongside a high single-digit rate of inflation, also between 5 per cent and 10 per cent a year. These, however, were countries that started their development from a lower level than the CEEC-5. This, in line with the notion of convergence, created conditions for more rapid economic growth during the period when the economies were benefiting from integration into the global economy.

Among the CEEC-5 countries, the lowest rate of inflation is recorded in Slovakia and the Czech Republic. As Table 3.1 indicates, three countries in this group have single-digit inflation, namely the Czech Republic, the Slovak Republic and Slovenia, but these levels are still high by the standards of advanced market economies. The 1997 average inflation rates in Slovakia, the Czech Republic and Slovenia, measured by consumer prices, were 6.1 per cent, 8.5 per cent and 8.9 per cent, respectively. In Poland and Hungary they were still in the region of 15 to 18 per cent. In view of the price and wage rigidities outlined above, reducing single digit inflation further is much more difficult than reducing inflation down from the original two-digit level.

In the Czech Republic, the growth of consumer prices peaked in 1991 at 57 per cent and again at 21 per cent after a tax reform introducing VAT in 1993. There are, however, powerful influences blocking a further reduction to much below 10 per cent. The rate of inflation measured by a consumer price index decreased from 9.1 per cent in 1995 to 8.8 per cent in 1996 and 8.5 per cent in 1997. That based on producer prices in industry has fallen by much more, from 7.6 per cent to 4.8 per cent. The currency depreciation together with an increase in the prices still controlled by the government, accounting for about 20 per cent of personal expenditure, halted a downward trend in inflation which had been strong in the first half of 1997.

Further moves towards full price deregulation in housing and a spontaneous adjustment of price relations of non-tradables to the level of tradables prices, which are now closer to foreign prices, will keep the inflation rate above the western European level for some time. The influence of rising imports in the total supply of goods and services declined somewhat in 1997, but is a continual source for the transfer of higher foreign price levels into domestic inflation. Its effect has been exhausted to a large extent by the convergence of domestic and foreign prices of tradables, but is still being transferred into the sector of non-tradables.

This puts into perspective arguments for placing priority on further reductions in the inflation rate. This has been a topical issue in the Czech Republic following an OECD criticism that a target of reducing the rate of inflation by one percentage point a year indicates a serious lack of ambition. Such a reduction could be achieved but, unless deregulation of controlled prices is stopped completely, the costs in terms of economic growth could be very substantial.

The point can be generalised to question whether the Maastricht criteria, which lay down the permissible rate of inflation on the basis of results achieved in the three most successful countries of western Europe, are acceptable for associated transition countries in the near future. As indicated in the preceding two chapters, the structural transformation of CEECs is still at an early stage and must be sufficiently deep to overcome the technological gap inherited from the period of central planning. The key point is to avoid high costs of disinflation which could hamper the restructuring of production and leave the economies unable to reduce the substantial lag behind the western European level. The extent and nature of this, in terms of a number of accessible macroeconomic variables, is discussed in the next section.

ECONOMIC LEVEL AND LABOUR PRODUCTIVITY

In 1996 the economic level of CEEC-5, as measured by per capita GDP and compared by purchasing power parity based on the 1993 comparisons, ranged from 32 per cent of the EU average for Poland to 59 per cent for the Czech Republic and Slovenia. The scatter is very substantial, with the span from the lowest to the highest amounting to 27 percentage points. Thus there is more scope for a catching-up effect in Poland than in the Czech Republic or Slovenia. This may partially explain the rather fast growth rates in Poland, as indicated in Table 3.1, which are associated with double the rate of inflation experienced in the Czech Republic. This could be taken as a direct indication that the priorities for economic policy differ with the different economic levels, with a greater emphasis in the Czech Republic, for instance, on anti-inflation policy, even at the expense of economic growth.

The first results from the European Comparison Project 1996 show a generally higher level of per capita GDP for CEECs. The main reason is a different method of calculation for non-market services. The results put Slovenia at 67 per cent of the EU average, followed by the Czech Republic at 64 per cent, Hungary at 47 per cent, Slovakia at 45 per cent and Poland at 35 per cent (Eurostat, 1998). Neither the newer nor the former method need be considered clearly superior. The general conclusions remain valid: there is a substantial gap between CEECs and the average EU level and a wide range of variation in levels across CEECs. The following discussion uses the 1993 comparisons as its base.

A comparison can be made of aggregate labour productivity levels using GDP per employed person as a proxy for productivity, and converting GDP from a national currency by PPP, so as to approximate comparable price levels. In transition countries exchange rates are grossly misleading owing to undervalued and widely fluctuating currencies. The resulting differences between the CEEC-5 and the EU are even bigger than those in economic level, because the transition countries still have, as a rule, a higher rate of participation and different population structures. The relative positions of CEECs are shown in Table 3.2, although using a methodology that cannot be compared directly with EU statistics.

Table 3.2 Participation rate in the CEEC-5, 1994–6

Year	Czech Republic	Hungary	Poland	Slovakia	Slovenia
1994	63.3	57.1	60.2	61.7	57.6
1995	62.8	56.1	58.8	61.6	58.7
1996	62.6	55.6	58.2	61.4	57.6

Note: Figures follow the ILO methodology showing total labour forces as a percentage of total populations aged 15 years and over, in Hungary 14 years and over.
Source: Statistical Bulletin CESTAT, 1996, No.4.

The divergence between labour productivity and economic level is greatest in the case of the Czech Republic: its rate of participation is the highest while its rate of unemployment is exceptionally low. As Table 3.3 indicates, its GDP per occupied person is 14 percentage points below its GDP per capita level, at 45 per cent of the average for EU in 1996. The gap is explained by a rate of participation that was 72 per cent against 65.5 per cent in EU, using the OECD's methodology, a rate of unemployment that stood at only 3.4 per cent against 10.9 per cent in EU and a high proportion of the population in the working age range.

There is a reservation here as GDP per occupied person is more difficult to calculate than GDP per capita. The figures reported by the individual countries on the total number of workers, including the self-employed, are not fully comparable. Nevertheless, calculations carried out by the Vienna Institute for Comparative Economic Studies pointed to similar tendencies. The Institute compared GDP per occupied person in the CEEC-5 to Austria, using information from ECP 93.

The results confirmed that labour productivity generally lagged further behind developed countries than did the economic level. At the same time, however, differences in GDP per occupied person are smaller than those in GDP per capita among the countries of the CEEC-5. When compared to Austria, the calculations by the Vienna Institute showed the 1993 relative GDP per occupied person ranging from 28 per cent of the EU level in Poland, through 40 per cent in the Czech Republic to 50 per cent in Slovenia (Havlik, 1997a). The interval between the lowest and highest levels of the CEEC-5 was thus 22 percentage points, smaller by 5 percentage points than that for GDP per capita. Fassmann (1997) came to similar conclusions, when comparing GDP per occupied person in 1995 to that in Germany, with figures of 27 per cent for Poland, 32 per cent for Hungary, and 38 per cent for the Czech Republic.

Table 3.3 Economic level, labour productivity and wages in the Czech Republic compared to the EU average

| | 1995 | | 1996 | |
	US dollars	EU=100	US dollars	EU=100
GDP per capita				
– by PPP	10724	57.6	11328	58.3
– by exchange rate	4954	21.7	5475	23.6
GDP per occupied person by PPP	21442	45.4	22255	45.5
Average annual compensation of employees	5345	15.5	6104	17.8
Average annual wage compared				
– by exchange rate	4050	14.7	4629	16.7
– by PPP	8793	38.5	9567	41.1
Unit labour costs	0.25	34.7	0.28	39.2

Note: Compensation figures include employers' contributions to social security, according to national accounts statistics. Unit labour costs are derived from row 4 divided by row 3.
Source: Calculations of the Economic Analytical Laboratory of the Czech Statistical Office on the basis of ECP-93, using extrapolations on the basis of GDP deflator differentials.

All of these comparisons of labour productivity use purchasing power parity. Although that is more appropriate than using current exchange rates, it does not fully reflect differences in the quality of products in the widest sense of the word. It does not allow for the competitive advantages derived from the latest innovations, after-sales and other service, modern marketing methods, well-known brand names or access to multinational sales networks, all of which are areas in which the transition countries lag behind. The prices received for exports of the same kind of products are therefore lower than is suggested from comparisons through PPP. In the Czech Republic this is made even worse by limited access to credits for exports of industrial equipment. The existence of these quality gaps means that physical productivity, and productivity measured from PPP, in transition economies is substantially higher than productivity measured from value added or current exchange rates. Neither can be taken as a completely adequate measure on its own, but the gap between the two demonstrates the extent to which improving competitiveness requires more than just the expansion of the real volume of output per occupied person.

The importance of different elements of competitiveness, and therefore also differences in labour productivity between the transition and EU countries, varies across sectors of the economy. Using percentage of white-collar employees as an indicator of the sophistication of production, Pick and Fassmann (1996) have shown an important relationship between sophistication and labour productivity and unit costs in different industries and branches of the Czech economy. The most favourable levels of labour productivity and unit labour costs, henceforth ULCs, occur in branches at the middle level of sophistication, such as metallurgy and heavy chemicals, where selling costs are minimal and product development easily accessible. It cannot compete in those at the lowest levels, such as standard textiles and footwear, due to much lower wage and other costs in countries of East Asia. It cannot compete in more sophisticated branches, or in the most modern and fashionable products even for those generally less-sophisticated branches, as its productivity, which should be understood to incorporate the non-price elements referred to above, is much lower and ULCs therefore substantially higher than in advanced economies.

A similar situation can be assumed to exist in the other countries of the CEEC-5. While some of the prerequisites exist for shifts from less to more sophisticated production, such as the strong industrial traditions and a reasonable education and skill level of the population, the 40-year isolation from world development constitutes a difficult gap to bridge. Moreover, development of the most sophisticated branches depends on an environment of much stronger support, including a substantially higher level of education, training and R&D activity. If anything, especially in the Czech Republic, the trend has been in the opposite direction, exemplified by the decline in vocational education that had been well-developed before. The extent to which the shift in the structure of production and exports has also been in the 'wrong' direction is discussed in detail in Chapter 1.

AVERAGE WAGES AND UNIT LABOUR COSTS

It has been widely assumed that low productivity in the CEEC-5 is more than compensated for by low wages. This conclusion, however, is heavily dependent on how the comparisons are made and need not be considered a permanent advantage. Average wages in the CEEC-5, converted by current exchange rates, certainly are only a fraction of wages in EU advanced economies. Low labour costs, accentuated by undervalued currencies, can therefore appear as the single most important comparative advantage of the CEEC-5. There is a more than tenfold difference between the lowest average wage in the CEEC-5 in Slovakia, and the highest in an EU country.

According to calculations made by the Vienna Institute for Comparative Economic Studies (Havlik, 1997a) the average monthly gross wage in 1996 amounted to only ECU 210 in Slovakia, ECU 250–280 in the Czech Republic, Hungary and Poland, and to about ECU 760 in Slovenia. In Austria, France, western Germany and the Netherlands it was more than ECU 2000. Slovak wages in 1993, including indirect costs, were only 6.6 per cent of the Austrian level. For the Czech Republic the figure was 7.5 per cent, while for Poland, Hungary and Slovenia the figures were 8.4 per cent, 10.8 per cent and 20.6 per cent respectively. Since 1993 trends in real wages have diverged, with growth of 27 per cent in the Czech Republic from 1993 to 1996, against a decrease in Hungary of 8.5 per cent over the same period, following the austerity measures of March 1995. This, however, still left the substantial gap in relation to the advanced countries of the EU and did not alter the ordering of wage levels among the CEEC-5. Czech wages moved a little closer to the Hungarian level, moving slightly ahead in 1997.

Unit labour costs (ULCs), defined as a ratio of wage costs to labour productivity, are also lower in the CEECs than in EU countries. The most appropriate methodology for the international comparison of unit labour costs uses the calculation of nominal wages by means of the exchange rate and GDP per occupied person by means of PPP (Oulton, 1994, and Havlik, 1997a). The results show the gap in ULCs to be slightly greater than the gap in price levels.

Comparisons of unit labour costs carried out by different institutions are more or less in agreement as far as relations between different countries of the CEEC-5 are concerned, although the precise figures for ULCs do differ between the studies. That by Havlik mentioned above used Austria for the comparisons, for which the ULC level is lower than that of western Germany, Sweden and Denmark, but above the average for the EU as a whole. Havlik reports that average PPP-based ULCs even in high-wage Slovenia were only about 70 per cent of the Austrian level in 1996, or 50 per cent when indirect wage costs are included.

Poland followed after a large gap with figures of 40 per cent and 35 per cent respectively. Next came Hungary on 33 per cent and 27 per cent, the Czech Republic on 31 per cent and 26 per cent and Slovakia on 24 per cent and 20 per cent.

A study by Fassmann (1997) makes comparisons with western Germany, which is the part of the EU with the highest ULCs, apart from those in eastern Germany. The author compares wages, including indirect labour costs, to 100 units of PPP based GDP measured in Deutschmarks. The resulting unit labour costs in 1995 stood at 18.8 in the Czech Republic, 20.1 in Poland and 23.3 in Hungary, while the ULCs for western Germany were 58.6. This comparison suggests that, in relation to the lands of western Germany, the ULC levels in the Czech Republic, Poland and Hungary were 32 per cent, 34.3 per cent and 40 per cent, respectively. This implies that, in relation to Austria, ULCs stood at 38 per cent for the Czech Republic, 41 per cent for Poland and 48 per cent for Hungary. These results differ significantly from those obtained from Havlik's study.

Fassmann is showing ULCs higher by 5 percentage points for Poland, by 12 percentage points for the Czech Republic and by 21 percentage points for Hungary. This also changes the order of the countries. Both studies show the Czech Republic to have the lowest ULCs of the three countries compared. The second lowest ULCs according to Fassmann are in Poland while, according to Havlik, they are in Hungary. Fassmann does not have figures for Slovakia or Slovenia, the two countries that had the lowest and highest figures in Havlik's study.

There are some obvious possible explanations for these differences. The calculation of the relationship between labour productivity, measured by PPP in that year, and the indicator of compensation of employees per occupied person is heavily dependent on the choice of year. Havlik uses 1993 PPP, whereas Fassmann uses 1995 PPP. Due to the large differences in inflation levels in CEEC-5, ULCs will take a higher value if prices from the latter year are used. Indirect wage costs also pose a problem. For example, charges on employers per employee, such as employers' contributions to social security, take somewhat different forms across different countries. It is not certain, however, whether they are included in the same way in indirect costs across all countries.

Although both studies show ULCs substantially below the western European level, the differences in the results are potentially quite important, for reasons explained below. A study by the Czech Statistical Office's Economic Analytical Laboratory, covering only the Czech Republic, gives a result much closer to Fassmann's. It uses figures for national accounts harmonised to the methodology used in EU. This makes possible a calculation of total labour costs per occupied person, including the self-employed, measured as the ratio of earnings per occupied person, exchange rate adjusted, to GDP per occupied person, PPP adjusted. In 1996 earnings per occupied person reached 17.8 per cent of the EU average while GDP per occupied person was 45 per cent, meaning that ULCs in the Czech Republic were equivalent to 39 per cent of the EU average. The striking conclusion is that the labour productivity lag is little different from the wages lag, when both are measured in real terms. This differs from the usual situation in less advanced countries, where the purchasing power of wages typically lags further behind than labour productivity. Using the new ECP-96 figures would show a GDP per occupied person of 55 per cent and ULCs of 33 per cent of the EU-15 level in 1996, but the overall trend would still be in the same direction.

In this sense, the Czech Republic is either exhausting, or has already exhausted, its 'wage cushion'. It appears to have flattened off as growth rates in labour productivity have fallen well behind those of average wages. Indeed, following the dramatic drop of unit labour costs in 1990 and 1991, they grew by about 30 per cent a year in the 1992–1993 period and by 12–17 per cent a year in the 1994–1996 period, using Havlik's calculations with wages converted into ECU by the exchange rate and labour productivity compared by PPPs. In other transition countries – Poland, Hungary and Slovakia – internationally comparable ULCs exhibited much slower growth.

Many foreign experts have concentrated on the faster growth in Czech wages and unit labour costs than in other transition economies of Central Europe. Although this might seem to point to a rapid weakening in the competitiveness of the Czech Republic, it cannot seriously be argued that the country has excessive wage levels when unit labour costs are not even 40 per cent of those of EU countries. That might even understate the level as that method of international comparison assumes away differences in the quality of products and services which, as mentioned earlier, are not fully reflected in the choice of comparable baskets of goods and services used to derive the PPP of a currency. Even though the annual rate of growth in wages in the Czech Republic has recently been around 18 per cent in nominal terms, or between 8 per cent and 9 per cent in real terms, according to consumer price index, Czech wages converted by the exchange rate remain slightly below one eighth the level of the most developed countries of the EU.

Thus when set against the different starting conditions, with initially much lower ULCs in the Czech Republic than in other transition countries, this should rather be seen as a process of catching up, unavoidable in the period of the preparation for full membership in the EU. Moreover, concentration on the appearance of high wages makes little sense for a long-term perspective. In the long run, the Czech Republic cannot survive as a low-wage economy, in view of potential competition from countries with even lower labour costs further to the East. The really remarkable point is that wages rank second lowest, ahead only of Slovakia, among the CEEC-5.

Three conclusions follow from this. The first is that wage and labour costs vary considerably across the CEEC-5, depending on past histories. The second is that in all cases they are below the EU level, but in no case so far below as to give an advantage in the simplest production processes over the very low wage countries of Asia or even the former Soviet Union. The third conclusion is that results vary depending on how international comparisons are made, but results suggesting the exhaustion of the 'wage cushion' should be taken as indicative of the limited scope for low wages to compensate for low productivity: that is a possibility increasingly limited to a narrow range of products.

This should therefore be interpreted as a firm warning that economic growth is becoming increasingly dependent on raising the level of productivity, understood in the broadest sense to include all indicators of product quality, rather than on restrictions on wage levels. In the short term, the restoration or maintenance of external balance in the economy of transition countries may be helped by wage restraint, but only as a means to restrict demand. In the longer-run it is hardly realistic to hope to keep real wages so far behind the levels achieved in neighbouring countries.

COMPARATIVE PRICE LEVELS

A very similar message emerges from a study of comparative price levels. As with the levels of unit labour costs, initial price levels were generally much lower in the CEEC-5 than in EU countries. At the same time, however, they differ very much from one central European country to another. Comparisons have become possible thanks to the European Comparison Programme of 1993.

Comparative price levels are defined as ratios of purchasing power parities to the exchange rate, using costs of an internationally comparable basket of goods and services at national currencies in the countries under comparison. They are calculated by means of the Fisher index, meaning the geometric average of weights of the individual expenditure groups in the respective country and the country of comparison. The reciprocal value is referred to as the Exchange Rate Deviation Index, or ERDI.

Multilateral comparisons, which were linked to other both European and non-European countries, were published by the OECD in preliminary form in February 1996 and in an official publication at the end of 1996 (OECD, 1996a and b). Their results could be used to derive, in appropriate form via the Austrian PPP in relation to the average of OECD and EU countries, ratios of PPPs of the currencies of individual CEECs to the average for the EU and to the USA. Using a differential of GDP deflator related to the USA and the EU, the 1993 PPP data could be extrapolated to 1996 and compared with the trend of the average annual exchange rates of CEECs which are published on a routine basis. This leads to the price level relations, or ERDI coefficients which are reciprocal values of the comparative price levels shown in Table 3.4.

The results recorded in Table 3.4 show Slovakia and the Czech Republic with the lowest price levels of the CEEC-5, reaching only 36 per cent and 38 per cent respectively of the EU average price level. Poland, with its 46 per cent, is somewhere in the middle. The highest price levels are revealed for Hungary and Slovenia, at 53 per cent and 74 per cent respectively. Thus the difference between the countries with the lowest and highest price levels is very substantial. Calculations based on ECP-96 narrow the range to some extent, with Slovakia on 34 per cent, the Czech Republic on 37 per cent, Hungary on 41 per cent, Poland on 43 per cent and Slovenia on 60 per cent of the EU average.

Hungary and Slovenia diverged less from the EU countries even in the pre-transformation period, as closer trade contacts with western Europe caused a tendency towards price convergence in tradables. The risk of a price shock in these countries as they join the EU is therefore much smaller than with the Czech and Slovak Republics. This points to the need for substantially different economic policies during the process of preparing for full membership in the EU.

Table 3.4 Price levels in CEEC-5 compared to EU average and the USA in 1996

	Czech Republic	Hungary	Poland	Slovakia	Slovenia
EU=100	40.5	53.0	48.6	37.1	70.5
USA=100	48.3	63.2	57.9	44.2	84.1

Source: author's calculations on the basis of ECP-93, extrapolated by GDP deflator differentials and nominal exchange rate changes.

The starting conditions rather than subsequent exchange rate policies are the most important factor in explaining differences between countries. Thus the relative positions of the Czech Republic and Slovakia in terms of comparative price levels remain remarkably stable. The rate of real appreciation of the Czech and Slovak currencies, even with the stable nominal exchange rate, have been no higher than in other countries from the start of the transformation period. The Czech Republic and Slovakia enjoyed substantially lower rates of inflation while in Poland and Hungary vigorous currency devaluations were compensated by high inflation differentials.

The most rapid appreciation of the real exchange rate was a figure of 9–10 per cent per year achieved in Poland and Slovenia in the early 1990s. The appreciation was also rapid in Hungary, with an annual average figure of 7.4 per cent over the 1991 to 1994 period. It subsequently decelerated due to the Hungarian austerity package aimed at reducing the trade deficit. Over the whole 1991–5 period it reached an average level of 6.5 per cent. The Czech Republic maintained a fixed exchange rate in the 1991–5 period, while Slovakia implemented a single 10 per cent devaluation in July 1993. This stability contributed to the lowest real exchange rate appreciation among CEECs, at around 5 per cent over the same period. Nevertheless, even in these two countries there have been serious problems with the current account balance.

In 1994 Hungary experienced the lowest ERDI of all the CEEC-5 countries. Its figure of 1.4, based on the US dollar, was the same as that of Portugal at the time. However, this relatively hard exchange rate policy caused very serious difficulties in the balance of payments, and a further real appreciation of the Hungarian Forint was brought to an end in 1995. The forint was devalued in March 1995 by 9 per cent with further monthly devaluations of 1.9 per cent until June and then of 1.3 per cent over following months. Overall, the rate of devaluation increased from 15.6 per cent in 1994 to 27 per cent in 1995, falling back to 18.5 per cent in 1996. Real wages decreased by 12.6 per cent in 1995, after their 7 per cent increase the year before, and continued falling by 2.6 per cent in 1996. The austerity package of March 1995 included severe enough measures to cause a depreciation by 5 per cent in 1995. In the following year, however, the Forint resumed its appreciation, when the real exchange rate rose 3.6 per cent using the PPI, the Producers' Price Index in manufacturing.

Thus even the continual devaluation of the nominal exchange rate was not enough to compensate for the inflation differential which was itself stimulated by devaluation. Calculations by the Hungarian organisation the Kopindatorg Foundation for Economic Research show that the rate of inflation measured by PPI in manufacturing grew from 12.8 per cent in 1994 to 26.1 per cent in 1995 – a 13.3 percentage points increase – while the rate of devaluation grew by 11.4 percentage points only. When measured by consumer prices, the inflation rate increased from 18.8 per cent to 28.2 per cent, almost as clearly cancelling out the effects of devaluation. Thus any pro-export and anti-import effects of the devaluation were swallowed up in a few months by an increase in inflation, which was well above that in the country's main trading partners. The main impact of the March 1995 policy package should therefore be seen as the dramatic decrease in real wages and the deceleration in economic growth, down from 2.9 per cent in 1994 to 1.5 per cent in 1995 and 1.3 per cent in 1996. Thanks to the depression of domestic demand, the country managed to reduce the trade balance deficit from $ 3.6 billion in 1994 to $ 2.5 billion in 1995 and to $ 1.7 billion in 1996. The resulting current account balances are referred to in Table 3.1 and discussed in a different context in Chapter 1.

This Hungarian experience is important in demonstrating how rapidly devaluation can lead to an acceleration of inflation in transition countries. The clear message is that devaluation can only be a short-term solution to a balance of payments current account deficit. The long-term solution depends on raising the level of competitiveness by the production of higher quality products. At the same time, the Hungarian attempts at maintaining a hard exchange rate proved untenable. Although the extent of undervaluation of the PPP-related exchange rate has differed across the countries of east-central Europe, the core of the problem is the same in all cases: the aim for the future is to achieve a gradual real appreciation of currencies, but this has to be based on more rapid labour productivity growth.

There is a danger that accession to the EU may be accompanied by rapid adjustments in CEEC-5 price levels, culminating in a repeat of the east German experience. It would clearly be preferable to ensure a gradual convergence of price levels accompanied by some convergence in real productivity levels. Portugal's experience indicates the kind of time scale that might be appropriate. The annual real appreciation of the Portuguese Escudo against the ECU was 4.5 per cent over the 1988–95 period. The ERDI in relation to the US dollar fell from about 2.6 in 1985 to 1.4 in 1994 and 1.2 in 1995. For comparison, the dollar-based ERDI coefficient in the former Czechoslovakia was 2.8 in 1990 and decreased to 2.1 in 1996 for the Czech Republic. Portugal's experience suggests that reducing the ERDI coefficient to a more 'normal' value of about 1.5 in a mid-developed country may require decades.

This, however, should not be seen as a simple process with uniform consequences across the whole economy. Both the process of price level convergence and its effects are somewhat complicated by divergences in the extent to which prices of individual expenditure items of GDP differ from foreign prices. Table 3.5 shows the position. According to the European Comparison Programme of 1993, price relations of capital goods were higher in all transition countries than price relations of the other components of GDP.

Thus the price levels of gross fixed capital formation in machinery and equipment ranged between 81 per cent of the Austrian level in the Czech Republic and 139 per cent in Hungary. There were also particularly low relative prices of non-tradable goods and services. The biggest price disparities are in the area of housing, with Czech prices one tenth the Austrian level when compared by the current exchange rates. Thus the deviation of the GDP price level, indicated by the ERDI value of 3.3, represents an average of widely divergent positions for different products. The prices of plant and machinery for investment were approaching Austrian levels, with Table 3.5 indicating an ERDI of 1.2 for transport equipment and 1.1 for electrical machinery.

Table 3.5 PPP and ERDI of GDP expenditures in the Czech Republic in 1993 compared to Austria

	PPP	ERDI
GDP total	0.75	3.32
Individual consumption by households	0.67	3.76
of which		
food, beverages, tobacco	0.89	2.81
clothing and footwear	0.93	2.7
gross rents	0.25	10.1
household equipment and operation	0.98	2.54
personal transport equipment	2.05	1.22
Collective consumption by government	0.81	3.08
Gross fixed capital formation	1.05	2.38
of which		
construction	0.57	4.42
machinery and equipment	2.17	1.16
of which		
transport equipment	2.02	1.24
non-electrical machinery	2.32	1.08

Source: OECD, 1996a.

The higher relative prices of machinery for investment partly reflect the high level of imports of such products. Czech imports of engineering products – SITC Group 7 – which contain these capital goods, account for one third of total imports in 1996, as in Slovenia. In Slovakia and Hungary, imports of products classified in this Group account for a quarter, in Poland for one fifth. This comparatively high proportion of imports in domestic investment also affects the prices of domestically-produced machinery, which were already high relative to the prices of other goods before 1990. In fact, the price gap is much larger for construction investment, which is largely of domestic origin.

These differing price relations mean that the shares of individual expenditure components of GDP calculated in terms of domestic currency diverge substantially from those calculated in PPP. For instance, the rate of fixed investments in the Czech Republic, which at 33 per cent in 1996 was as high as in the Asian tiger economies, would be significantly lower if expressed in terms of the price relations of EU countries. The high savings rate, which is needed to provide sufficient resources for investment, is thus linked to high relative prices of machinery for investment. New technology is 'costly' for transition economies and currency devaluation makes it even more costly, meaning that the same real investment calls for a higher volume of savings.

Thus the ideal development of the exchange rate would avoid two extremes. Devaluation offers no long-term solution, but a sudden adoption of western European price levels would also bring serious dangers. The evidence for that is clear both from east German experience and from developments in Hungary where real appreciation of the currency was held in check. A gradual appreciation is the preferred option for the long term, but it must be accompanied by improvements in the level of productivity. Moreover, especially for those countries with the most undervalued currencies, revaluation brings the prospect of a relative cheapening of capital goods, which could significantly stimulate a faster structural transformation by reducing difficulties in the financing of investment discussed in the next section.

SAVINGS AND INVESTMENT

Investment in modernisation is a prerequisite for the structural transformation of production, but the levels of domestic saving have not matched the financial demands and this has been a major contributory factor behind the balance of payments difficulties across much of the CEEC-5. The usual relevant indicators are the investment ratio and the rate of gross domestic savings. The latter is calculated as the share of the difference between gross capital formation and the current account deficit in GDP. To be more exact, this difference should be related not to GDP but to gross disposable national income, but such an indicator is not published in national statistics. The current account deficit includes not only the balance of imports and exports of goods and services, but also the income balance and transfers from abroad. 'National' savings would therefore be a more exact term than 'domestic' savings in this case.

Both of these indicators show wide divergences across the individual countries of the CEEC-5. As Table 3.6 indicates, the Czech Republic and Slovakia have high rates of both investment and savings. Those levels have been maintained over significant periods among the Asian tiger economies, but in Europe they are extremely rare. Hungary, Poland and Slovenia have rates of investment and saving close to or under the EU average, which was about 20 per cent in the 1990s. Czech rates of both investment and saving fell in 1997, but were still well above the European average.

Table 3.6 Investment and savings ratios in the CEEC-5 as percentages of GDP

	Gross capital formation		Current account	Gross domestic savings
	fixed	total		
1995				
Czech Republic	32.8	34.0	−3.8	30.2
Hungary	20.0	23.9	−5.6	18.3
Poland	16.9	18.0	4.5	22.5
Slovakia	27.4	28.4	2.2	30.6
Slovenia	21.2	23.2	−0.1	23.1
1996				
Czech Republic	33.0	35.5	−7.6	27.9
Hungary	21.5	26.8	−3.7	23.1
Poland	19.0	20.2	−1.0	19.2
Slovakia	36.9	39.4	−11.2	28.2
Slovenia	22.3	23.2	0.2	23.4

Source: *Statistical Bulletin CESTAT*, 1997, No. 3, author's calculations.

The high rate of domestic saving in the Czech and Slovak Republics has generally been overlooked by foreign analysts, possibly because internationally comparable data are only now becoming available. The European Commission's *Agenda 2000* document somewhat misleadingly refers to the Czech Republic's 'very low domestic savings rate', contrasted with the rapid growth in wage and non-wage incomes: the country was assumed to exhibit 'the very high propensity to consume rather than to save' (EC, 1997, p.25).

The figures provided here point to the opposite conclusion. The Czech Republic has had an unusually high savings rate and a low propensity to consume. While this rate dropped somewhat in 1997, 27.8 per cent against 27.9 per cent in the previous year, it is still clearly above the European average. The error probably relates an over-emphasis on savings out of personal incomes and on the recent rapid growth of wages. It takes account neither of the wage level, nor of the share of wages in value added, both of which are low. Thus a high savings rate for the economy as a whole is consistent with a relatively low rate of savings out of earnings.

The position of the Czech Republic is clarified in Table 3.7, showing detailed data on the rate of investment and saving over the 1994–7 period prepared by the Economic Analytical Laboratory of the Czech Statistical Office. This used revised figures on national accounts and the central bank's revised balance of payments figures. These revisions, made in June and September 1997, including the removal of various anomalies in the calculation of changes in inventories, increased the savings figures considerably pointing, contrary to the EU claims, to record levels in international terms.

Table 3.7 also shows that the high rate of domestic savings in the 1994–5 period was enough to cover the high rate of investment without any large contribution by foreign savings. In 1996, however, the share of gross fixed capital formation in GDP climbed to 33.0 per cent: when the change in inventories is included, gross capital formation reached 35.5 per cent of GDP and this could not be financed by domestic savings alone. The result was a deficit of the balance of payments current account. Thus the problem could be seen as one of 'over-investment' by the Czech economy rather than a low rate of savings.

Table 3.7 Savings and investment in the Czech Republic 1994–7

	Gross capital formation	Gross fixed capital formation	Balance of current account	National savings	
				Kč billion	% of GDP
1994	30.1	29.6	–1.9	324.2	28.2
1995	34.0	32.8	–3.8	407.2	30.2
1996	35.5	33.0	–7.6	428.0	27.9
1997	33.9	30.7	–6.1	458.8	27.8

Note: Figures are percentages of GDP, unless otherwise stated.
Source: ČSÚ and OECD, 1997.

Nevertheless, the high rate of fixed investment is not reflected in rapid economic growth rates. This can be explained partly by the relative prices of investment to consumption goods, as discussed above. A further important reason is the high weight in total investment for infrastructural projects which yield no rapid returns. In 1995 these made up 46 per cent of total investment by the non-financial business sector, although during 1996 and 1997 their share dropped somewhat to 42 per cent and 41 per cent respectively. Within these figures are the construction of new motorways, the Ingolstadt oil pipeline system connecting Czech oil refineries to a west European supply network, a new gas pipeline system, railway corridors, the modernisation of telecommunications, and heavy investment in the energy industry in desulphurisation systems for coal-fired power stations plus the construction of the Temelín nuclear power station. By way of contrast, investment in manufacturing accounts for only a small part of the total from non-financial enterprises, with a share that grew slightly from 33 per cent in 1995 to 35 per cent in 1996, although in 1997 it fell back to 31 per cent.

The need for infrastructural investment is strongly emphasised by the EU, even though it brings no speedy returns. In this respect, the Czech Republic appears to have done well at following outside advice, as can be illustrated by the very high Incremental Capital Output Ratio which stood at 7–8 over the 1995–6 period, compared with a figure of about 3 for Poland. It is therefore not surprising that foreign savings are needed to cover the gap between investment and domestic savings to a greater extent in the Czech Republic than in Poland. This is one of the factors behind the variations in balance of payments current account deficits across the five countries. It is clearly not the only factor, as one of the highest deficits occurred in Hungary in 1994 at 9.4 per cent of GDP, but it was a major contributory factor in two other record figures of 7.6 per cent of GDP in the Czech Republic in 1996 and 11.2 per cent of GDP in the Slovak Republic in the same year.

Such big deficits cannot be maintained over a long time period without an impact on foreign exchange reserves and currency stability, leading Hungary to adopt the austerity package in March 1995. In 1997 the Czech Republic followed Hungary into currency problems associated with an excessive external imbalance and two government austerity packages were adopted in April and June 1997, directed at restoring external balance in the short-term by means primarily of fiscal restrictions. However, the degree to which a balance of payments deficit leads into a crisis itself depends to a significant extent on how the gap between domestic savings and investment has been covered.

The Czech economic difficulties of 1997 were partly linked to a previous inflow of short-term capital, reaching 16 per cent of GDP in 1995, which helped cover the current account deficit for a time. An outflow of this speculative capital in early 1997 pushed the Czech central bank into allowing the Kč to float. The danger of such a destabilising exodus of foreign capital is at its lowest with foreign direct investment which can also bring clear benefits of investment and modernisation in the domestic economy.

CONCLUSIONS

The macroeconomic analysis of the five Central European countries points to four broad conclusions. The first is that standard predictions of uninterrupted growth, permanently above the levels reached in the advanced western European countries, need not be confirmed in practice. The process of economic transformation is proving to be more difficult and more gradual than expected at the beginning of the 1990s, with a clear barrier emerging in the trade-off between growth and external balance.

The second is that the rates of growth in the individual countries, and their relationship to other macroeconomic variables, may differ substantially from each other. Thus the strength and relative weights of different causal factors behind the balance of payments constraint vary across the five countries. Both Czech and Hungarian experiences have demonstrated the vulnerability of even the most advanced transition economies. In the former case the structure of investment and relative price of investment goods, partly stemming from an exceptional undervaluation of the currency, were of greater importance. In both cases, however, drastic measures to suppress domestic demand inevitably hit investment and led to lower growth rates.

Even the more protectionist policies pursued in Poland and Slovakia have not prevented rising trade deficits, with the high price of investment goods contributing to a particularly serious situation in Slovakia. Poland has been much more successful at controlling imports, but the maintenance of the relatively high rates of economic growth there can also be partially explained by the fact that the country has the lowest economic level of the CEEC-5, leaving greater scope for a catching-up effect.

The third broad conclusion, following from the previous two, is that macroeconomic policy objectives should not be based on criteria set for countries with per capita GDPs two or three times higher than those in the CEEC-5. Nor should the same targets be set for all the countries of the group when rapid adjustments can themselves bring negative consequences. Nevertheless, the comparisons do make possible some generalisations on key indicators. In particular the inflation rates within the range experienced across the CEEC-5 do not seem to present a major barrier to growth, while attempts to suppress inflation rapidly could have negative consequences. It is reasonable to aim for a reduction as price levels harmonise with those of the EU and as rising productivity leads towards a harmonisation of economic levels. Similarly, changing exchange rates, in isolation from other measures, carry as many dangers as benefits. The effects of devaluation can rapidly be swallowed up by inflation while revaluation leads into risks of balance of payments difficulties.

The most general conclusion is that no single macroeconomic problem can be resolved in isolation from a number of others and, above all, that macro-economic performance cannot be improved substantially by measures aimed at macroeconomic indicators alone. The experiences of the CEEC-5 give no support to the notion that a stable macroeconomic environment can be created by adherence to a few simple policy rules and that it alone is enough to ensure economic growth. Harmonisation with the EU requires a gradual harmonisation of price levels accompanied by a progressive revaluation of the currency. This, however, depends on measures to increase personal savings, to encourage inward investment and, most important of all, to improve productivity across the economy. Thus the only long-term solution requires an improvement in competitiveness in more sophisticated branches of industry with greater growth potential which is in turn dependent on targeted support to further development of the educational level, training, innovation, science and research.

REFERENCES

ČSÚ (Český statistický úřad) and OECD (1997), *Národní účty 1993-1994 Zdroje, metody, výpočty,* Prague.

EC (European Commission) (1997), *Agenda 2000 – Commission Opinion on the Czech Republic's Application for Membership of the European Union,* Brussels.

Eurostat (1998), *Statistics in Focus. Economy and Finance,* No.28.

Fassmann, M. (1997), 'Mezinárodní srovnání úrovně mezd (nákladů práce) a produktivity práce s vyspělými evropskými zeměmi', (International Comparison of wage levels (labour costs) and labour productivity with advanced European countries), Pohledy, No.6.

Havlik, P. (1997a), 'Labour cost competitiveness of Central and Eastern Europe', in Wolfmayr-Schnitzer *et al., The Competitiveness of Transition Countries,* WIFO/WIIW study prepared for the OECD.

Havlik, P. (1997b), *Transition Countries Outlook Falters in 1997: Some Stumble and Recover, Some Have Problems Ahead.* Vienna Institute for Comparative Economic Studies Research Report, No. 239.

IMF (1996), *World Economic Outlook,* Washington, D.C.

OECD (1996a), *ECP results 1993,* Press Release, Paris.

OECD (1996b), *Purchasing Power Parities and Real Expenditures,* Volume II, Paris.

Oulton, N. (1994), 'Labour Productivity and Unit Labour Costs in Manufacturing: the UK and its competitors', *National Institute Economic Review*, May.

Pick, M. and M. Fassmann (1996), 'The social market economy in the industrial and post-industrial era – the social market economy in the CEEC and in the European Union', in *Economic Policy Framework in CEEC for the Process of Moving towards the European Union*, Prague: The Foundation for the Study of International Relations.

Statistical Bulletin CESTAT, 1996, 1997, 1998, Statistical Offices of the CEFTA countries.

UN (1997), United Nations Statistical Commission, *International Comparison of Gross Domestic Product in Europe 1993*, New York and Geneva.

4. Financing Enterprise Restructuring

Petr Chvojka

This chapter concentrates on the problem of financing restructuring in the Czech Republic, Poland and Hungary. This appears as one of the most important issues, but one that has been rather neglected amid a one-sided concentration on privatisation as the core policy measure for the micro-sphere. The central argument (cf. Chvojka, 1997), is that privatisation should not be viewed in isolation – either for analytical or for policy-making purposes – from a range of other measures. It is not synonymous with restructuring and neither does it lead automatically to the latter.

In fact, restructuring should be understood as a broad and complex process. The general restructuring of the former centrally-planned into market economies should be conceived as proceeding at two distinct levels – that of the national economy and that of the individual enterprise – and with two distinct aspects, the real and the financial one. Thus real restructuring at the level of the national economy incorporates the changing branch structure and the possible disappearance of some old, alongside the appearance of new, enterprises. Real restructuring at the enterprise level refers to the optimal utilisation of its resources around an appropriate strategy for meeting both domestic and external demand. These processes have a number of preconditions, including the development of modern management methods, the creation of new distribution and sales networks and, above all, investment in new technology and product development. Whether these take place and are successful depends on the abilities and motivation of management. It also depends on the availability of financial resources.

Financial restructuring refers to the shifting of financial resources between sectors and enterprises and to the possibility of finding the necessary financial resources at the enterprise level to enable the real restructuring to take place. Both the levels and aspects of restructuring should be in harmony if the process is to lead to sustainable growth and improved competitiveness. Both also depend on a number of identifiable elements in the macroeconomic and institutional environments. While some changes can be rapid, others, particularly those involving investment in new production processes, take substantially longer to achieve. The industrial legacy of the decades of the command economy cannot be overcome in only a few years. Moreover, an effective system of corporate governance and a stable institutional environment, including a satisfactorily functioning financial, legal and regulatory framework, also take a long time to develop.

The macroeconomic environment is important in creating favourable conditions for restructuring and there are broad similarities in the key macroeconomic reform steps which, despite some differences in ordering and timing, have led to fairly similar results across the three countries. Price and foreign trade liberalisation have been at the core of a process creating the preconditions for the emergence and growth of a new private sector, both competing with and complementing the state sector. The previously under-developed service sector, neglected for many years as a 'non-productive' activity, has expanded rapidly in all the countries concerned, while the share of agriculture has shown a similarly clearcut decline.

It is, however, clear that fully successful restructuring processes can be achieved only if the critical micro-level constraints are also given due attention (Asaf, 1995). Indeed, the limitations of the transformation process are most clearly visible from the changes in industry where restructuring in the Czech Republic, Hungary and Poland has embodied a shift towards the export of raw materials and semi-finished products. The pressures for restructuring have therefore not resulted in a process spread evenly across the whole economy.

This points to a striking feature of the transformation process in east-central Europe. Success appears to have been greatest where the restructuring needed was the least. The activities that have been the most successful are precisely those that needed to innovate the least. The results are the least impressive where the greatest changes were needed, meaning in sectors that depend on the development of new products and the adoption of new technology. It is here that change is the most dependent on substantial external sources of funding. This is consistent with the argument that one of the key barriers to restructuring is the limited ability of enterprises to finance the necessary investment. In purely theoretical terms it can be argued that any worthwhile investment project should find a satisfactory source of finance, but the realities of east-central Europe are very different from such an ideal picture. As the next section shows, privatisation itself can create obstacles as well as opening up possibilities for the restructuring of production.

PRIVATISATION AND RESTRUCTURING

An important element in the relationship between ownership change and restructuring is the ordering of the two key elements, meaning whether or not companies are restructured before they are transferred to private ownership. In cases where 'ownership restructuring' preceded the 'production-related' restructuring, the form of privatisation and the identity of the owner were important in influencing the course and results of restructuring. Standard methods, such as direct sales, public tenders and auctions, often led to a relatively rapid and effective restructuring, including innovations in production, the formulation of a new corporate strategy, improvements in technology and in the quality of production. That at least is the typical result of sale to a foreign owner. However, the need to finance purchases by means of credits typically prevents a domestic owner from investing in further development. Restructuring can therefore prove extremely difficult.

It is, however, more difficult to generalise on the consequences of mass privatisation through the non-standard form of more or less cost-free transfer of shares of the company to citizens. The supreme example is 'voucher privatisation' as practised in the Czech Republic which led at first to the dispersion of shareholding among individual investors and investment funds. Owners could have, at best, a limited influence on company managements. Moreover, voucher privatisation provided no new sources of finance for 'production-related' restructuring. It did not bring in new capital, as it amounted to no more than a reallocation of property that already existed.

It should be clear from this that the relationship between privatisation and restructuring is at best ambiguous. Once the problem is posed as one of creating scope for the financing of restructuring, then privatisation can often appear to be playing a negative role. It would, however, be too simple to suggest that privatisation in any general sense acts as an obstacle to restructuring. A more precise view of the relationship is developed in the following two sections, the first of which outlines differences between the countries.

THE RESULTS OF PRIVATISATION

Comparisons between countries do not produce simple and unequivocal answers. The scope for raising additional financial resources for enterprises depends partly on the form of the privatisation adopted, including the speed and the methods of property transformation, and the types of new owner. Variations between countries in these elements are relatively clear. However, it also depends on the broader framework of institutional and legal conditions. There are substantial variations in these factors across east-central Europe, stemming from different historical and national conditions. It is difficult to separate these possible influences to allow a full comparison of individual aspects. This section therefore provides an overview of the likely key factors, without being able to reach a definite conclusion on their relative importance.

The Czech Republic

From its start in 1991, privatisation has been considered the key to transformation of the economy by Czech governments. It began with 'small' privatisation in which, over a two-year period, 21,357 small trade and manufacturing units passed to private hands, mostly by auctions. This raised a total sum of Kčs 29 billion, a figure equivalent only to about 6 per cent of state revenue in 1992. In three quarters of the cases only leases were sold, restricted to a two year period, although these were later extended to five years.

'Big' privatisation, which at the start included the whole former federation, meaning both the current Czech and Slovak Republics, combined standard methods with voucher privatisation. In some cases state property was sold to domestic or foreign investors through public auctions and tenders, with no particular ownership concessions to insiders. There were also direct sales to a designated owner, free transfer of property to municipalities, pension funds and the like and restitution to the original owners and their heirs. The bulk of property was transferred to private ownership following the transformation into a joint-stock company with the subsequent sale of shares to private investors, or their distribution in exchange for voucher points. In all, the 'big' privatisation programme involved property valued in excess of Kč 950–1,000 billion, equivalent to more than $35 billion, in the period up to 1996. About one third of this was exchanged for voucher points and therefore contributed no income to the state.

The initial goal had been to privatise about 80 per cent of the country's assets by the middle of 1996 and the Ministry for Privatisation was abolished on 30 June 1996, with claims that it had fulfilled its key task. In fact the 'completion' of privatisation was still incomplete. The National Property Fund was left as the sole institution responsible for its final stages and as the government's depository of shares to the value of Kč 193 billion in partially privatised joint-stock companies. Kč 156 billion relates to equity of 56 strategic companies, such as public utilities, the fate of which was still to be decided in 1998. Kč 12 billion were in the category of 'reserves' or 'temporary possession', again with an uncertain future. A further unsolved issue was the privatisation of the remaining state share in three of the four largest banks, the market value of which was estimated at more than Kč 54 billion in 1996.

Voucher privatisation itself, involving the exchange of shares of state-owned enterprises for vouchers bought at a nominal price, was a novel Czechoslovak solution to a familiar problem in east-central Europe. The aim was to accelerate the privatisation process, even when the population did not have sufficient savings for acquisition of property by purchase. Moreover, voucher privatisation was considered politically desirable. By maximising the participation of the widest possible range of the population, it was hoped that it would ensure mass political support for the privatisation process and for the idea of economic transformation in general.

Voucher privatisation was implemented in two waves. The first, initiated on 1 October 1991, covered the whole of the former federal republic. The second wave began on 11 April 1994 and was implemented in the Czech Republic alone, after the break-up of the Czechoslovak Federation. The number of enterprises on offer and the possible number of participants was therefore smaller than in the first wave, although the level of interest in privatisation had if anything increased, in the sense that the number of citizens taking part in the Czech Republic was higher. The broad relationships are indicated in Table 4.1.

Table 4.1 Voucher privatisation in the Czech Republic

	Value of property (Kč bn)	Number of enterprises	Number of shareholders
First wave	213	988	5,977,466
Second wave	108	676	6,074,000

Note: Figures for the second wave exclude enterprises the shares of which were left from the first wave.
Source: Fond národního majetku (National Property Fund).

The most frequent criticism of voucher privatisation is the resulting dispersion of shareholding among individual investors and investment funds. This was slightly less marked in the first wave in which almost 74 per cent of the total number of Czechoslovak citizens registered allocated their vouchers through one of the 436 investment privatisation funds that emerged. The relevant figure for the second wave was only 49 per cent of participants, pointing to a still greater dispersion. This had important consequences in limiting the impact of the new owners on the management of companies they had acquired and hence in reducing their potential power to force changes. This, however, as indicated earlier, should be seen as only one element in the restructuring process and the Czech privatisation process had a number of further characteristics.

In terms of the chronological order of privatisation and restructuring, the philosophy was to privatise all assets before they were restructured. This was the result partly of the emphasis on speed and partly of the conceptual and ideological starting points. Apart from the political reasons for this choice, the domestic policy makers were convinced by the neo-liberal economic theory that the state is simply unable to make correct entrepreneurial decisions. New owners were left to solve the problems of financing substantial restructuring and of establishing effective control over their firms as part of a future system of corporate governance.

There has been a considerable concentration of the 'dispersed' shareholding in the wake of voucher privatisation with the so-called 'third wave'. Individual share-holders and many of the investment funds have eagerly sold their shares. Buyers have emerged often from rather unclear origins, creating and consolidating the power of various financial groupings, often riding roughshod over the interests of smaller shareholders. There is no evidence that it has led to improved performance through effective corporate governance (Carlin and Landesmann, 1997, p.2). The new owners seem in many cases to be interested purely in short-term financial gains and to have contributed little or nothing to improving the work of man-agement.

Thus the capital market, as it has developed up to now in the Czech Republic, has not led to the kind of ownership transfers that could lead to an appropriate ownership structure for stimulating a full, 'production-related' restructuring. Over-all, then, the choice of maximum speed and participation in privatisation has meant a resignation from full restructuring. In essence it created the conditions for nothing beyond a 'restructuring of ownership'.

Nor was there much direct impact on the state budget. The possibility of rais-ing revenue played a minimal role in decisions over the forms of Czech privati-sation. A substantial part was implemented free of charge. This was most obvi-ously true of voucher privatisation, but cost-free transfers were also made to municipalities and various funds. The main source of revenue has in fact been foreign investors, from which the National Property Fund received in 1992–6, or will receive in the future, the total of $4.6 billion. Despite the fact that foreign par-ticipation represented only 1.2 per cent of all privatisation projects, it has been the source of more than half of all proceeds from large-scale privatisation (Zemplínerová, 1997, p.19). Within this a few big deals have dominated, such as Volkswagen's takeover of the Škoda car manufacturer or Philip Morris's takeover of the only substantial Czech cigarette manufacturer, Tabák of Kutná Hora.

Poland

The privatisation process was off to a quick start in Poland with the Law on the Privatisation of State Enterprises of 13 July 1990. This created legal preconditions for a wide variety of forms, including mass privatisation using vouchers. The bulk – approximately 20,000 – of the small retail, wholesale and building enterprises were privatised by local governments early in the reform programme. The follow-ing years, however, saw a slow and cautious period of implementation of the priva-tisation of bigger enterprises. The initial aim was to sell 50 per cent of the 8,000 enterprises within five years. By the end of 1996 the first steps had been taken towards privatisation of 3,770 enterprises, but the process had been completed for only 1,872.

Privatisation has been proceeding along the following main routes. The first is direct privatisation or liquidation, covering small and medium-sized enterprises. The assets and liabilities have often been leased to insiders, as the first step towards an eventual purchase. The second is, indirect, or capital, privatisation, concerning larger firms. Following an initial 'commercialisation' stage, with transformation into a state-owned joint-stock company, shares can be sold to a strategic outside investor. The third, also following commercialisation, involves offering shares for sale to private investors. The fourth is 'mass' privatisation, involving the distribution of ownership rights to all citizens.

This last programme was subject to repeated delays and took off only in 1995 with the transformation of state enterprises into private joint-stock companies under conditions set by the government. Share certificates of one of 15 National Investment Funds (NIFs) were bought by Polish citizens for privatisation vouchers, the issue of which was closed in November 1996. These private NIFs, with managements reinforced by the involvement of prominent international consultancy firms and banks, selected by the Polish government, gained control over 512 large state-owned enterprises with assets valued at about $5.2 billion. The idea was that the NIFs would be able to ensure restructuring before the full transformation of enterprises into independent companies.

In all 25.7 million inhabitants participated in this form of mass privatisation, meaning 98 per cent of the eligible population. Already during 1996, however, 50 per cent of Poles resold their vouchers leading to estimates that in April 1997 about 40 per cent of the vouchers were held by foreigners and 10 per cent by Polish institutional investors, mainly insurance companies. In mid May 1997 a start was made to the exchange of share certificates of NIFs for shares of those enterprises that had already been restructured. This was to be completed by November 1998. In the meantime both the share certificates of NIFs and the shares of the respective enterprises were traded on the stock exchange.

There were clear similarities in the thinking behind Polish and Czech privatisation. Both have been influenced by considerations of widening political support and by a belief that private ownership alone should lead to improved performance. In Poland, however, an early enthusiasm was tempered by elements of caution from the government such that the respective places of privatisation in both economic and political thinking have been somewhat different. Above all, it has not maintained a position as an objective in isolation from other aspects of economic transformation.

The difference is reflected in practical terms in two elements. The NIFs differ in conception and role from the investment funds in the Czech Republic which emerged without government encouragement. The former have the task of encouraging restructuring in the production sphere. The foreign partners were selected by the government on the basis of their likely ability to achieve this. The Czech investment funds are concerned only to earn the greatest possible profit for the original voucher holders or subsequent share owners. They achieve this by purely financial activities, such as trading in shares, and by exerting pressure on enterprises to pay out dividends. They can therefore appear as a barrier to the restructuring of production in some enterprises by restricting the amount of finance available for investment.

The second element distinguishing the place of privatisation in Poland from that in the Czech Republic is the active role of the Polish state, basing itself partly on the experience of the market-oriented reforms of the 1980s, in initiating significant enterprise restructuring. It has achieved large productivity gains with its economic policy since the beginning of privatisation such that it is possible in many cases to refer to a government-led restructuring. This goes beyond the 512 large enterprises now being restructured by NIFs, as referred to above. The state also retained partial or complete ownership of 3,700 enterprises, the value of which is estimated at about $50 billion, or 38 per cent of GDP. At the end of 1996 about one half of total production and transport services still belonged to the public sector, although a substantially lower figure can be obtained by counting as already private all assets on the way to privatisation, such as those held by NIFs, as in Table 4.3. Moreover, despite a 27 per cent fall in production for the public sector in the years 1990–95, state enterprises still contributed 85 per cent of all tax revenues from enterprises.

This continuing strength of the state sector means that, according to an assessment by the EBRD (1997), the growth of the private sector and restructuring of the economy in terms of ownership have been the result largely of the emergence of new firms. This may appear paradoxical for a country where private ownership played an important role even before the fall of the Communist system. Thus, for example, 85 per cent of agricultural production was generated by private farmers. It partly reflects some definite policy decisions about the extent of privatisation. Above all privatisation of the strategic industries, such as coal mining, oil refineries, power plants, railways and air transport, was postponed to some unspecified future date.

It also reflects a number of further political influences. There were divergent views on the importance of ending state ownership, in contrast to the consensus in policy-making circles in the Czech Republic, and various degrees of distaste for allowing foreign investors to play too great a role in the economy. Only the sales of the state stakes in privatised banks in 1997 marked a departure from the previous practice of restricting foreign holdings to minority stakes. However, with the completion of mass privatisation, Poland can be expected to attract increasing amounts of foreign capital.

A number of other differences from the Czech political climate influenced the Polish privatisation process. There were various forms of preferential treatment to enterprise insiders, including the possibility for employees to block the privatisation of their enterprise. The Law on the Commercialisation and Privatisation of State-Owned Enterprises, passed in 1996, ended this veto right. However, even under this law the employees of an enterprise undergoing privatisation have the right to 15 per cent of the shares without charge, compared with a right beforehand to 20 per cent at half price.

A further decelerating factor was the fact that in Poland there was for a long time no law on business property restitution. Although relatively small in its overall impact, returning property or compensating former owners whose assets had been confiscated during the period of Communist rule was agreed to in the Czech Republic before mass privatisation began. In Poland, by way of contrast, there were lengthy arguments and a lack of consensus among politicians. The possibility that one would at some time be agreed was a source of uncertainty hampering some privatisation deals. Under the 1996 law referred to above 'restitution vouchers' were introduced with the stipulation that 5 per cent of the capital of the firms undergoing privatisation must be set aside for restitution purposes.

One final significant point is the interconnection between Polish privatisation and the development of a new pension system. Part of the remaining state-held equity is to be used for financing new pension funds. This contrasts with the Czech Republic where, having implemented mass privatisation prior to reforming the pension system, such possibilities for financing pension funds were very limited. The slower pace of privatisation in Poland, apart from its direct impact on enterprise restructuring, may even have advantages for the reorganisation of social policy, an area that has aroused a great deal of recent controversy and worry in the Czech Republic.

Hungary

Small-scale privatisation was implemented very early in the Hungarian reform process. Of 10,423 state-owned small enterprises and businesses in 1990, almost 10,000 had been transferred to private hands in the period up to March 1995. Large-scale privatisation, however, followed a significantly different course from that in Poland or the Czech Republic. The crucial distinction was that Hungarian governments never entertained the idea of mass privatisation at all and focused instead on 'classical' forms, especially cash sales. The emphasis was on finding strategic investors.

This was effective as a means to raise finance for the state budget and for the enterprises themselves and it could improve corporate governance by bringing in an owner with a direct involvement in company management. It also, however, meant that privatisation proceeded more slowly than in neighbouring countries at least at the start. Then, in 1995, the two main privatisation agencies, the State Property Agency and the State Holding Company, were merged into the State Privatisation and Asset Management Company and a transparent legal framework was created with the enactment of a new privatisation law in May 1995. This laid the basis for a speedier privatisation of state assets.

In 1990, 1,857 companies were in state hands. By January 1996, 1,074 companies, 58 per cent of the previous total, had been privatised, in the sense that they had been transferred into majority private ownership. In 1996, there were still 356 companies – 19 per cent of the initial number – in majority state ownership, out of which 89 are to be excluded from privatisation for the foreseeable future (Bager, 1996). By that time some 70 per cent of all state property had been sold off, raising in total $6 billion.

Despite the changes in institutional arrangements, the principal means of privatisation have remained unchanged since 1990. Direct sale has been the preferred method for disposing of state-owned property and in such a way that both domestic and foreign investors have faced nominally the same conditions. In practical terms, of course, in view of the shortage of domestic capital, this has given preferential treatment to foreign buyers. The sale of energy utilities and telecommunications, pharmaceutical and other firms led to record privatisation revenues of about $3.5 billion (Ft 450 billion) in 1995, of which $3 billion were represented by foreign investment.

The sale to foreign investors was, as Table 4.2 indicates, substantially more important in Hungary than in Poland or the Czech Republic. Apart from other macroeconomic benefits, referred to in Chapter 3, this helped Hungary in repaying foreign debt inherited from the communist past that had reached $21 billion by 1989. Thus, for example, the proceeds from the sale of the large utilities in late 1995 were used to finance the repayment of $1.5 billion in 1996. Further prepayments totalling another $1 billion were planned for 1997. Some foreign sources refer even to repayment of around $4 billion. Such figures have enabled the National Bank to sterilise the inflows from foreign direct investment and avoid currency appreciation while the level of net foreign debt was estimated at only $9.6 million in June 1998.

Moreover, the emphasis on selling to foreign owners provides a clear example of macroeconomic and microeconomic concerns coming together (Carlin and Landesmann, 1997). Alongside the impact on debt repayment, it could lead to effective corporate governance and access by privatised firms to external sources of funds for investment. Moreover, pressures for a speedy process of enterprise restructuring, running in parallel with privatisation, were increased by the enactment and enforcement of the Bankruptcy Act of 1992. A substantial proportion of companies, estimated at about 16 per cent, went into liquidation or closed down completely. It should be added that, although there clearly are benefits in eliminating chronically inefficient enterprises, financial difficulties were exacerbated at the time for many enterprises by depressed demand conditions. There was therefore probably a significant loss of capacity that might under different circumstances have been profitably saved (Bager, 1996, p.1).

Table 4.2 Foreign direct investments in CEECs, 1989–1997

	Inflow, 1997		Stock	
	total $bn	per capita $	total $bn	per capita $
Czech Republic	1.00	97	8.12	789
Poland	4.50	116	9.90	256
Hungary	2.10	206	15.36	1,506

Note: Polish figures show only project with capital of at least $1 million.
Source:. European Bank for Reconstruction and Development.

In some other respects too, Hungarian privatisation has gone further than in the other east-central European countries. The formerly state-owned banks were sold after a long period of hesitation. Some had been privatised in 1994. The government decided on full privatisation of the whole banking sector in 1995 and all apart from two specialised institutions were transferred to the private sector in 1997. The problem of property restitution has also been resolved with the distribution of 'compensation vouchers' to about 1.2 million citizens as a result of the May 1995 privatisation law. They have in practice been usable mainly for purchase of land. Overwhelmingly, however, the striking features of Hungarian privatisation remain the extent to which it was implemented as a part, rather than being conceived as the whole, of a wider transformation process and the resulting scope this has given to foreign capital to play a crucial role in the restructuring and modernisation processes of the economy.

A COMPARISON OF RESULTS

When assessed in the simplest quantitative form, the results of privatisation appear very similar across the three east-central European countries. Table 4.3 shows the growing share of the private sector. The results in the Czech Republic look particularly favourable in view of its relatively late start. There were already substantial private sectors in Poland and Hungary before 1989, but the Czech Republic had a 96 per cent share of state ownership in GDP at that time.

Table 4.3 Percentage share of private sector in GDP

	Czech Republic	Poland	Hungary
1991	17	42	30
1996	74	78	75

Source: Statistical office publications of individual countries.

However, the key question is how far the privatisation process has led to the desired changes in the sphere of production. It is not self-evident that a privatised enterprise will show better results than a state-owned one (Pöschl, 1997) and certainly not self-evident that all forms of privatisation will produce the same results. Indeed, a comparative study in 1997 for the North Atlantic Assembly, effectively the parliament of NATO countries, comparing privatisation in the candidate countries for NATO membership, evaluated Hungary the most positively and the Czech Republic the most negatively. The author, K Zijlstra, considered direct sales to be the best method of privatisation while criticising the voucher privatisation practised in the Czech Republic on the familiar grounds that it has led to fragmented ownership under which the desirable restructuring has not taken place. Claims of fragmentation may miss the point, but doubts about the extent and depth of Czech restructuring are discussed in more detail in Chapter 7.

A detailed inter-country comparison is very difficult despite, or perhaps precisely because of, the fact that the literature on these themes is already very extensive. There is a body of valuable comparative evidence showing the relationship between privatisation and restructuring, but the conclusions are not always unequivocal and in some cases studies point to very different conclusions. Although a major part of the central argument here is that privatisation should not be the sole focus of attention, the available literature means that the most accessible starting point is a comparison beginning with the process and methods of privatisation itself.

An EBRD analysis (EBRD, 1995) distinguished five main types of ownership and governance structure in the economies of east-central Europe. These are state ownership with control exercised by insiders, meaning managers and employees, inside ownership with control exercised by employees, inside ownership with control exercised by managers, domestic outside ownership, such as individual voucher holders, and foreign investor ownership, which can mean an individual investor, a firm or investment fund.

These ownership structures, and the governance they generate, lead to different restructuring outcomes. The objectives of relevant subjects, and also of course the possibilities for financing investment, vary considerably, leading also to variations in the extent and effectiveness of restructuring. There now appears to be considerable agreement around the conclusion that mass privatisation programmes, which have diluted ownership and control among voucher holders, have so far produced only limited, primarily 'reactive', restructuring. On the other hand, a privatisation with dominant and concentrated outside ownership, especially when combined with direct foreign capital inflows, appears to generate 'deeper' restructuring, involving substantial new investment and subsequently significant performance improvements.

The pace of privatisation raises somewhat more complex issues. The attempt to privatise into domestic ownership as quickly as possible by the voucher method creates only the 'primary', fragmented set of owners of shares, the concentration of which – as a precondition and a sign of completion of the privatisation itself – takes place slowly and imperfectly. It is dependent on the functioning of the secondary capital market. The concentration of ownership can stimulate interest from foreign entrepreneurs, or can be brought about by them. Again, however, a portfolio investment inflow is dependent on the functioning of the capital market which, as is argued below, is not satisfactorily fulfilled at least in the case of the Czech Republic.

By way of contrast, capital acquired from standard privatisation methods, such as direct sales and auctions, comes into the economy from the moment the transactions are completed. Thus the standard methods, unlike the voucher system of 'accelerated privatisation', points to more rapid overall economic development. The same point can be put in reverse with the formulation that 'voucher privatisation postponed foreign participation in the short term, but should allow for a substantial capital inflow in the form of portfolio investment in the long run' (Hunya, 1997b, p.144). However, when that will happen depends on the satisfaction of other preconditions.

There are, however, clear disadvantages to delays in privatisation. Postpone-ment, as in Poland up to 1995, leaves enterprises in a stage of 'pre-privatisation agony'. Unsure of their fate, they may resign themselves to passivity. Even this, however, is by no means clearcut, with evidence of cases where state-owned enter-prises feel under strong pressure from tighter budget constraints and a denial of access to subsidies or soft loans to finance losses (Carlin and Landesmann, 1997, p.8).

On one point, however, there is less scope for equivocation. The benefits of privatisation do depend on how the acquisition is financed, or more precisely on the access to financial resources on the part of the new owners. The difficulties for new domestic owners in financing further investment seem to be universal pheno-mena across east-central Europe while foreign ownership seems almost invariably to provide a solution. Even if the foreign capital inflow is used purely for the pur-chasing of pre-existing assets, it usually opens the door to large volumes of follow-up investment, suggesting that foreign investors typically restructure rapidly the firms they acquire (Hunya, 1997a, p.290).

There is a possible problem in the interpretation of evidence here. The potential for modernisation and investment in new technology is greatly enhanced by foreign ownership. At the same time, foreign investors have naturally tended to target the most promising enterprises for purchase. Although there are cases of outside acquisition being a consequence rather than a cause of an enterprise's suc-cess, there is also an enormous body of evidence across all the three countries of the benefits of foreign capital. Its role as the precondition for successful restruc-turing is so important that there are even references to a segmentation of the econ-omy between foreign-owned and domestic firms with few areas of overlap (Carlin and Landesmann, 1997, p.36).

The conclusion on any general causal relationships between privatisation and performance has to be expressed carefully. Any such relationship is far less clear and consistent than in the case of a comparison of a foreign with a domestic in-vestor. Indeed, many studies 'fail to find any systematic relationship between ownership type and enterprise performance' (Carlin and Landesmann, 1997, p.15). Hunya (1997a, p.295) has reached three general basic conclusions from these comparative studies. The first is that there is great diversity of performance between individual companies, irrespective of their ownership. The second is that the difference in restructuring between state-owned enterprises and domestic private companies is not very large. The third is that restructuring in foreign-owned companies is much more significant than in domestically-owned com-panies.

FINANCE AS A DETERMINANT OF DEVELOPMENT

The failure of studies to reveal a clear, consistent and precise relationship between privatisation and restructuring stems partly from the oversimplified nature of the question asked. As argued earlier, the simple transfer into private ownership is not sufficient to ensure the complex and multi-faceted process of restructuring, even when understood as confined to a single enterprise. A summary of the relationship between restructuring and privatisation is shown in Table 4.4, which illustrates also how different forms of privatisation lead to different requirements and possibilities for additional funds for financing of restructuring.

This is one of the key factors in determining the success of enterprise restructuring. Various forms of privatisation have been associated with a failure to bring the required increase in financial means for enterprises. In many cases it seems to have led to very negative results. With privatisation the enterprises released themselves not only from state control, but also from the state's financial resources. However, with the limited funds channelled into enterprises, full restructuring was rarely possible even for those enterprises under domestic ownership that had the managerial motivation and ability.

Unable to adopt strategies for full restructuring into the kind of successful enterprises found in advanced market economies, they have sought various alternative solutions, a point pursued further in Chapter 7. Some have reacted by discontinuing inefficient production, laying off excessive manpower: that is frequently the logical response to the market signals for an independent unit in a market economy. Many others, however, have benefited from a soft policy framework that has enabled them to raise prices, protect employment and lobby heavily for government support and assistance (Hunya, 1997a).

These points illustrate a crucial test for a judgement on different methods of privatisation. They should ideally be part of a policy framework that serves to open up new possibilities for funding and that simultaneously exerts pressure on enterprises to abandon hopes of salvation from a soft approach from governments.

The situation therefore varies both with the methods of privatisation adopted and with the specific national situations and policy frameworks that create the conditions under which a deeper restructuring may or may not be possible. Thus the effects of privatisation are influenced by the general approach of governments towards loss-making enterprises, by the strength of bankruptcy laws and by the nature and role of the banking system and the capital market. A number of other institutional and legislative factors, often ignored in economic analyses, can also prove very important. Thus the extent to which the 'rules of the game' are guaranteed, observed and enforced has important implications in generating investor

Table 4.4 The basic relations between privatisation and the restructuring process

Privatisation method	New owner	Advantages/disadvantages for state	Advantages/disadvantages for enterprise		Next aims	
Standard methods, characterised especially by outside ownership	domestic investor	withdrawal from ownership responsibilities, budget revenues	defined corporate governance		enterprise restructuring	mobilisation of required sources
	foreign investor	as above, (usually) higher degree of efficient linkages to world market	defined corporate governance	modern management, organisation, know how, new technologies	enterprise restructuring	possibility of utilising foreign sources
Mass privatisation (vouchers)	individual voucher- (then share) holders	withdrawal from ownership responsibilities, usually minimal direct economic effect, important political and social aspects, speed	absence of stimulating corporate governance with all the related consequences		further ownership restructuring through capital market	effective corporate governance, parallel inflow of portfolio investment

confidence and hence in the functioning of the financial system as a whole. The following subsections address some of these issues around the central question of how enterprises can raise the necessary funding.

Unfortunately, the variety, incompleteness and mutual incomparability of relevant data on enterprise funding in individual CEECs, makes it impossible to compare reliably the importance of the various alternatives. Nevertheless, it is useful and possible to provide a rough picture of the alternative forms of enterprise financing and the main differences across east-central Europe. The following sections therefore do not provide a conclusive analysis of the financing of restructuring, but they do summarise the possibilities and obstacles enterprises have to face.

Self-Financing by Enterprises

Privatisation brought both the costs and the benefits of financial independence for enterprises. They had, at least in theoretical terms, the option of relying on resources they could create themselves or on external resources. The role of internal savings has proved extremely important with a share in the financing of investment similar to that of industrial countries such as Japan or Germany (EBRD, 1995, p.97). This, however, may not be associated with such efficient mechanisms for the allocation of capital in the investment decisions of individual enterprises, in view of the ownership structures, lack of financial discipline and habits and techniques inherited from the past.

Table 4.5 indicates the strong bias towards internal sources of funding in the Czech Republic. The table shows all disposable sources of finance for enterprises as it is impossible in practice to separate out investment from other uses of external finance. Even some credits given explicitly for investment may be used for totally different purposes, such as paying wages. Nevertheless, these figures show the closest approximation available to identifying the sources of finance for investment.

A high rate of self-financing, or lower requirements for external sources, is characteristic of those large enterprises that have survived from the past, in so far as they have continued to be profitable. These are typically the ones that have continued with the same products, providing electricity, steel or other goods that require little adaptation for the new market environment. There are, however, much greater problems for small and medium-sized enterprises which could be the most dynamic element within a broader transformation process. These have the greatest difficulties in gaining access to external sources of funding and also the lowest level of internal resources.

Table 4.5 Sources of finance for non-financial enterprises in the Czech
Republic as percentage of the total

	1994	1995	1996
Available profit	25.0	27.2	21.8
Depreciation	32.9	34.4	35.2
Issue of bonds	1.5	3.2	4.1
Subsidies from state budget	1.7	1.7	1.3
Total internal sources	61.1	66.4	62.4
Increase of credits:			
– in Kč	24.3	15.8	21.2
– in foreign currency	4.3	11.6	7.1
– foreign loans and credits	10.3	6.1	9.3
Total increase of credits	38.9	33.6	37.6

Note: Figures refer to non-financial organisations with over 25 employees and, in the case of industry, with over 100 employees.
Source: Czech National Bank.

Thus the heavy reliance on internal sources of funding can be seen as a source of structural inertia, tending to restrict the scope of restructuring to changes within a particular group of enterprises only. It is significant that although there has been a rapid expansion in small enterprises, especially in the service sector, this has generally been in activities that require low levels of investment. A serious gap persists with the very poor representation of small, or even larger, enterprises in modern sectors of manufacturing.

A similar classification of sources of investment financing in Hungary, restricted only to 'large' investments of over Ft 50 million, shows a similar bias towards internal sources of financing. Thus, as Table 4.6 shows, this covered 60 per cent of investment. The figure was probably even higher for the economy as a whole, because the data in the table do not contain small investments where self-financing is probably even more dominant (Szangi & Czemlér, 1996). There is, however, a relatively high share of financing from government funds and from the state budget which is connected with investment in the underdeveloped infra-structure, especially transport. The very low share of domestic credits clearly points to major problems in channelling savings into investment, resulting in high interest rates on domestic credits, a point taken up in the next section.

Table 4.6 Sources for investment finance for all enterprises in Hungary as percentage of total

	1992	1995	1992–5
Total	100.0	100.0	100.0
Own sources	60.1	48.2	54.6
External sources from the government			
funds	6.9	18.0	9.2
state budget subsidy	9.2	16.9	16.6
domestic credits	4.3	6.3	5.0
World Bank and other international credits	8.1	6.1	8.7
other financial sources	11.4	4.5	5.9

Note: Only projects of over Ft 50 million are included.
Source: Hungarian Statistical Office, quoted in Ujházy, 1997.

Such complete data are not available for Poland, but the financing of investment is again heavily dependent on enterprises' internal resources. There is also a substantial role for subsidies to large enterprises still under state ownership. This is connected with the government-led restructuring efforts, where state enterprises are leading the process of consolidation in the oil and chemical industries. The restructuring of the coal and steel sectors is next on the agenda. The share of credit-financed investment was reported to be about 10 per cent in 1995.

Bank Credits

As Tables 4.5 and 4.6 indicate, domestic credits have been substantially less important than self-financing of investment in the Czech Republic and Hungary. The somewhat higher figure in the Czech case needs to be interpreted carefully, partly because of the rather special role played by banks in the Czech economy. Commercial banks in the Czech Republic have been actively engaged in the privatisation process, in other words in 'ownership restructuring', as well as in the subsequent process of 'production-related' enterprise restructuring. In the former they provided credits to clients for the purchase of property.

Beyond this, however, commercial banks played an important – maybe even a dominant – role in voucher privatisation as founders of investment companies and investment privatisation funds. A large number of voucher holders entrusted their voucher points, which were exchanged for shares during the two privatisation waves, to a relatively small number of such funds. In the first wave thirteen investment companies, each controlling one or more investment funds, acquired 55 per cent of all voucher points. Nine of these 13 companies were founded by banks.

There are, then, important links between commercial banks and enterprises, which go beyond the standard financial ones. They involve a relationship of indirect or secondary ownership. Commercial banks, as founders and administrators of investment funds, could influence the fate of up to two thirds of the property of privatised enterprises, the shares of which they purchased for investment vouchers entrusted to them (Chvojka, 1996).

They are, however, rarely involved in corporate governance or concerned with active restructuring of production. In practice, the credits they grant may be used not to support restructuring but to prop up those enterprises that fail to restructure. Banks are reluctant to take a tough line and press to initiate bankruptcy proceedings as these would not yield any significant return. The disappearance of firms that owe large sums to banks would only damage the latters' balance sheets. Their role as secondary owners either makes no difference to this or marginally strengthens the tendency to let failing firms lumber on.

Thus the role of banks in financing production-relevant restructuring of the Czech economy has been rather less impressive. They have granted credits, but these, amounting for example to Kč 1,035 billion in 1996, were mainly short-term and medium-term. The share of long-term credits, which are the most useful for financing investment projects, remained on a low level, accounting for only about 30 per cent of total credits granted. Several factors lie behind this unsatisfactory trend, including the limited volume of long-term funds held by commercial banks, prudence on the part of banks when issuing credit, the quality of projects for which long-term applications were made, and the creditworthiness of applicants.

There is a similar time structure in credits granted by Hungarian banks. These, however, played a much less important role in the financing of enterprise investment than the credits in the Czech Republic. This difference has been attributed to the current collateral requirements which are viewed by many potential borrowers as excessive: collateral worth three times the amount of the loan could be demanded (OECD, 1997a). There may also be a crowding-out effect related to state securities. The banks not only had to finance the state budget, but also had to earn more on corporate lending in order to compensate for the low profitability of state securities. Thus the interest rates on credits had to be high, meaning that private investment was easier to finance from internal sources or from abroad (OECD, 1997b).

The financing of restructuring by means of credits has followed a slightly different course in Poland. Slower and state-driven privatisation was accompanied by relatively modest demand for credits. Moreover, scope for credits was influenced by the Law on Financial Restructuring of Enterprises and Banks, adopted in February 1993 which included provision for solving the problem of so-called bad loans built up before 1991.

The exact scale of the problem is difficult to determine precisely and exact comparisons between countries are impossible. The debts are partly the result of investment financed by credits under central planning, when enterprises did not have responsibility for their own financial affairs, and partly the result of further losses built up during and after the transformation recession. In Poland banks were required to find solutions in one of a number of possible ways, including repayment of the loans, agreement on a gradual settlement between a bank and an enterprise, initiation of a bankruptcy procedure, liquidation of an enterprise or the sale of debts.

This was intended to help the restructuring process as a whole by freeing the financial system of a burden that was tying up bank credits in loss-making enterprises. Its elimination would, it was hoped, enable credits to be redirected towards the development of new enterprises and sectors. In practice the results of this process have been judged positively, although there are a number of reservations (Provazník, 1997). Thus although the law prohibited banks from granting further credits to enterprises the debts of which were classified as bad by international auditing firms, about one eighth of the enterprises acquired further new credits or the postponement of repayment. Moreover, even among the 40 per cent of enterprises that repaid their old debts, only a part used internal sources for this purpose, while 28 per cent used further credits. This was inconsistent with the programme, as it effectively side-stepped the aim of eliminating debts from the past.

Where agreements were reached between banks and enterprises, further restructuring of production was often delayed. The latter generally found a 'breathing space' during which pressure was weakened. The financial restructuring in the form of agreement between a bank and an enterprise similarly led to little change in ownership relations. The initiation of a bankruptcy procedure generally had little positive effect. Creditors received only a small percentage of their claims with banks receiving 17 per cent and suppliers only 5 per cent. The procedure itself lasted on average up to three years while in the meantime the book value of the enterprise decreased significantly.

Thus conditions for a better restructuring and for improving the competitiveness of enterprises were at best only partially created. Nevertheless, the whole programme meant an important step and impulse towards recovery of the respective institutional and functional framework. Its course and results drew attention to the need to amend the Bankruptcy Law and for reform and privatisation of banks. These are points of general significance across CEECs.

Further Sources of Credit

There are a number of other sources of credit to enterprises, one of the most important of which is direct credits to enterprises from abroad. In view of the limited availability and high cost of long-term loans from domestic commercial banks, foreign loans and credits have become increasingly important since 1992. Their volume increased after the individual CEECs relaxed their foreign exchange restrictions and moved to free currency convertibility. Unfortunately, data allowing a full comparison of their importance across the different countries is not available, but the enterprise sphere in the Czech Republic owed over $9 billion abroad by the end of 1996. This had by then become the most important source of long-term capital inflow.

Another form of credit for financing investment is leasing. This is indirectly linked to credits from commercial banks which are the source of over 90 per cent of the funds for leasing companies. Across western Europe 20–25 per cent of investment is financed through leasing. It also covered about 20 per cent of corporate investment in fixed assets in the Czech Republic in 1996, with the total volume of goods in lease after depreciation exceeding Kč 100 billion. Its importance, however, has varied with the precise rules applied by governments. Thus, for example, it lost importance in Hungary after some changes in the accountancy regulations and in customs rules in 1993 (UN 1995, p.13).

For completeness, mention should also be made of mutual enterprise indebtedness, or the reduction of financial difficulties by failing to pay bills when due. The levels of inter-enterprise arrears in CEECs have been estimated to be no higher than levels of trade credit in advanced economies. However, they are significant in the Czech Republic, reaching about Kč 132.4 billion at the end of 1996, and are a particularly serious and unwelcome problem for enterprises in view of the cash-flow problems that may be experienced due to difficulties with other forms of credit.

The Domestic Capital Market

Generally, commercial banks play the central role in the reallocation of financial resources in countries at an early stage in the development of financial structures.

In more developed economies, specialised financial institutions and equity markets become more important, as do bond issues. The development of the stock exchange as the supreme organisational expression of the capital market allows for the emergence of additional processes of the issue and trading in bonds and shares. The importance of the stock exchange for enterprise finance can be exaggerated. Studies show that even in developed countries, only a small part of productive investment is financed by new share issues. In the Anglo-Saxon world, the stock market serves rather as a control over management (Pöschl, 1997, p.5). It therefore does not replace banks which continue to play both a large and a specific role, although they are no longer so dominant within the financial system as a whole.

There are substantial differences between the financial markets across CEECs, reflecting partly historical differences connected with when the individual countries embarked on systemic transformation, with Hungary and Poland in the lead. However, the subsequent development of the securities market depends primarily on the differences in the character of privatisation. In those countries that have pursued a selective approach both to privatisation and to listing companies on the stock exchange, such as Poland, the capitalisation of the market remains small relative to the size of the economy, but liquidity of the stocks is higher relative to total capitalisation. In those countries that pursued mass privatisation, such as the Czech and Slovak Republics, the total stock market capitalisation is high relative to the size of economy, but the liquidity of these markets is low relative to their total capitalisation. As argued earlier, this lack of market liquidity in those countries that pursued mass privatisation programmes can pose a serious impediment to the post-privatisation restructuring of enterprises (cf. EBRD, 1995).

This is particularly true of the Czech Republic. It has in effect three capital markets. There is the official Prague Stock Exchange alongside trading through the so-called RM-System – an automated trading system established in 1993 enabling the new, small share holders to enter the securities market without an intermediary – and the Securities Centre for direct, over-the-counter sales. The Securities Centre was originally only a registration point for confirming transfers of ownership of securities between individuals, but it grew in importance. It is estimated at one time to have accounted for up to 80 per cent of the total equity transactions volume concluded, but the prices may diverge widely from those on the Prague Stock Exchange. This fragmentation of the capital market means that there are no uniform prices for company shares and must cast doubt on the meaning of any published figures. Some efforts were made by the Prague Stock Exchange in 1997 to reduce trade via the Securities Centre and, in 1997, the former increased its share of the total trade to 59.6 per cent, against 11.6 per cent for the RM-System and 28.8 per cent for the Securities Centre.

The important point, however, is that this capital market could not provide any possibility of an alternative source for financing restructuring which could compete with or supplement credits from the banking sector. This follows from the process of voucher privatisation which has left an abundance of shares available for sale, reducing any possible interest in buying new issues. The Czech market has therefore remained primarily a secondary market. The point is made clear in Table 4.7. Voucher privatisation led to an enormous number of issues, of which only about 200 proved to be active and truly liquid in the market. During 1997 the Prague Stock Exchange put out of operation the shares of 1,301 companies that were either untradable or only rarely traded.

Table 4.7 Comparison of equity markets in CEECs in 1996

	Czech Republic	Poland	Hungary
Companies listed	1,700	84	48
Market capitalisation ($bn)	19.9	7.9	5.3
Daily volume ($mil)	29.0	41.6	10.0
Return, IFCI (per cent)	16.9	75.0	102.6
Earning per share (growth in per cent)	−7.8	14.2	9.4

Source: *Emerging Market Investor*, March 1997.

Apart from its segmentation and non-transparency, the Czech capital market, when compared with similar institutions in Poland and Hungary, has suffered from a number of weaknesses in regulation and in the legal framework which have further contributed to a lack of public confidence and limited its potential to develop beyond a poorly-functioning secondary market. More detail on this is provided in Chapter 7. As Table 4.7 indicates, the Czech Republic was characterised by an enormous number of listed companies alongside a relatively small daily volume of trading.

Bond markets have developed somewhat more smoothly and are now functioning well across the CEEC. Market capitalisation is higher than in the equity markets and turnover is sufficiently high to make them attractive to foreign investors. The greater importance of bond markets in Hungary and Poland is shown in Table 4.8. Most outstanding bonds in the CEECs are short-term maturities or treasury bills, with fixed income securities constituting the largest market segment.

Table 4.8 Comparison of domestic bond markets in CEECs in 1996

	Czech Republic	Poland	Hungary
Market volume ($bn)	12.0	15.5	10.0
– as per cent of GDP	24	11	21
Return of domestic investors (in real terms, per cent)	2.8	2.5	2.9
Return of foreign investors (in dollar terms, per cent)	9.0	5.9	7.4

Source: Dresdner Bank.

Bond markets are primarily dependent on the financial needs of the governmental sector, but are increasingly also encompassing private debt. Nevertheless, this still accounts for no more than 8 per cent of the market in Poland. The Czech Republic is something of an exception owing to the maintenance of a broadly balanced state budget up to 1997 and to the exceptionally limited scope for enterprises to raise finance by other means after voucher privatisation. About 60 per cent of the Czech bonds are issued by private companies. Indeed, during the first quarter of 1997 Czech enterprises gained about Kč 4 billion on the capital market. This is hardly negligible when set against the Kč 19.5 billion credit increment provided by commercial banks in the same period.

Foreign portfolio investment

Outside participation in trade on domestic capital markets can constitute another form of financing of domestic enterprises. This includes both the purchase of shares of domestic enterprises by foreign investors and the placing of domestic currency bonds on the Eurobond market. Thus, for example in 1996, the value of outstanding Eurobonds issued by Hungarian borrowers totalled $15 bn: this was almost 80 per cent of the whole Euromarket volume in east-central Europe as a whole.

In the Czech Republic at the end of 1996, portfolio investments by foreign subjects amounted to $5.3 bn, of which $4.6 bn concerned securities denominated in Kč and sold in the domestic market. Of these 73 per cent were shares and 27 per cent bonds, with 42 per cent of the latter corporate bonds, 39 per cent bank bonds and the remaining 19 per cent government bonds. During the course of 1996 the issue of Kč Eurobonds by foreign banks increased in importance under the stimulus of a high interest differential and a low exchange-rate risk. The financial means in Kč acquired by the issuers were reallocated in the Czech market, both in the form of deposits and by the purchase of domestic bonds. Issues of these Kč instruments were realised in the value of Kč 35 bn in 1996. The majority of issues were carried out by German and Austrian banks.

Foreign direct investment

Comparative figures for foreign direct investment have been provided in Table 4.2. Analogous comparisons of other forms of foreign investment are not available. The relative importance of direct and portfolio investment probably varies between countries. Table 4.9 shows the changing situation in the Czech Republic. The growth in portfolio investment was clearly related to voucher privatisation. Domestic individual owners and many investment funds could sell their shares relatively easily and quickly, but it is far from clear how the inflow of capital was used. Much was undoubtedly absorbed in personal consumption, often contributing to the worsening trade balance. It is not obvious that much found its way into financing restructuring. Moreover, the negative figure in early 1997 demonstrates another danger with this kind of capital inflow. Investors can pull out relatively easily, when they lose confidence in the possibilities of short-term gain, thereby threatening a foreign-currency crisis.

Table 4.9 Annual increase of foreign investments in the Czech Republic in Kč billion

	direct	portfolio	total
1993	16.6	46.7	63.3
1994	24.8	24.6	49.4
1995	67.0	36.1	103.1
1996	37.7	19.7	57.4
1997	40.5	34.4	74.9

Source: Czech National Bank.

Such dangers are very much less with direct foreign investment, although the boundary between direct and portfolio investment is not absolutely rigid. A slightly arbitrary cut-off is used setting direct investment as the acquisition of a share of 10

per cent or more in a company. There are also different categories of direct investment, including investment on green-field sites, the establishment of joint ventures
and purchases of shares in existing companies. Nevertheless, all these forms of
direct capital participation have generally had striking implications for
restructuring. There is a possible causal relationship in both directions such that
foreign direct investment stimulates successful privatisation and restructuring
while successful privatisation and restructuring can stimulate further foreign direct
investment.

There are some possible well-known dangers attached to a high degree of
foreign penetration and foreign control of manufacturing industries. The country's
development may become completely dependent on foreign companies which
could use their subsidiaries purely as suppliers of simpler components or ecologically undesirable products, bringing only limited long-term benefits to the host
country. There have also been more specific references to a possible 'time' relevance of the foreign capital inflow. The importance of foreign investment in
bringing success in rapid restructuring at an early stage need be no 'guarantee of
future success' (Hunya, 1997a, p.298). These partial reservations may point to the
need for a more systematic analysis of the impact of foreign investment, but they
do not invalidate the fundamental point. This has proved to be the nearest to a sure
method for achieving a satisfactory level of real restructuring at the enterprise
level.

CONCLUSION

The success of the transformation process of CEEC economies is dependent on a
complex combination of factors. The methods used to privatise state property
determine the type and nature of the new owners. This in turn affects both their
attitude towards future restructuring and their ability to gain access to the financial
resources necessary for the restructuring of production.

Despite problems of comparison and interpretation, the current literature points
to the conclusion that the speediest form of privatisation was associated with the
deceleration of restructuring. Apparently promising initial results were paid for by
a subsequent decrease in growth rates. Moreover, the impact of privatisation
cannot be viewed in isolation from other aspects of both the macroeconomic and
microeconomic environment. Above all, successful enterprise restructuring is only
possible when privatisation is accompanied by the development of a satisfactory
institutional and legal framework, including the development of an appropriate
financial system and capital market, and possibly also by the application of appropriate economic policies. The need to set privatisation in this wider context could

be seen as a further reason for the problems associated with undue emphasis on the pace of ownership transformation alone.

Hungarian experience serves very clearly to illustrate these points. Irrespective of ownership, enterprises faced substantially tougher conditions than in the other countries. They were not protected by the 'foreign-exchange cushion' in the initial stages of restructuring. They had to endure hard budget constraints and to repay debts under the threat of bankruptcy. They had to adapt quickly to new conditions which in practice meant an orientation to foreign sources.

The bank-led privatisation in the Czech Republic, and to a certain extent also Poland, was characterised by a regime of softer budget constraints. Enterprises were frequently allocated new funds, enabling them to survive. Their restructuring has been and is slow also as a result of the absence, or relative weakness, of the threat of bankruptcy. Banks are the institutions best placed to begin bankruptcy proceedings against enterprises, but have shown little enthusiasm for using the existing legal powers. The principal reasons for this reluctance are the losses they would have to acknowledge, with only a small proportion of their debts recoverable, and the length of the proceedings involved. Contrary to widely held suspicions, their role as 'indirect owners' is of little significance in this context.

The widely differing numbers of bankruptcies, according to EBRD data for 1996, 725 in the Czech Republic, 984 in Poland and 3007 in Hungary, can be seen as an indication of weaknesses in the restructuring processes at least in Poland and the Czech Republic. It is consistent with the view that a substantial proportion of the funds flowing from banks to the enterprise sphere are used to protect enterprises against collapse rather than for financing a purposeful restructuring. In so far as bank credits are used to prop up inefficient and over-indebted enterprises with no long-term perspective, they are effectively being wasted on holding back the required restructuring process. In this context, the completion of bank privatisation could be a crucially important step, creating sound governance.

It is, however, not for commercial banks alone to ensure and allocate the necessary resources for investment. Other possibilities also exist, at least at the theoretical level. Moreover, the capital market, as one of the important channels, has a twofold role with respect to the processes of privatisation and restructuring, especially in the Czech case. The primary market can act as an external capital source for enterprises, while the secondary market can be the vehicle for overcoming the fragmentation resulting from voucher privatisation.

Even this, however, has not proved to be a simple process. Recent Czech analyses suggest that at least 60 per cent, and possibly up to 80 per cent, of firms which passed through voucher privatisation, now have majority owners. However, the functioning of the capital market in its present state, despite this ownership concentration, has not brought anything positive as far as the character and impact of corporate governance is concerned. The results of industrial enterprises have, on the contrary, worsened significantly since 1996. There is therefore every prospect of a further 'fourth' wave, which will mean bankruptcies and liquidations of enterprises. Many have been hit by the form concentration of ownership has taken with funds siphoned out by their new, but clearly only temporary, owners.

This points again to the importance of setting privatisation within the context of the creation of a satisfactory legal and institutional framework. Contrary to a view from within the Czech government in the past, privatisation cannot be accompanied by the government abdicating responsibility for economic processes. To quote from the analysis of the Czech capital market, completed by the Czech Ministry of Finance in October 1997, 'The state has initiated the transformation of the economy, and its role must be strong also in the post-privatisation period.' (*Hospodářské noviny*, 8 November 1997).

REFERENCES

Asaf, G.B. (1995), *The Economies in Transition: The Challenge of Restructuring and Economic Recovery*, Vienna: UNIDO.

Bager, G. (1996*), Restructuring of the Hungarian Economy*, Budapest: Ministry of Finance.

Carlin, W. and M. Landesmann (1997), *From Theory into Practice? Corporate Restructuring and Economic Dynamism in Transition Economies*, Vienna Institute for Comparative Economic Studies, Research Report No. 240.

Chvojka, P. (1996), 'The role of commercial banks in the Czech economy transformation process', *Prague Economic Papers*, December.

Chvojka, P. (1997), 'Banking sector's role in restructuring of CEEC economies (Case Study of the Czech Republic)', *Ekonomický časopis*, **45**, 511–545.

EBRD (European Bank for Reconstruction and Development) (1995), *Transition Report 1995, Investment and Enterprise Development*, London.

EBRD (European Bank for Reconstruction and Development) (1997), *Transition Report Update*, London.

Hunya, G. (1997a), *Large Privatisation, Restructuring and Foreign Direct Investment*, Vienna Institute for Comparative Economic Studies, Reprint Series, No. 166.

Hunya, G. (1997b), *Foreign Direct Investment and Its Effects in the Czech Republic, Hungary and Poland*, Vienna Institute for Comparative Economic Studies, Reprint Series No. 168.

OECD (1997a), *Economic Survey of Hungary*.

OECD (1997b), *Economic Survey of Poland*.

Pöschl, J. (1997), 'Successful transitions: Czech Republic, Hungary, Poland, Slovakia, Slovenia', Vienna Institute for Comparative Economic Studies, Members Seminar, March.

Provazník, D. (1997), *Poland: Impact of Banks on Enterprise Restructuring* (in Czech), Prague: Czechoslovak Trade Bank Internal Study.

UN (United Nations Economic Commission for Europe) (1995), *Survey of Europe in 1994–1995*, Geneva.

Szangi, M. and T. Czemlér, (1996), 'Investment patterns of Hungary 1981–1995', Paper for the ACE Project No. P-95-2226-R.

Ujházy, K. (1997), *The Role of the Banking Sector in the Restructuring of the Hungarian Economy* (in Czech), Prague: Czechoslovak Trade Bank Internal Study.

Zemplínerová, A. (1997), *The Role of Foreign Enterprises in the Privatisation and Restructuring of the Czech Economy*, Vienna Institute for Comparative Economic Studies, Research Report, No. 238.

5. Investment and Restructuring

Karel Ujházy and Karel Zeman

Investment, understood here as investment in fixed assets, is essential to the normal functioning of an economy. It is necessary both for the replacement of fixed assets that are physically worn out or obsolete and as a precondition for sustained economic growth. It is, quite obviously, likely to be of even greater importance in an economy undergoing, or hoping to undergo, a major structural transformation and hoping for a period of rapid and sustained economic growth. The experience particularly of east Asian countries suggests that high levels of investment are a precondition for moving from a 'middle' to a high level of economic development. Thus investment rates of over 30 per cent of GDP were recorded in the early years of the 1990s in South Korea, Malaysia, Singapore and Thailand, with the last two passing the 40 per cent figure in 1992.

This chapter aims to assess how far the levels and structure of investment being undertaken in CEECs are likely to be sufficient to ensure an analogous transformation. The argument requires an investigation of investment activities in some detail as international comparative studies have consistently shown that there is no simple relationship between the aggregate level of investment and the rate of economic growth. Growth accounting studies and modern theories of economic growth, referred to in Chapter 1, point in general to a surprisingly lowly role for investment in overall growth. A larger proportion is frequently explained by the 'residual' after the easily measurable increases in labour and capital have been taken into account.

Four broad explanations can be given for the weak relationship between investment and growth. The first is the variable returns to investment across different kinds of activities. In some sectors quick returns can be expected to the installation of new equipment. In some there may be no obvious return at all even after a long time period. Thus measurable returns may be very unclear for the creation of a modern transport network, at least within a short time scale, and this is an activity that can require enormous capital outlays. Different needs for transport investment, for example because of long distances involved and sparse population densities, are often suggested as an explanation for low returns to high volumes of total investment in some parts of the world. As will become clear, there are reasons why transport investment may be substantial in some, but not all, CEECs.

The second explanation is the quality of the investment work itself. 'Mistakes' may be made by undertaking investment in new capacity that may not be needed or there may be weaknesses in project organisation leading to delays and waste. That was a typical feature of investment under central planning where problems were exacerbated by restrictions on the import of modern technology, or even of particular materials when shortages appeared in the domestic economy. Similar difficulties have persisted with major investment projects, most notably the nuclear power programme in the Czech Republic. The Temelín power station, already well under way before 1990, remained some time from completion even in 1998 amid a strengthening body of opinion that it should simply be abandoned. Thus one of the main reasons for poor returns to investment under central planning have been reproduced at least in one important case.

The third explanation is the possible need for complementary investment in research, human capital or other less tangible assets. Thus fixed investment on its own need not ensure an increase in output if the skills and know-how are not available to use the new equipment to the full. This is not obviously a barrier in CEECs, although that is largely because investment has been undertaken predominantly in activities that do not need a strong accompanying research or education base. However, a shift towards more modern sectors would probably require a more vigorous creation of the necessary infrastructure.

The fourth explanation is the possibility of increasing output without increasing the volume of fixed assets. There has been plenty of scope for better organisation of work and for more sophisticated marketing to reach full utilisation of existing capacity. Output gains without much new investment have been an important factor enabling CEECs to rise from the depths of depression in 1991 and 1992. They are, however, not a satisfactory basis for sustained growth over a longer time period.

When set against this background, the following analysis of investment in four countries of east-central Europe must raise doubts about their ability to achieve and sustain high rates of economic growth. There seem to be remarkable divergences within the group, with Slovakia and the Czech Republic experiencing much higher investment rates than the other two, but not enjoying faster rates of growth. That becomes largely explicable in terms of the structure of investment in those countries. The general picture is of an absolute level of investment that cannot finance the technological advances needed to match the western European level. Moreover, the branch structures of investment are consistent with the structural weaknesses in the transformation process referred to in other chapters. There is a bias towards activities such as heavy industry and energy which were favoured under central planning. There is inadequate evidence of a shift towards newer sectors or towards modernisation in sectors with greater long-term prospects for expansion. These points are illustrated with comparative data for Germany, including references to the transformation that has taken place in eastern Germany.

COMPARISONS OF GROSS INVESTMENT

This chapter uses data published by the various countries' statistical offices over the period 1992–6. Unfortunately, these suffer from various weaknesses. It is not possible to compare investment levels with the needs of reproduction of the existing capital stock. There has been no full revaluation of the gross stock of fixed assets since 1990, despite the rapid inflation and changes in relative prices since that date. At present, however, the depreciation allowances in companies' accounts do not provide sufficient resources for reproduction at current purchase prices of new equipment. Thus, for example, rough estimates for the Czech Republic indicate a shortfall in 1993 of Kč 90–120 billion for the requirements of simple reproduction of fixed assets. A survey conducted in 1996 for the main representative body for Czech large-scale business, the Union of Industry and Transport, showed that 71 per cent of enterprises had not undertaken a major modernisation since 1991 and 50 per cent of enterprises had not even undertaken a minor investment project with a value of up to Kč 50 million (Maruton, 1996).

The position is broadly similar for Slovakia, albeit with steel and chemicals appearing as exceptions, and for Poland. In Hungary the only real exceptions are the firms under predominantly foreign ownership. The general picture, then, is one of a deepening obsolescence that threatens still greater difficulties in the future, especially in terms of the stock of machinery.

The situation is particularly serious when set against the background of the recent past. Two elements are important here. The first is the general slowdown across all countries of east-central Europe in the 1980s. Increasing economic difficulties and creeping stagnation were met by an 'investment fast' as governments tried to maintain some increase in personal consumption levels. Thus recorded real investment grew over the whole 1980 to 1990 period by 13 per cent in the Czech republic and by 10 per cent in Slovakia while it fell by 9.9 per cent in Hungary. In Poland the dramatic fall at the start of the 1980s was roughly made good by the end of the decade. The 1980s were characterised across all the countries by a tendency towards general stagnation at a technological level that had already been obsolete before the start of the decade.

The first stage of the transformation could do little to improve this situation. Table 5.1 shows the changes in investment levels during the period of the 'shock' as macroeconomic policies were tightened and trade within the CMEA collapsed. The fall came slightly sooner in Poland, a country that imposed harsh policies of demand restraint before the others. Recovery really began in 1992 but still left investment at a level below that of 1980.

Table 5.1 Annual percentage changes in investment, 1989–92

	1990	1991	1992	1989–92
Czech Republic	6.5	–33.5	16.6	–17.4
Slovakia	5.0	–27.6	9.2	–17.0
Hungary	–9.8	–12.3	–1.5	–22.1
Poland	–10.1	–4.1	0.4	–13.4

Source: *WIIW Handbook of Statistics*, 1996.

Table 5.2 Annual percentage changes in investment, 1993–6

	1993	1994	1995	1996	1989–96
Czech Republic	8.0	17.0	14.8	9.1	30.6
Slovakia	13.1	2.1	20.0	37.8	58.4
Hungary	2.5	12.3	–5.3	6.3	–9.8
Poland	2.3	8.2	17.1	23.0	38.0

Source: Statistical Yearbooks of CEECs.

Table 5.3 Percentage shares of gross fixed investment in GDP in CEECs

	1992	1993	1994	1995	1996
Czech Republic	25.4	28.1	25.2	31.2	32.1
Slovakia	29.8	31.3	28.3	30.9	41.7
Hungary	18.9	18.0	19.3	18.0	18.9
Poland	17.5	15.9	16.1	13.5	14.0

Source: Calculated from figures in Statistical Yearbooks of CEECs.

The following years have seen a considerable acceleration in investment activity, as shown in Table 5.2. The big exception was Hungary, which suffered from the sharp drop in 1995 associated with the macroeconomic restrictions referred to in Chapter 3. The other countries, however, clearly surpassed the investment levels of 1989. Moreover, even these figures could understate the extent of the improvement. Investment could now take greater advantage of imports of modern equipment and could therefore have a greater effect on improving output.

This growth in investment activity has been accompanied by a tendency in some of the countries for the share of investment in GDP to rise to apparently very high levels. Table 5.3 shows the gap between those with high levels, the Czech republic and Slovakia, and those with levels close to, or slightly below, the EU average of 18.6 per cent in 1996. Even these high figures need to be treated with some caution for three reasons. The first is that a high share in GDP need not point to a high absolute level. With a per capita GDP slightly under 60 per cent of the EU average, even the Czech investment ratio of slightly under 30 per cent for the 1992 to 1996 period points to a per capita investment level below the EU average. The second is the differing relative prices of investment, referred to in Chapter 3. The third is the structure of investment, a point taken up below.

Changes in the composition and structure of investment can be followed at two levels. The first is the technological structure. There have been substantial shifts from construction towards machinery in the Czech Republic, with the former declining from 50.4 per cent to 40.7 per cent of the total between 1992 and 1996, and in Poland, with a similar fall from 57.4 per cent to 35.8 per cent. In Hungary and Slovakia the share of the construction investment increased slightly, from 50.0 per cent to 53.6 per cent in the former case and from 44.6 per cent to 48.3 per cent in the latter.

There is a general tendency to view investment in machinery as more likely to lead directly to more rapid economic growth, but there are also variations in its importance between branches, such that the technological structure largely reflects the sectoral structure. The significance of this is expanded below with relevant data especially in Tables 5.7 and 5.9. The growth in construction work in Slovakia stemmed from the high share of investment in energy. This included the controversial Gabčíkovo project for redirecting the Danube and generating peak-time electricity which was originally agreed between the Czechoslovak and Hungarian governments in 1997 and completed after the break-up of Czechoslovakia in 1993 as well as other hydro-electric projects. Hungary's figure was influenced by high investment in transport and communications which counterbalanced a low figure for electricity generation. Poland's figure looks the most favourable, although it partly stems simply from a relatively low absolute level of investment in infrastructure.

Construction investment is, in almost all cases, covered by domestic production, for which capacity is adequate. Thus the share of imported construction investment in the Czech Republic fell from 6.8 per cent in 1992 to 3.7 per cent in 1996. There are, however, substantial differences in the share of imports in machinery investment. Unfortunately, figures for directly comparable time periods are not available, but some general indication is possible. The share of imports in machinery investment grew in the Czech Republic from 31 per cent in 1992 to 36 per cent in 1996. The figure for Slovakia over the same period was around 29 per cent, reflecting the slow pace of industrial modernisation and a slightly different orientation of investment within industry. In Hungary it increased from a figure of 51.2 per cent in 1991 to 61.9 per cent in 1992 and 58.6 per cent in 1994. For Poland the available data show a 47 per cent increase in imports of investment machinery in volume terms between 1993 and 1995 and a 107 per cent increase in current prices, which together must imply a rise in the share of imports in total machinery investment.

The very high figure for Hungary can probably be related to the important role for foreign-owned companies and could suggest a greater degree of modernisation of the industrial capital stock. Indeed, imported machinery investment as a share of GDP is slightly higher in Hungary than in the Czech Republic, despite the much higher rate of total investment in the latter case. This matches the argument in Chapter 1 that Hungary may be the most successful of the CEECs in beginning a clear move towards a more technologically-advanced economy.

Table 5.4 Percentage shares of total investment by broad sector

	1992		1995	
	Production	Services	Production	Services
Czech Republic	54.8	45.2	49.1	50.9
Slovakia	53.5	46.5	46.2	53.8
Hungary	40.1	59.9	40.8	59.2
Poland	50.7	49.3	40.3	59.7

Source: as Table 5.3.

The second level for following the composition and structure of investment is its allocation between sectors. Table 5.4 uses the broadest division, between production and services, and shows that the general trend has been towards a growth in the shares of services. The relative stability of the structure in Hungary – in line with the stability in other structural features referred to in Chapter 1 – is partly a consequence of the high share of investment in services already achieved in the 1980s. The changes in the other cases reflect a genuine structural reorientation, following the neglect of service sectors in earlier decades. A precise interpretation depends on a more detailed look at changes within these broadly defined sectors.

However, a comparison with advanced market economies rather suggests that the structural reorientation is still at an early stage. Figures for Germany in 1994 show 23.7 per cent of total investment in the 'productive' sector and 76.3 per cent in services, with a large part of the latter accounted for by housing construction and public services. Similarly, the proportions in the total coming from construction and machinery were heavily dependent on this broad sectoral breakdown. Thus machinery investment in Germany accounted for only 36.4 per cent of the total in 1994, below the level of any CEEC, but for 70.3 per cent of investment in productive activities against 25.9 per cent for investment in services. This comparison rather suggests that the CEECs have a bias away from investment in services and hence from construction investment in general.

The changes in eastern Germany are a warning against interpreting all structural changes as favourable if they move towards the statistical position of advanced economies. They suggest a somewhat more rapid move towards a 'western European' structure, but a move that has 'over shot'. The share of machinery in total investment fell from 45.6 per cent in 1991 to 36.8 per cent in 1992 and then on down to 29.2 per cent by 1994. This was associated with a share of investment in production activities that actually rose from 30.4 per cent in 1991 to 40.7 per cent in 1992 and peaked at 45.2 per cent in 1994 before declining slightly. This, however, was associated with an unfavourable allocation of investment within the productive sector with a bias towards construction-intensive branches.

Nevertheless, the comparison between the CEECs and Germany as a whole points both to a fall in, and a low level of, housing construction and to a failure to develop adequate education, research and other services that may be crucial to improving competitiveness. These seem to be treated as 'luxuries' that can only be afforded by countries that already have highly efficient productive activities that could be expected somehow to develop without the need for those service activities. Needless to say, reaching the level of an advanced economy is hardly possible without the associated service infrastructure. It is clearly noteworthy that the structural changes across the CEECs have still left an investment structure that differs markedly from that of advanced market economies.

COMPARISONS BY SECTOR

In this section the comparison is deepened by setting the changing shares of various sectors in total investment against the shares of those sectors in total GDP across the CEECs. These data do not allow for a comparison of absolute levels of investment, or even of absolute levels of investment per employee. They therefore do not indicate whether investment in any sector is likely to be adequate for reaching the technological level of an advanced market economy. Nevertheless, they do indicate the sectoral biases in investment, how far these are similar across the CEECs and how far they are similar to, or likely to be leading a sectoral shift towards the structures of, western European economies.

Table 5.5 shows the comparison for agriculture. There has been a general trend across the CEECs for a sharp fall in both output and investment. Hungary and Poland stand out as the cases where this has been particularly severe. There are common factors at work here in falling domestic demand and in a degree of lasting uncertainty in the sector. Agriculture in western Europe has received considerable government help that has both bolstered investment and given farmers greater confidence about their futures. These features are lacking in the CEEC countries.

Table 5.5 Percentage shares of agriculture in GDP and investment in CEECs

	GDP		Investment	
	1992	1995	1992	1995
Czech Republic	5.8	5.2	4.3	3.4
Slovakia	6.5	6.1	5.0	4.0
Hungary	7.3	7.2	2.9	3.0
Poland	7.1	7.9	3.3	3.3

Source: as Table 5.3.

In Hungary agriculture consistently accounted for over 10 per cent of investment in the 1980s, but the figure had fallen to about 3 per cent over the 1992 to 1995 period, reflecting a drop of approximately two thirds in total volume. That is roughly in line with the fall in the share of output in GDP. The drop has been particularly severe because agriculture had previously been a major export sector, but rapidly lost both export and domestic markets in face of western European competition.

In Poland investment in agriculture accounted for 14.1 per cent of the total in 1989, but only 3.2 per cent by 1992, from which level it has hardly increased at all. This also reflects falling domestic and export demand, but the striking feature of Polish agriculture is the continuing high level of employment, at 26.7 per cent of the labour force in 1995, alongside an exceptionally low level of investment per employee. This is only 13 per cent of the average for the Polish economy as a whole. Thus, partly as a continuation of a structure inherited from the past and partly as a result of financial difficulties imposed during the transformation process, the small individual farms that dominate Polish agriculture have been able to undertake only an extraordinarily low level of investment.

Table 5.6 Percentage shares in GDP and fixed investment of service sector activities in CEECs

	GDP		Investment	
	1992	1995	1992	1995
Non-market services				
Czech Republic	13.5	10.1	8.7	11.0
Slovakia	11.7	11.6	7.3	2.2
Hungary	17.3	16.8	10.9	8.3
Poland	15.4	13.4	5.6	6.4
Finance and insurance				
Czech Republic	8.2	10.0	7.2	6.6
Slovakia	4.4	6.2	5.2	7.2
Hungary	4.1	5.4	4.5	3.9
Poland	0.5	1.3	3.9	4.9
Other market services				
Czech Republic	25.2	27.4	22.1	19.5
Slovakia	21.1	33.7	18.9	17.2
Hungary	28.9	28.9	31.3	31.5
Poland	28.2	28.9	34.0	27.3

Source: as Table 4.5.

In the other three countries investment per employee is around 50 per cent of the average. While playing a much smaller role in total GDP and even total investment, agriculture in advanced market economies is a more modern and investment-intensive sector. Thus in Germany it accounted for 1.6 per cent of total investment against 1.1 per cent of GDP in 1994 with investment per employee at 98.2 per cent of the average for the economy as a whole. This comparison gives further weight to the widespread concerns from within the agricultural sector in the CEECs over their ability to cope with the greater competition to be faced within the EU. That is a common problem across all countries, although probably more severe in Poland than elsewhere.

A further common feature across east-central Europe is the very low share, relative to Germany, for most branches of services in both investment and GDP. Table 5.6 shows the broad position across the four CEECs. Comparable figures for Germany in 1994 show finance and insurance accounting for 5.6 per cent of GDP and 2.3 per cent of investment while other services, predominantly non-market activities, accounted for 44 per cent of GDP and 60 per cent of investment. There are variations between countries but, apart from the finance sector which is referred to below, they are generally minor in comparison with the gap between CEECs and advanced market economies. The most striking point is the poor representation of service activities such as education, health and housing. In this respect eastern Germany appears to have moved rapidly towards the all-German structure.

One of the important elements in CEECs has been the near collapse of housing construction. The number of completed dwellings per 1,000 inhabitants was already relatively low in 1990, ranging from 3.4 in Poland to 4.4 in Slovakia. By 1995 the figures ranged from 1.1 in Slovakia to 2.4 in Hungary. That can be set against figures of 5.4 for Austria, 5.3 for Finland or 7.4 for Spain. The German figure had risen from 4.1 in 1990 to 8.7 by 1994. Precise comparisons are difficult because the countries use different methods of classification, but there is every indication also of a relatively low level of investment in education, health and public administration across the CEECs.

The finance and insurance sector reveals a remarkable contrast. The Czech Republic is an extreme case in terms of share in GDP although not in investment. Investment per employee in the Czech Republic, Slovakia and Poland is almost three times the average for the economy as a whole, compared with a figure of little over half the average in Germany and only 20 per cent for Hungary. These enormous differences cannot be explained by differences inherited from the past, such as the start made to banking reform in Hungary in the 1980s. They must reflect either a lack of comparability of data or the quite exceptional position of the finance sector in three of the CEECs.

The low shares in investment for most services and for agriculture are balanced to differing degrees in the CEECs by higher shares for energy, water and gas, extractive industries, transport and communications and manufacturing. Tables 5.7, 5.8 and 5.9 show the high representation of the 'infrastructure' sectors. Transport and communications are generally well represented in both GDP and investment.

There are some yearly fluctuations, but the only real difference is the somewhat lower level for transport, although not telecommunications, in Poland. This is due in part to the special pressures on the other three countries from their geographical positions on routes both from East to West and from North to South. This encourages the maintenance of, and investment in, motorways, railway links and pipelines for gas and oil from the East. Comparable figures for Germany in 1994 show a share in GDP of 5.5 per cent alongside a share in investment of 8.4 per cent. These are investment-intensive activities, but the bias in their direction is higher than in western Europe. The point is that once investment is to be undertaken its absolute cost is fairly similar between countries, so that the CEECs have to tie up a greater share of their resources in these kinds of activities.

Table 5.7 Percentage shares in GDP and fixed investment of transport and communications sector in CEECs

| | GDP | | Investment | |
	1992	1995	1992	1995
Czech Republic	6.5	6.3	11.2	5.8
Slovakia	9.4	10.1	8.7	12.5
Hungary	9.3	9.8	15.9	19.3
Poland	6.5	6.5	8.7	10.8

Source: as Table 5.3.

Table 5.8 Percentage shares in GDP and fixed investment of extractive industries in CEECs

| | GDP | | Investment | |
	1992	1995	1992	1995
Czech Republic	4.6	2.6	3.6	2.1
Slovakia	1.2	1.1	2.7	3.3
Hungary	1.2	0.4	0.6	0.4
Poland	3.6	4.6	4.4	3.5

Source: as Table 4.3.

The extractive industries have tended to decline across all the CEECs, although they continue to account for a significant percentage of investment in Poland. Figures for investment per employee are consistent with this. They have been around the average for the economy as a whole in the Czech Republic, below the average in Hungary and well above in Poland and Slovakia, rising to 270 per cent of the average in the latter case in 1995. This indicates how far the restructuring process in these latter two countries has been accompanied by a renewed emphasis towards, rather than away from, some of the most basic industries. A major reason behind the different trends in Hungary and the Czech Republic has been the progressive exhaustion of reserves of coal, uranium and, in the Hungarian case, bauxite.

Table 5.9 Percentage shares in GDP and fixed investment of electricity, water and gas in CEECs

	GDP		Investment	
	1992	1995	1992	1995
Czech Republic	7.8	5.5	14.0	16.5
Slovakia	7.8	5.1	16.6	19.3
Hungary	3.9	3.4	7.2	9.0
Poland	4.0	4.0	12.4	14.4

Source: as Table 5.3.

The share in GDP of electricity, water and gas – electricity is the most important of these – and related branches has tended to decline across the CEECs, while the share in investment has risen in all cases, reaching very significant levels. The comparison with Germany suggests that this is one of the major and most consistent differences from western European economies. Precisely comparable figures are not available, but mineral extraction and energy together accounted in 1994 for 2.8 per cent of German GDP and 6.3 per cent of investment. These are investment-intensive activities and the levels of investment per employee were between 7 and 10 times the average for the whole economy as a whole in Poland, the Czech Republic and Slovakia over the 1992–5 period. The figure for Germany in 1994 is similar even for the combined sector of energy plus extractive industries. Hungary, however, shows a considerably lower figure for investment per employee in energy at only 357 per cent of the average for the economy as a whole, in line with the lower share of energy in investment as a whole. These figures are consistent with the CEECs feeling obliged to invest in energy generation to an absolute level that is in line with the advanced countries of western Europe. In view of their more limited resources, the overall share is very much higher.

There are differences in the importance of the energy sector among the CEECs with particularly high shares in Slovakia and the Czech Republic and a relatively lower share in Hungary can be explained partly by decisions inherited from the past. Both Slovakia and the Czech Republic have been undertaking investment in nuclear power which has been subject to lengthy and expensive delays. Slovakia has also been investing in the Danube project around Gabčíkovo. Hungary was undertaking no new investment in nuclear power over the period studied. It stopped work on its part of the Danube project as long ago as May 1989 amid criticisms of its environmental consequences and did not proceed with expensive work to reduce the environmental damage from coal-fired power stations.

INVESTMENT IN MANUFACTURING

The shares of manufacturing in GDP and investment are shown in Table 5.10. The equivalent figures for Germany in 1994 were 25.3 per cent of GDP and 14 per cent of investment. Thus manufacturing's share in GDP has fallen to an even lower level in both Hungary and Poland, but remains better represented in the Czech Republic and Slovakia. The share of manufacturing in investment is higher across all the CEECs although, in view of the substantially lower level of per capita GDP, the level of per capita investment remains somewhat higher in Germany.

Table 5.10 Percentage shares in GDP and fixed investment of manufacturing in CEECs

	GDP		Investment	
	1992	1995	1992	1995
Czech Republic	32.3	26.8	26.7	19.6
Slovakia	31.0	28.3	32.0	21.1
Hungary	22.2	23.1	24.8	22.1
Poland	28.2	22.6	22.7	24.9

Source: as Table 5.3.

The changes in the 1992–5 period point to a dramatic fall in the overall share of manufacturing in total investment in the Czech Republic and Slovakia, a slight rise in Poland and a slight fall in Hungary. This follows a drop in the years prior to 1992 and shows that the transformation has not been accompanied by general recovery in this sector. The differences between the countries should not be exaggerated. The stability of the shares in Hungary and Poland are based on a significantly lower starting level. The shares for investment should also be set against the lower overall investment ratios in those two countries. The general picture, then, is of a very low absolute level of investment in manufacturing.

Table 5.11 Structure of investment in manufacturing in the Czech Republic, Slovakia by percentage shares of sectors, 1995, compared with Germany, 1994

	Czech Republic	Slovakia	Germany
Food and tobacco	15.8	11.1	11.3
Textiles and garments	4.8	3.5	1.8
Leather and footwear	0.5	1.0	0.2
Woodworking	1.7	3.0	2.0
Paper and printing	6.9	7.8	6.6
Coke, oil refining and nuclear fuels	4.2	4.1	3.3
Chemical and pharmaceutical	8.3	8.1	12.9
Rubber and plastics	3.5	4.7	5.0
Glass, ceramics and building materials	12.2	4.7	7.0
Metallurgy and metal products	13.2	24.5	10.8
Machinery for further production	7.1	5.2	9.2
Electrical and optical equipment	6.0	5.1	10.9
Transport equipment	12.4	13.8	16.5
Other	3.2	3.5	2.2

Source: as Table 5.3.

Tables 5.11 and 5.12 show the bias in investment within manufacturing towards the investment-intensive sectors, representing the 'middle' level of sophistication, such as chemicals, oil refining, rubber and plastics, glass and metallurgy. These are generally over-represented in terms of the comparison with Germany. Detailed figures showing changes over time confirm that, with the exception of Poland, there is a clear trend for the CEECs to move towards these kind of products, although the exact ones vary between countries. For Slovakia the move is towards metallurgy and paper. For Hungary there has been a bias towards investment in the coke and oil refining branch. For the Czech Republic there is a strong bias towards the branch that includes glass and building materials and towards rubber and plastics.

Table 5.12 Structure investment in Hungary and Poland in manufacturing by percentage shares of sectors, 1995

	Hungary	Poland
Food and tobacco	23.9	24.0
Textiles and garments	2.6	4.8
Leather and footwear	0.4	0.7
Woodworking	1.5	4.3
Paper and printing	3.3	6.3
Coke, oil refining and nuclear fuels	17.8	6.0
Chemical and pharmaceutical	11.8	10.1
Rubber and plastics	2.7	4.6
Glass, ceramics and building materials	4.7	7.2
Metallurgy and metal products	7.3	12.2
Machinery for further production	3.9	5.0
Electrical and optical equipment	8.8	5.5
Transport equipment	10.7	5.9
Other	0.7	3.4

Source: as Table 5.3.

The point can be amplified with the figures in Tables 5.13 and 5.14. The ratios of investment to the value of output across manufacturing are fairly similar in the CEECs and often close to the German levels. This could be expected as sectors do vary consistently across countries in their levels of investment intensity. Marked divergences from the international norm would therefore suggest a structural shift towards, or away from, that sector. Significantly, such exceptions tend to be in the investment-intensive branches where each CEEC shows a substantially higher figure in one or more specific sectors. Each country has used its past heritage as a basis for developing export-orientated sectors further and the revenue from sales has enabled enterprises to finance further investment.

Table 5.13 Percentage share of investment in value of output in manufacturing industry as a percentage of the average for that country, Czech Republic and Slovakia, 1995, and Germany, 1994

	Czech Republic	Slovakia	Germany
Food and tobacco	94	71	95
Textiles and garments	65	83	70
Leather and footwear	49	60	60
Woodworking	99	162	138
Paper and printing	191	120	115
Coke, oil refining and nuclear fuels	65	51	60
Chemical and pharmaceutical	218	80	119
Rubber and plastics	210	108	118
Glass, ceramics and building materials	181	110	197
Metallurgy and metal products	74	123	96
Machinery for further production	78	68	75
Electrical and optical equipment	68	104	88
Transport equipment	103	172	110
Other	68	150	84

Source: as Table 5.3.

Figures for the food, drink and tobacco sector are remarkably similar across all the countries. The share of investment is high in comparison with Germany, but the ration of investment to output is close to the German level. Changes over time have also been relatively small. These sectors are strongly oriented towards domestic markets and enterprises have been earning enough to undertake investment.

By way of contrast, figures for light industry indicate low levels of investment which have tended to decline. Some of these sectors have already practically disappeared in Germany so that this could be seen as a gradual move towards the structure of a more advanced country. There are, however, important reservations. As indicated in Chapter 1, the CEECs have been able to expand exports of textile and footwear products into western Europe and this has made an important contribution to trade performance. The low levels of investment are consistent with the observation that this is based largely on existing – and often obsolete – equipment. It cannot represent a basis for long-term sustained growth. The general decline of these sectors, and reports that many enterprises are on the brink of collapse, show that the advantages gained from lower wage costs are not enough to assure a future.

Table 5.14 Percentage share of investment in value of output in manufacturing industry as a percentage of the average, Hungary and Poland, 1995

	Hungary	Poland
Food and tobacco	96	89
Textiles and garments	59	79
Leather and footwear	42	54
Woodworking	96	134
Paper and printing	66	113
Coke, oil refining and nuclear fuels	248	93
Chemical and pharmaceutical	111	127
Rubber and plastics	74	123
Glass, ceramics and building materials	132	166
Metallurgy and metal products	63	100
Machinery for further production	68	77
Electrical and optical equipment	107	93
Transport equipment	93	86
Other	52	95

Source: as Table 5.3.

Nor is there evidence of a basis for growth in the most modern sectors, which are broadly those coming towards the end of the tables. Representation is consistently higher in Germany and, in a number of cases, the trend in the CEECs has been away from these branches. The machinery sector has either stagnated at a low level or has been in continuing decline. Electrical and optical goods have shown some increase in Hungary as has transport equipment in all cases. Inward investment is undoubtedly crucial particularly in the latter of these cases, but it remains noteworthy that the share in total manufacturing investment even in this branch appears to be significantly below the German figure. Data on investment as a proportion of output confirm that there is no consistent basis for a structural shift towards these sectors. The figure is similar to that for Germany in 1994 reflecting, in view of the low level of productivity in CEECs, a substantially lower absolute level of investment per employee.

CONCLUSIONS

The comparison across CEECs fits remarkably well with the generalisation that there is no precise relationship between the share of investment in GDP and the rate of economic growth. In terms of the four points explaining the weakness of the relationship at the start of the chapter, a major role is played by the differences in sectoral structure of investment with the strong bias towards energy and transport in the Czech Republic and Slovakia. It is not possible on the evidence in this chapter to identify differences between countries in the extent of sources of growth without investment or in the quality of organisation of investment projects. The energy sector, however, is one in which poor organisation of very complex investment projects is particularly likely.

More generally, the key question over investment in the CEECs as a whole, or indeed in any individual CEEC, is whether the level and structure is adequate for achieving rapid and sustained growth. The evidence above must raise doubts in two respects. The first relates to the absolute volume which is low in per capita terms, partly reflecting the relatively low level of per capita GDP. Those that do not have high levels of investment in the infrastructure have rather low overall investment ratios. The second relates to the structure which, even apart from the investment in energy and transport, tends to favour sectors that were strong in the past. Thus there is a bias towards investment-intensive branches producing semi-manufactures that were well-established before 1989. These are themselves frequently energy-intensive creating the demand for investment in the energy sector to which the Czech and Slovak governments have been responding.

This is consistent with the argument in Chapter 4 on the weakness of capital markets and the heavy dependence of enterprises on self financing. Investment has been undertaken on a substantial scale where it can be financed by governments or by enterprises that have been able to earn revenue from exports or from stable domestic sales. There is little evidence of a reallocation of resources towards sectors and activities that are likely to provide a basis for rapid and sustained growth.

Thus, despite variations that reflect specific conditions in individual countries, investment has tended to be conservative and backward-looking in its impact on the sectoral structure. Structural change has been most marked where large volumes of investment are not needed, such as in small-scale services. However, any attempt to rush towards a western European structure – and the 'infrastructure-led' east German experience could be characterised that way – seems to carry enormous dangers. Moreover, in so far as it has depended on subsidisation from western Germany as discussed in Chapter 8, it is not applicable elsewhere. The problem, then, is to find the institutional and policy framework that can make possible a sustained reorientation of resources towards the key activities for long-term prosperity without, as in eastern Germany, destroying valuable elements inherited from the past. The role of governments should therefore be to find the means to improve the working of capital markets, to stimulate adequate levels of domestic savings to finance higher investment, to encourage greater inward direct investment and to develop the necessary education and research infrastructure.

REFERENCES

Maruton Consulting and Rating (1996), *The Development of Investments in the Period of Economic Transformation.*
WIIW Handbook of Statistics, 1996, Vienna: Vienna Institute for Comparative Economic Studies.

Statistical Yearbooks;
Statistická ročenka ČSFR, Czechoslovak Federal Statistical Office, Prague, 1992.
Statistická ročenka České republiky, Czech Statistical Office, Prague, 1993–7.
Štatistická ročenka slovenskej republiky, Statistical Office of the Slovak Republic, Bratislava, 1993–7.
Rocznik statystyczny, Main Statistical Office, Warsaw, 1992–7.

6. Towards a Competitiveness Policy in Slovakia

Richard Outrata

This chapter lays the basis for an assessment of the point reached by the structural transformation of the Slovak economy and the first attempts to develop a comprehensive competitiveness policy. That transformation is interpreted as covering the shifts in the sectoral and branch structure of the economy and in the size distribution, management and control of enterprises.

This, then, is not a complete account of all aspects of the Slovak transformation as it does not cover macroeconomic policy issues or a number of other changes to the institutional environment in which enterprises operate, such as the creation of an independent banking sector or of a wide variety of governmental and non-governmental organisations. Nevertheless, the concluding part of the contribution, dealing with the development of policies aimed specifically at industrial enterprises, does point to some of the problems of trying to treat competitiveness policy in definable packages. The wider institutional changes are clearly important for the effectiveness of policy measures adopted.

SLOVAKIA'S MACROECONOMIC PERFORMANCE

When measured by the familiar macroeconomic indicators Slovakia's economic results appear impressive. The average annual rate of growth of GDP in 1994–6 was the highest among the CEECs at 4.9 per cent in 1994, 6.8 per cent in 1995 and 6.9 per cent in 1996. Thus, by the end of 1996, Slovakia had reached 90 per cent of its pre-transformation level of GDP, with a forecast that it should finally surpass that level in 1998 by roughly 1 per cent. As indicated in Chapter 3, there have also been impressive results in other macroeconomic indicators, such as the inflation rate, ERDI development and the level of gross foreign debt per capita.

Table 6.1 Slovakia's macroeconomic performance

	1990	1991	1992	1993	1994	1995	1996	1997
Percentage change in GDP	−2.5	−14.6	−6.5	−3.7	4.9	6.8	6.6	6.5
Percentage change in consumer prices	10.4	57.8	10.0	23.2	13.4	9.9	5.8	6.1
Unemployment rate	1.0	11.8	10.4	14.4	14.8	13.8	12.8	12.5

Source: Slovak Statistical Office, various publications.

Table 6.2 Sequence of CEECs by selected macroeconomic indicators

Ranking	GDP1	GDP2	CPI	U	ERDI	Bud	Debt1	Debt2
1	Sk	Cz	Sk	Cz	Sl	R	R	R
2	P	Sl	Cz	R	H	Sl	Sl	P
3	R	Sk	Sl	H	P	Cz	P	Sk
4	Sl	H	P	Sk	Cz	H	Cz	Cz
5	Cz	P	H	P	Sk	P	Sk	Sl
6	H	R	R	Sl	R	Sk	H	H

Key: Cz; Czech Republic, H; Hungary, P; Poland, R; Rumania, Sk; Slovakia, Sl; Slovenia.
GDP1; Annual percentage change in GDP, 1994–6, GDP2; Per capita GDP compared by purchasing power parity, CPI; Percentage increase in consumer price level in 1996, U; Unemployment rate in 1996, ERDI; Exchange Rate Deviation Index in 1996, Bud; Budget surplus as percent of GDP in 1996, Debt1; Gross foreign debt as percent of GDP in 1996, Debt2; Gross foreign debt per capita in 1996.

Source: Calculated from various publications of the countries' statistical offices.

Tables 6.1 and 6.2 show Slovakia's macroeconomic position since 1989 and provide a comparison with other CEECs. Slovakia generally occupies a middle position when compared with other central European economies, coming last only in the percentage ratio of the state budget deficit to GDP. Some further indicators could strengthen the impression that this macroeconomic development is closely related to, or even a direct consequence of, a successful structural transformation.

The very favourable GDP growth rates after 1993 followed the low points of the transformation recession after a drastic slump in output across all sectors. They have been associated with a rapid growth in the service sector, alongside falling shares for production branches in GDP. Moreover, the contribution to GDP growth of the expansion in the service sector was particularly pronounced thanks to the high share of value added in its output. It reaches a figure of 53–55 per cent, compared with 27 per cent in industry and 31 per cent in construction.

Table 6.3 Share of sectors in value added in selected European countries

	Slovakia		Czech Republic	Hungary	Poland	Austria
	1989	1996	1996	1995	1995	1994
Primary	9.3	5.2	5.0	7.2	6.6	2.9
Secondary	58.3	31.0	40.6	31.8	34.1	37.1
Tertiary	32.2	63.8	54.4	61.1	59.3	60.0

Note: The Slovak figures are in current prices.
Source: Statistical Office of the Slovak Republic, *Statistical Bulletin, CESTAT*, 1996, National Information Centre of the Czech Republic.

The apparently dramatic nature of the structural transformation is shown in Table 6.3 with comparable data for other CEECs and also for Austria. From this it would seem that Slovakia has gone further than other CEECs, and even some in western Europe, towards the kind of economic structure usually associated with some of the most developed countries in the world. There are, however, very important reservations. The growth in the service sector in Slovakia has not been accompanied by labour productivity growth in industry and construction, as in advanced market economies. The rising share of services in GDP is partly a result of a rapid expansion to fill a gap in this sphere inherited from the past and partly a consequence of the substantial decline in industry during the transformation recession and its continuing low growth rate in the following years.

Thus, despite the similarity to advanced countries in a purely numerical indicator, the high share of the service sector has somewhat different causes. In some respects, the transformation process has moved Slovakia further from the structure of an advanced economy and this is particularly true of changes in the branch structure of industry itself. Table 6.4 shows this in a very broad form in comparison with Austria and the average for a group of smaller western European economies. The striking feature, as in other transition economies, is the high share of production in capital-intensive, rather than research-intensive, branches. The Slovak economy is strongly oriented towards the manufacture and export of semimanufactures, especially steel, paper and heavy chemicals.

Table 6.4 Industrial structure of selected countries by factor intensity and use of output (per cent of total gross output of industry)

Group of branches	Slovakia (1995)	Austria (1993)	Small market economies (1992)
Factor intensity			
Labour intensive	20.4	23.5	19.7
Capital intensive	53.7	44.4	49.4
R&D intensive	25.8	32.1	30.9
Use of output			
Foodstuffs	13.8	15.8	18.5
Semiproducts	42.9	27.7	27.5
Short-term consumption goods	12.7	10.9	11.6
Long-term consumption goods	14.9	19.5	17.4
Investment goods and components	15.7	26.1	25.0

Note: Factor intensity figures for small market economies show an average for Denmark, Finland, Austria, Sweden, Netherlands, Ireland, Spain and Norway. Use of output figures show an average for Denmark, Finland, Austria and Sweden.
Source: UNIDO, 1995 and author's calculation from material provided by Statistical Office of the Slovak Republic.

Table 6.5 confirms the low share of value added in gross output against the same comparators, a finding that seems to hold across all the broad groups of products. Thus even when classified as investment goods, Slovak products still have some similarities to semi-manufactures. In general, then, Slovakia has a capital- and material-intensive economic structure which corresponds to the middle rather than the highest level of economic development (cf. Outrata, 1997). In terms of Porter's (1990) classification, it is at the 'investment-driven' stage of development , but making little progress towards the 'innovation-driven' stage.

Table 6.5 International comparison of value added rate in industry by lines of output use

| | Value added as per cent of gross output | | |
	Slovakia	Austria	Small market economies
Foodstuffs	20.7	24.3	26.3
Semiproducts	20.2	32.3	33.6
Short-term consumption goods	30.3	34.8	32.8
Long-term and other investment goods	17.6	34.8	37.1
Total manufacturing	20.8	33.4	33.8

Note: The small market economies figures are averages for Denmark, Finland, Austria and Sweden.
Source: UNIDO, 1995 and author's calculation from material provided by Statistical Office of the Slovak Republic.

Moreover, the low shares of value added in industrial output across all branches can help explain the low contribution of industry to overall GDP and GDP growth. Thus, in so far as the rapid growth in services partly reflects a process of catching up with long suppressed demand, the implication from this industrial structure is that the rapid rates of GDP growth may not be sustainable in the future. The chosen transformation strategy would therefore appear, so far at least, not to have created a solid basis for assuring sustainable growth. As in other CEECs, one of the key policy measures that was to provide a basis for this was privatisation but, as argued in Chapter 4, its effects have been somewhat contra-dictory.

OWNERSHIP TRANSFORMATION

Privatisation in Slovakia began in 1991 within the Czech and Slovak Federation following the same principles: the voucher method was dominant for large enterprises. The first wave was completed at the end of 1993 with ownership transferred into private hands. However, in contrast to the Czech Republic, there was no second wave based on vouchers. After considerable hesitation and uncertainty, the Slovak second wave was implemented in 1995 and 1996 with the emphasis on direct sales, accompanied by the so-called bond privatisation concept. Moreover, the scope of privatisation was narrowed by the designation of strategic enterprises that were to be excluded.

The system of direct sales provides a mechanism for maintaining a greater initial concentration of ownership and for transferring the property to a more limited group of owners. It could, therefore, avoid some of the negative effects associated with the Czech privatisation process. The role of the National Property Fund has become more important in the privatisation process with the power to choose the new owners. Investment funds have been restricted to holding no more than 10 per cent of the shares in a single company, compared with 20 per cent at the time of the first voucher wave. Furthermore, emphasis was put on promoting local entrepreneurial expertise through sales to domestic managers and employees. Sales have been supported by advantageous financial terms, typically involving a down payment of 10–20 per cent with the balance to be paid off over 10 years.

The bond scheme was introduced at the end of 1994 as a substitute for the long-delayed and politically controversial second voucher wave. The government decided that individuals who were registered for the second round would instead receive a bond with a face value of Sk 10,000, maturing in 5 years and bearing an interest rate equal to the discount rate, 8.8 per cent in late 1997. This means that citizens have no ownership rights over the enterprises, but are at least guaranteed some form of payment, unlike the Czech case where, especially in view of the 'tunnelling' from some investment funds referred to in Chapter 7, they may receive nothing.

Nevertheless, there are a number of risks with the chosen approach. Initially selected owners may find it difficult to raise credits or equity finance for restructuring, partly because they are already indebted through the sale process and also because 'outsiders' may have little interest in providing capital if they are allowed only a minority stake. The consequence may be a very gradual process of adjustment, with the new owners doing just enough restructuring to survive, but not enough for substantial improvements in performance.

There have also been doubts about the emphasis on direct sales, relating to the limited transparency in the selection of successful purchasers and in the sales themselves. There is no officially published information on total revenues or individual prices. Nor have the names of purchasers been publicised by the government. The authorities appear to prefer to keep key companies in local hands, to promote the development of domestic skills and experience in business activity, and to be wary of foreign investment unless linked to clear long-term strategic promises. However, attempts to choose from among potential foreign investors have reduced the level of external interest and participation in the economy. Uncertainty over the privatisation process, including several important policy and legislative changes, have further contributed to a relatively low level of foreign direct investment in Slovakia.

Table 6.6 Employment by ownership in broad sectors of the Slovak economy as a percentage of the total

	1989	1991	1995	1996
Private	1.0	12.8	48.9	52.2
Cooperative	16.5	13.0	7.6	7.3
Public	83.5	74.2	43.5	40.5

Source: *Statistical Yearbook of the CSSR*, 1992, and *Bulletin of the Statistical Office of the Slovak Republic*, various issues.

However, the significance of eliminating strategic enterprises from privatisation should not be exaggerated. These were in a relatively limited number of branches and in some industries Slovakia moved more rapidly than other CEECs, for example privatising the Košice steel producer, the country's biggest exporter, over the 1991–5 period. Some shares were distributed in the first voucher wave, followed by employee privatisation and finally direct sale to the management. The privatisation programme was essentially completed in 1996 with the bulk of state property in industry transferred to private hands. Tables 6.6 and 6.7 show the process. Employment in the private sector increased up to 1991, largely thanks to the formation of new, small private firms. The big jump after that to 1995 primarily reflected the privatisation process.

As Table 6.7 shows, the percentage of firms privately owned is only slightly lower in Slovakia than in the Czech Republic. Moreover, it is far from clear whether the different approaches to privatisation in the two countries have led to differences in the performance and competitiveness of industry and to the development of the trade balance. The crucial question is whether, and to what extent, privatisation has been accompanied by, or led to, changes in the structure and management of enterprises.

Table 6.7 Profit-making organisations by basic forms of ownership as of the end of 1995

Ownership form	Slovak Republic		Czech Republic	
	Number of firms	per cent	Number of firms	per cent
Public	475	6.5	976	4.8
Private	6,843	93.5	19,427	95.2
Total	7,318	100.0	20,403	100.0

Source: Statistical Yearbooks of the Slovak Republic and the Czech Republic, 1996

THE STRUCTURE OF ENTERPRISES

The economic transformation has been accompanied by a reduction in the average size of enterprises. This stemmed partly from the new possibilities for business activities and partly from the separation of some sections of larger enterprises to become independent organisations. The result was a numerical strengthening of the weight of small and medium-sized firms in industry.

Table 6.8 shows the transformation as a progressive increase in the share of smaller units alongside a declining average size for all enterprises. Table 6.9 shows the comparison with the Czech Republic, indicating the slightly greater concentration into larger enterprises. In other respects too, such as export performance, they remain crucial to the success of the economy. Its transformation therefore depends heavily on the managements of these big firms. Although it is not a precise measure, changes in management personnel do give an indication of the extent and depth of that transformation.

The results shown in Table 6.10 are based on a survey across 86 medium-sized and large industrial enterprises. As can be seen, in more than half the cases the top management had not undergone any change before 1994, when compared with the period of central planning. The most frequent form of change affected only 10–20 per cent of management members. Even assuming that 'the old managements' could in many cases display the skills needed for a market economy, the extent of change does appear rather low.

Table 6.8 Development of the size structure of units in Slovak industry by percentage of firms in size ranges

Average number of employees	1991	1992	1993	1995
up to 500	65.7	82.2	87.6	91.2
501–1000	13.9	8.2	6.5	4.0
1001–2500	13.7	6.5	4.1	3.7
2501–5000	5.2	2.4	1.4	1.0
5001 and more	1.5	0.7	0.4	0.1
Average number of employees	751	512	417	227

Source: Statistical Yearbook of the Slovak Republic, 1996

Table 6.9 The size structure of industry by number of employees in 1995

Size group by number of employees	Share of employees, per cent		
	Slovak Republic		Czech Republic
	All enterprises	Enterprises with 100 or more employees	Enterprises with 100 or more employees
up to 99	12.8	–	–
100–499	25.8	29.6	31.7
500–999	12.7	14.5	17.8
1000 and over	48.7	55.9	50.5
Total	100.0	100.0	100.0

Source: Statistical Yearbook of the Slovak Republic, 1996.

The reasons for changes in top management personnel were, most frequently, the poor economic situation of the enterprise (56 per cent), followed by insufficient professional skills of management (26 per cent), resistance to the plans of new owners (11 per cent) and other grounds (7 per cent). These need not be mutually exclusive. A poor management could contribute to an enterprise falling into a weak economic situation. Nevertheless, economic results are also partly a question of luck and, above all, of the branch of industry concerned. The starting point therefore remains the small extent of change motivated by a search for more pro-fessional management. This is consistent with points made in Chapter 2 on the level of management across CEECs.

Table 6.10 Percentage distribution of management changes by the share in total number of top management members

| Percent of changed members | Share of change cases in per cent | | | | |
	1990	1991	1992	1993	1994
0	50.0	57.7	48.1	51.9	51.9
1–10	7.7	1.9	5.7	3.8	7.7
11–20	13.5	15.3	13.5	17.3	17.3
21–30	7.7	3.8	11.5	13.5	3.8
31–50	7.7	9.6	11.5	3.8	5.8
51–75	7.7	5.8	7.7	3.8	3.8
75 and over	5.8	5.8	1.9	5.8	5.8

Source: Brzica, 1996.

Investigation of the potential for changing management methods and perform-ance was pursued somewhat further around the issue of whether active owners had been created out of voucher privatisation. Managers were asked about their expe-rience with the representatives of investment funds on firms' statutory bodies. In 31 per cent of cases experiences were described as good, in 11.5 per cent as bad, 11 per cent had no response while in 46 per cent the representatives of funds were not present in statutory bodies.

In those cases where funds were represented they could play an active role. Questioned on how far they perform their ownership rights in strategic decisions of the board, the enterprise managers responding said that fund representatives initi-ated 35 per cent of decisions, other funds 32 per cent, managers of the enterprises 26 per cent and the National Property Fund 5 per cent. Evidently, then, the main responsibility for improving the competitiveness of Slovak industry continues to rest with managements, and largely with management personnel inherited from the past.

COMPETITIVENESS POLICIES

Slovakia is one of those transition countries that has at least at the formal level acknowledged the need for certain specific policy measures to support structural changes and the growth in competitiveness in industry. In 1994, the government approved the first document on industrial policy. That was a positive act, but the approach adopted was open to four main lines of criticism.

The first is that in practice the underlying conception was for 'vertical' rather than 'horizontal' support, meaning support for particular sectors or firms rather than general support for activities, such as R&D, irrespective of the sector. The document was presented as containing elements of both around a general aim of the revival and restructuring of industry towards a higher share of more sophisticated production with higher value-added ratios. The emphasis, however, was on the former and selectivity was defined so broadly as to include a very substantial share of the whole economy. Thus the relevant document from the start divided branches into three groups. The first were the 'strategic' branches, including fuel and energy, machinery manufacturing, transport equipment, metal and metal products and the chemical and pharmaceutical industries. Within these branches 38 enterprises were chosen as strategic enterprises. The two other groups were those based around domestic raw materials and the so-called perspective branches relevant to sustaining future industrial development. Among these were textiles and garments, leather goods, glass and jewellery and the manufacture of electrical and optical equipment. The branch programmes included the conversion from military production and general support for metallurgy, mining, chemicals, light industry and engineering.

Horizontal programmes, conceived as complementing the vertical element, included programmes for promotion of SMEs, for energy conservation, for helping enterprises through temporary crises, for promoting R&D, for use of ecologically less harmful equipment and for helping exporters. The striking point, however, as shown in Table 6.11, is the far greater share spent on the branch than on the horizontal programmes. The imbalance in practice was even greater than that accepted within the government's original assumptions on how money would be spent. In reality, then, the focus was on a general revival across industry as a whole rather than on stimulating or supporting desirable changes in industrial structure.

The second criticism is that the industrial policy was not formulated as part of a coherent package of policies. Thus, for example, it was not coordinated with foreign trade policy, which remained a distinct policy area. Nor was it coordinated with financial and credit policies and there was no notion of linking it to a policy for scientific or technological development. In fact, no policy at all was formulated for those areas.

Table 6.11 Financial means spent on realising industrial policy programmes in manufacturing 1991–6

	Total in Sk bn	State budget subsidies	Domestic and foreign bank credits	Tax allow- ances	PHARE	Other foreign sources
Horizontal programmes						
assumed	5.2	2.5	1.4		0.9	
realised	2.045	0.9	1.1		0.045	0.4
SME support						
assumed	2.2		1.3		0.9	
realised	1.14		1.1		0.04	
R&D support						
assumed	0.9	0.8	0.1			
realised	0.9	0.9				
Export support						
assumed	1.5	1.5				
realised	0.005				0.005	
Ecology						
assumed	0.4					0.4
realised						
Branch programmes						
assumed	20.2	6.7	13.5			
realised	49.0	6.7	35.8	6.5		
Total manufacturing						
assumed	25.4	9.2	14.9		0.9	
realised	51.045	7.6	36.9	6.5	0.045	0.4

Source: author's calculation from data from Ministry of Economy of Slovak Republic.

The third criticism follows on from this. Export support measures were adopted by the government as a quite distinct package from the document on industrial policy. They were actually in conflict with any notion of progressive structural change by giving blanket support across all export projects. Thus, for example, there was no preference to the export of products with high value added or a high dependence on education and research.

The fourth criticism is that both industrial and foreign trade policies tended to focus on the identification of objective problems rather than on working out how the general policy objectives could be achieved by the development of instruments appropriate to an advanced market economy. It would not be true to say that nothing was done, but the measures were in general insufficient and relatively ineffective.

These, however, need not be the principal reasons for the failure to influence structural changes. More important was the absence of two key ingredients. The first was the simple lack of finance from both government and banks. The second was the inadequate number of genuinely promising projects from the enterprise sector that could have justified support.

A NEW APPROACH?

Over the years 1995 and 1996, the government adopted a range of measures which started to overcome many of the weaknesses of the first document. In mid 1997 the government adopted a further comprehensive document updating industrial policy in line with a general forecast of economic development for the period 1998–2005. With this the Slovak government had created the outline for a relatively comprehensive framework for the support of industrial competitiveness.

The measures either already in place or planned for the future span general legal changes and specific measures aimed to promote regional development, investment, exports, inward investment, technological development, growth of SMEs and environmental improvements. The attempt at such comprehensiveness and at coordination between these diverse policy areas appears impressive, but there are a number of weaknesses in the measures that have been proposed and there are grounds for doubting whether the programme will be implemented in full in its current form.

New Laws and Tax Changes

A key element in the new framework is the general Draft Law on the Development of Industry, in preparation during 1997, which is conceived as a legislative measure determining the overall framework of competences and activities of all participants in industrial development. In this sense it is concerned with the acceleration of industrial adjustment to structural changes, support to business activities accentuating small and medium-sized enterprises, support to cooperation among enterprises, support to innovation, research and technological development and support to regional development. It is assumed that the appropriate financial resources will be made available.

This is backed up by the Law on the Structural Fund for Industry which should provide legislative coverage for issues relating to the elimination of differences in regional development levels. It should also cover support for the implementation of development programmes adopted by the government, which can be seen as participation of the state in industrial restructuring. The main financial sources for this fund are to come from the state budget, with bank credits supported by state guarantees. The fund will be at the disposal of the Ministry of the Economy with the aim of stimulating the entrepreneurial sphere towards substantial changes. The precise extent of financial resources was not specified while the law was being prepared.

There are also plans within the proposed framework for increasing resources available for investment. The current propensity to save, as indicated in Chapter 3, has been insufficient to match the country's investment needs, posing obstacles to restructuring of industry. The policy up to 1997 had been based essentially only on tax-credit and depreciation schemes. Support under the new policy framework was to be directed towards decreasing the overall tax burden on enterprises. The tax system was also to be used to encourage collective investment in preference to individual investment and to savings in banks.

Support to Exporters

There are also proposals for a more systematic approach to export support. Export promotion had, up to 1996, been dependent on bill of exchange credits. Within the scheme that operated the central bank was able, up to a set limit, to buy the bills of exchange from commercial banks that had insufficient liquidity. In practice the increasing liquidity of commercial banks has meant that this scheme has been of only limited significance. The amount of credit under these terms was Sk 15.4 bn in 1993 falling to Sk 2.3 billion at the end of 1995.

The picture so far is therefore of a poorly organised system for financing exports with little use of credits on advantageous terms. To overcome this shortcoming, the Foreign Trade Support Fund was established, starting operating on 1 January 1997, followed by the Eximbank, effective as of 1 July 1997. These steps amounted to a slightly belated catching up with the Czech system of export support. It is somewhat paradoxical that the verbal commitment to an active approach in Slovakia was often not reflected in individual measures while the verbal opposition to an active approach in the Czech Republic was accompanied by some relatively systematic individual steps, such as the creation of an institutional framework for guarantees and credits to exporters.

The Foreign Trade Support Fund, as a non-state specialised fund, should assist enterprises in funding expenses connected with participation in fairs and exhibitions either at home or abroad. It is intended to play a role in settling debts on customs duties for the import of modern technology. It can fund trade missions abroad and cover expenses for the acquisition of foreign trade information. The aim is that it should help predominantly small and medium-sized enterprises.

It is funded from compulsory contributions from all enterprises, both exporters and importers, to the extent of 0.1 per cent of foreign trade turnover. The obvious drawback, especially at a time when the hope has been to reduce tax obligations, is that enterprises may see this as another form of taxation without any more significant benefit. Moreover, this method of securing resources means that this fund has no particular incentive to seek cheaper sources of finance on the capital market at home or abroad.

The Eximbank is similar to the standard institutional instruments of export support found in advanced market economies. Its existence is justified within any comprehensive system for supporting competitiveness. In the Slovak case, however, it suffers from two weaknesses. The first is that it was established so late on. The second is that, instead of being subordinated to the banking supervision of the National Bank of Slovakia, it falls under the authority of the Ministry of Finance. This direct subordination to a government body may mean that it enjoys less independence.

More generally, the system being created for export support involves specific roles from a number of organisations, including the Eximbank, the Agency for Export Support and the Agency for Industrial Development and Revitalisation. With this comes the danger of excessive institutionalisation and administrative complexity. Moreover, the means of finance, requiring payments from enterprises, could appear to be taking resources from them while giving very little in return.

Moreover, some important areas are given only limited attention. Provision of information for foreign trade activities is regarded as one of the key factors of export performance in advanced market economies. In Slovakia, despite the proliferation of other institutional forms, there is still no clear responsibility for this activity. It is taken up sporadically in the Agency for Export Support, in the Foreign Trade Support Fund and sometimes in the Eximbank. There is no Slovak institution analogous to the Infocentrum at the Ministry of Industry and Trade of the Czech Republic, although the case for its creation is very strong. Thus, despite the development of an institutional framework for export support, there are still weaknesses in this element of the overall framework for supporting competitiveness.

Inward Investment

A further important element in the overall framework for enhancing industrial competitiveness is support to the inflow of foreign capital and know-how. The main institutional element here is the Slovak Agency for Foreign Investment and Development, established in 1991 but with only 15 employees in 1998. In addition, the import of modern technology is supported by favourable customs duties only in the case of foreign investors. This appears as a rather odd form of additional help to inward investment: it would seem logical to apply this measure also for domestic investors.

A further intensification of the foreign investment inflow might be helped through the privatisation of more state property, either in the form of direct sales, increasing the equity capital, or by managers' contracts. A standardisation of the capital and financial markets, by amending the law on investment corporations and investment funds and by creating a commission for securities, could also help to encourage confidence for potential inward investors. The situation is slightly different from that in the Czech Republic as controls on some big investment funds were tightened at the beginning of 1995 by measures taken by the Ministry of Finance. The problem of regulation is therefore less serious. Nevertheless, the inflow of foreign capital is strongly influenced by perceptions of political stability and by the existence of a stable macroeconomic environment. Slovakia needs to present itself to the world as a country in which investors would not be taking un-reasonable risks.

There is also an absence so far of any attempt on the government's side to map out priorities and criteria for the kind of inward investment it is seeking. Thus it could be making particular efforts to link inward investment to desirable structural changes such as strengthening sophisticated production in machinery and electrical engineering and in more modern branches of industry. Ideally, inward investment should be oriented towards export, bringing technological and managerial know-how and enabling sales participation in distributional networks of mother companies. At the moment, however, there is no clear conception of how inward investment could realistically contribute to industrial restructuring. Nor is there a vision of how it can be achieved, while a number of aspects of the Slovak framework act to discourage rather than encourage potential inward investors.

Support for New Technology

There is, however, at least some progress in support to innovation and technology which appeared as a new element in the government's updated industrial policy. The absence of innovation or technology policies within the whole previous transformation period can be partially excused in terms of the lack of finance. Nevertheless, the failure to maintain and support the research base from the past has made an already unfavourable situation even worse. As in other transition economies, the restrictive budgetary policy and the weak financial position of enterprises led to a marked fall, and often a complete collapse, of research and development. The change since 1989, in terms of the total employment and spending on research, is shown in Table 6.12.

Table 6.12 Number of employees and expenditure on R&D in Slovakia

Indicator	1989	1991	1995	1996
Number of R&D employees as per cent of total employment	2.49	1.86	1.56	1.18
R&D expenditure as per cent of GDP	3.7	2.2	1.0	1.0

Source: *Statistical Yearbook of the Slovak Republic*, 1994 and 1996.

The government's intention is to support innovation and technology development predominantly around specific programmes. These are to be sponsored by the Ministry of the Economy, and the Office for Strategy for Society, Science and Technology Development of the Slovak Republic. This latter body, with about 80 employees, was established in 1995 with the role of elaborating conceptual documents for the government. The two bodies together are to create commissions to decide which enterprises' projects to adopt for financial support.

The government plans to base this around four broad programmes. These are the Technology and Innovation Development Programme, the Quality Upgrading and Industrial Design Programme, the Human Capital Development Programme and the Development and Use of Biotechnology Programme. Their fulfilment is to be financed mainly from the normal sources of enterprises and bank credits, covering 96 per cent of the needs, with only 4 per cent from the state budget. These programmes are to be realised through technical centres representing a special-interest association of research and development institutes. This is essentially a development of ideas applied elsewhere for 'incubators', supported at the regional level. The individual technical centres are to be coordinated by the Science and Technology Agency at the Ministry of Economy.

Although it appears that an impressive institutional framework is being created for supporting technological advance, there are two serious weaknesses that could greatly reduce the effectiveness of the programme. The first is that the programmes are oriented practically to all branches without any effort at concentration into selected areas, where the desirable level of competitiveness should be achieved. The second is the absence of clear institutional and financial instruments for the implementation of the policy approach and for ensuring the diffusion of research knowledge into the enterprise sphere. This is a problem well-known in other countries where an apparently very impressive effort can lead to very little in terms of practical results. Specific institutional forms need to be created to bridge that gulf.

SMEs and Environmental and Sectoral Policies

Support to small and medium-sized enterprises has been a part of the government industrial policy practically since the beginning of the transformation process. The Agency for SME support was established in 1993. Its first activities were the provision of credit guarantees, small loans and support to spin-offs. A further significant instrument of SME support was The Employment Fund established at the Ministry of Labour, Family and Social Affairs which changed its name on 1 January 1997 to the National Labour Office.

In 1997 small and medium-sized enterprises, including tradesmen, produced about 40 per cent of gross output in industry, while accounting for about 46 per cent of employment. Nevertheless, those in retail trade and the smallest businesses generally assess the government support programmes rather negatively. The main barrier, according to a poll with 124 respondents conducted from the Economics Institute of the Slovak Academy of Sciences in 1996, was the heavy financial burden. More than 50 per cent of respondents mentioned this, referring to income taxes and insurance premiums. The next biggest concern was the lack of clarity in the legislative framework and its frequent amendments, mentioned by 32 per cent of respondents. The shortage of bank credits was the main source of complaint for 16 per cent of respondents.

To some extent the government has tried to respond to these concerns in its programme for state support up to the year 2000. Plans include amendments to the system of income tax and of tax allowances, better use of the resources of the National Labour Office, and an improved credit programme called 'Support', to be implemented by the Slovak Guarantee Bank, a body already created under previous government programmes. It will be able to guarantee up to Sk 1.1 billion of credits.

The government also proposed more active support to environmentally beneficial programmes in industry. These were linked to competitiveness for the first time in Slovakia, following developments in the EU where environmental policy is seen as a means to improve the quality of life. It may also enhance industrial performance more directly, for example through finding means to reduce the energy intensity of production. It is to be implemented within the framework of two programmes. These are the Programme of Support to Environmental Management and Audit in the Industrial Sphere and the Programme of Support to Recycling.

A final element in the government's framework is support to selected industrial sectors. This is a vertical element within the updated version of the government's industrial policy. Support is to come under specific programmes for the motor industry, for the machinery and armaments industries and for the development of industries using wood, a plentiful raw material in Slovakia.

Table 6.13 Slovak government's estimate of financial needs for development programmes 1998–2005 in SK million

Horizontal programmes	6,071
of which	
technology and innovation	3,300
quality and industrial design	40
export of investment projects	2,400
capital risk use	330
human resources development	1
environmental control	80
recycling	400
biotechnology	300
Vertical programmes	1,125
of which	
automobile programme	na
other engineering programme	325
wood-processing programme	800

Source: Updated industrial policy of the Slovak Republic, discussed by government July 1997.

Overall, however, the Slovak Ministry of Economics foresaw a much greater emphasis on horizontal than vertical support over the 1998-2005 period. Table 6.13 shows the intended breakdown with the strong emphasis on technology and innovation and the export of investment projects. These are activities in which substantial government support is common in advanced market economies.

CONCLUSION

Despite the appearance of very positive results, the Slovak transformation suffers from severe limits especially in the development of new sectors dependent on the most modern technology. Policies up to mid 1998 have not addressed this fundamental problem. The government's updated industrial policy does represent an attempt to formulate a completely new conception around a comprehensive framework of support for improving the level of industrial competitiveness.

However, apart from criticisms of specific elements, there are more general doubts about the programme as a whole. These relate in part to the nature and complexity of the administrative structures that are being created around the large number of programmes. It is far from clear that these new bodies can develop beyond the status of administrative units and achieve a genuine impact on the restructuring process. When enterprises experience difficulty in gaining support for their ideas, as is likely within this potential maze of administrative complexity, they may themselves lose interest in entrepreneurial activity.

There are also doubts relating to the isolation of ideas on industrial, innovation and foreign-trade policy from considerations of financial policy. As a result promising programmes are not guaranteed financial support and may remain on paper only. This too may discourage interest from managements who anyway may in many cases lack the capacity to elaborate and present quality projects which could justify state support.

Thus in some respects the Slovak policy approach appears as an attempt to take ideas from EU and OECD thinking on competitiveness policy. It differs, however, in a number of respects, including the greater emphasis on elements of detailed centrally-determined tasks for individual branches. Differences can certainly be justified due to the specific problems faced by the transitional economies, but the weaknesses in the Slovak approach referred to above may mean that it contributes far less than it could to the restructuring process.

REFERENCES

Porter, M. (1990), *Competitive Advantage of Nations*, New York: The Free Press.

Brzica, D. (1996), 'Empirical analysis of the selected problems of corporation management in the Slovak Republic', *Ekonomický časopis*, **44**, 359–370.

Bulletin of the Statistical Office of the Slovak Republic, Bratislava.

Outrata, R. (1997), 'Structural changes and competitiveness in Slovak industry', *Ekonomický časopis*, **45**, 480–499.

Statistical Bulletin CESTAT.

Statistická ročenka ČSFR, 1992, Prague: Federal Statistical Office.

Statistical Yearbook of the Czech Republic, 1996, Prague: Czech Statistical Office.

Statistical Yearbook of the Slovak Republic, 1994 and 1996, Bratislava, Statistical Office of the Slovak Republic.

UNIDO (United Nations Industrial Development Office) (1995), *International Yearbook of Industrial Statistics.*

7. The Transformation of Czech Enterprises

Martin Myant

The original philosophy behind the Czech transformation stemmed from a familiar criticism of central planning. Enterprises, so it was argued, had been able to manipulate the planning system to their own advantage. In effect, they set their own plan targets and naturally chose an easy life in which they were free from direct pressures to improve efficiency. The Hungarian economist János Kornai (1980) found an analogy with the position of favoured firms in a market economy referring to a 'soft' budget constraint. Transformation of the economic system therefore required the reimposition of hard constraints on enterprises through the threat of bankruptcy for the enterprise as a whole and the threat of removal for managers. That pointed to tough financial and macroeconomic conditions followed by speedy privatisation to bring the benefits of active, profit-oriented owners. This, it was assumed, would force enterprises to improve their efficiency and competitiveness.

Much of the academic research on enterprise transformation in CEECs has also been built around this framework. The key questions have concerned the establishment and effects of hard budget constraints and the consequences of different forms of privatisation. The argument in this chapter is that such a framework can only provide a partial basis for understanding the changes in the enterprises inherited from central planning. Hard budget constraints and private ownership are not sufficient conditions to ensure a successful transformation. The first part of the chapter argues this around critical comments on past work while the later parts of the chapter are based on case studies of changes in selected sectors of Czech manufacturing. The conclusion is that some of the most important preconditions for a successful transformation at the enterprise level have frequently been underestimated and this has important implications for the appropriate policy framework for advancing the level of industrial competitiveness.

ECONOMIC THEORY AND PRIVATISATION

The neo-classical framework

Placing the hard budget constraint and private ownership at the centre of the analysis fits easily into the world of neo-classical economic thinking. However, it means playing down other important issues. A satisfactory institutional environment – including a legal framework that can ensure formal rules are applied – is taken for granted. Economists have traditionally not concerned themselves with how it might be created or what difference it makes if actors are not obliged to stick rigidly to the 'rules of the game'.

The simple theory of the firm in basic economics textbooks also tends grossly to oversimplify the decisions and choices confronting individual firm managements. It is implicitly assumed that all the necessary information and expertise are fully and freely available and that managements then need only make a relatively simple calculation to achieve profit maximisation. The key factor differentiating the performance of firms then becomes the structure of incentives. Transformation of the economic system is conditioned primarily on a 'modification of incentives' so that the most important corporate actors would 'look to the benefits of enhanced economic efficiency' (Frydman, Gray and Rapaczynski, 1996, Vol.I, p.2). As will be argued, these assumptions are not realistic and once they are abandoned the issue of incentives appears as only one – and often not the most central – of the preconditions for enterprise adaptation.

Researchers in the field may acknowledge that ownership is 'certainly not all there is to enterprise restructuring' (ibid., p.3), but that needs to be matched with an attempt to put this in the context of what these other elements might be and to assess their relative significance. Instead, the 'orthodox' approach has found a welcoming environment in the debates that have developed in recent years within the much narrower framework of comparisons of systems of corporate governance. Key questions tend to relate to the system of ownership, meaning the role of banks as in Germany or of capital markets as in the Anglo-American system, and how they affect incentives. There is a frequent preference for 'outsider' control, rather than giving ownership to management or employees, as the best means to ensure that pressure is kept on managements and that they can be removed if found to be incompetent (Frydman and Rapaczynski, 1997, p.266).

Set in this context Czech privatisation as outlined in Chapter 4 could be expected to lead to highly favourable changes in enterprise behaviour. There had always been doubts about the novel and untried voucher method, but it was rapid and no formally privileged position was given to insiders. Private owners quickly emerged and fears of excessive dispersion were dispelled by the strong position of investment funds. The author of one thorough study concluded that 'the leading current issue in [Czech] privatization is ... how it can be emulated' (Coffee, 1996, p.113).

Events have not been kind for the Czech economy since the completion of voucher privatisation, but there is a great reluctance to break free from the established paradigm. Even the disappointments, it seems, can be accommodated within the same theoretical framework with the problem identified as the failure of a satisfactory system of corporate governance to emerge. Thus, it is argued, an adequate incentive structure has still to be imposed on enterprises and many can continue as before with little need to adapt to market conditions. Weak bankruptcy laws and subsidisation protect the inefficient. A picture has also been painted of dispersed and interlocking ownership which in some versions can appear as a pyramid leading back to the state. Thus big companies are typically owned predominantly by investment funds the largest of which are controlled by big banks. Banks in turn are owned partly by investment funds and partly by the state. A pessimistic view could point to the conclusion that privatisation had not really taken place at all and that only 'quasi' rather than 'real' owners had been found (Mlčoch, 1995). This, or very similar, lines of argument are taken very seriously across a wide range of economic opinion and have influenced international agencies such as the IMF and the OECD (eg OECD, 1996).

Cases are cited below of enterprises that have stubbornly failed to undertake the appropriate restructuring, but they are not typical and changes at the enterprise level cannot be adequately explained within the kind of framework outlined above. A substantial body of survey and case-study research across east-central Europe (eg Carlin, Van Reenen and Wolfe, 1994, and Aghion and Carlin, 1997. See also Chapter 4) shows 'reactive' restructuring taking place across all enterprises irrespective of ownership type. This means primarily defensive measures aimed at survival. The most important are the shedding of labour, the closing down of some production for which markets had disappeared and the selling-off of social activities inherited from central planning. These are the sort of changes that the textbook firm of neo-classical theory could be expected to make when confronted with a hard budget constraint and a cut in demand. The need is for little more than an incentive to survive and an ability to undertake some basic calculations. However, 'deep' restructuring, involving investment, modernisation and the launching of more advanced products, has occurred with any regularity only in foreign-owned firms.

The consistency of these empirical results points to the need to review the theory. The principal inadequacies in the exclusive focus on corporate governance are, as already indicated, its assumption of a stable institutional and legal framework and its oversimplification of the role of management.

'Tunnelling'

The importance of the institutional framework has become increasingly clear with the phenomenon of 'tunnelling'. Czech voucher privatisation was rushed through without the consolidation of a satisfactory legal system. This reflected the firm belief of its architects, such as the then Federal Minister of Finance Václav Klaus, that regulation in any form was an unwelcome restriction of the free market. However, the lax system of controls left scope for widespread abuse.

The extent of this is difficult to estimate. An interim report for the Ministry of Finance produced in September 1997 catalogued 1,420 cases of 'tunnelling out' of wealth in 1996 and estimated 892 in the first half of 1997 (EIU, 1998). A report by the Ministry of Finance (*Hospodářské noviny* 8 November 1997) cited as examples 15 ways in which the property of funds or enterprises could be transferred into the hands of controlling individuals. For the most part these were, strictly speaking, illegal, but laws were very difficult to enforce. Thus, for example, a law was belatedly passed in July 1996 to protect the interests of minority shareholders. In its absence those able to command a majority at a shareholders meeting could simply transfer the enterprise's assets to themselves. However, the law proved ineffective as courts were rarely prepared to intervene in advance to prevent such property transfers from taking place. The only protection, and one to which some shareholders actually resorted, was to take control of the meeting by force (EIU, 1998).

The most dramatic cases have occurred in investment funds. In one case a carefully prepared operation in March 1997 enabled the transfer of all of a fund's assets – estimated at Kč 1.3 billion – out of the country. Laws had been transgressed and the Ministry of Finance missed an opportunity to block the whole operation for reasons that remain obscure, but there seemed little chance that any of the investors would see their wealth again (EIU, 1998, pp.18-19).

Of still greater significance was the case of the Harvard group of investment funds. These had a special place in Czech privatisation history. They were set up by the then 28-year old former emigré Viktor Koženy at the beginning of the voucher wave. He built his success with the promise that those investing their voucher points, bought for Kčs 1,000, would be guaranteed ten times that much one year and a day later. Other emerging investment funds followed with similar offers and this was crucial in overcoming widespread apathy towards voucher privatisation in the early months of 1992 (Myant, 1993, pp.240-1).

The Harvard group continued as a pioneer developing some of the most imaginative methods of 'tunnelling' identified by the Ministry of Finance. They were very weakly penalised at the time. They included a series of manoeuvres that transferred assets into a Cyprus-based company that was safely beyond the reach of the Czech authorities (Wallace, 1996). The exact fate of the original investors' wealth was still unclear in mid 1998, but they may be left with nothing while Koženy enjoys his wealth abroad. This, and other cases of 'tunnelling' clearly have been harmful to the Czech economy, robbing firms of financial resources for investment and delaying the development of a stable capital market. The extent of that harm is impossible to quantify.

Management's Tasks

The second theoretical ground for reservations about the emphasis on corporate governance is, as already suggested, that the framework of neo-classical economics grossly over-simplifies management's tasks during enterprise restructuring. The firm of the basic economics textbook has no internal life or structure. Nor does it have a history with a body of experience built up over years. It is in effect an entity that does no more than undertake an arithmetical calculation so as to reach profit maximisation. This, of course, is an abstraction, but it is very difficult to use it as a basis for understanding the full complexity of the adaptation process in a real firm. Nor can it help explain the growth and existence of large, multi-product firms, bringing together R&D, marketing and other activities that are important for 'deep' if not for purely 'reactive' restructuring.

Once the complexity of the firm is recognised, the process of adaptation takes on a very different appearance. Firms face choices spanning technology, product range and market orientation. These require a longer-term perspective and involve the selection of a definite strategic orientation which may need to change as external circumstances alter. Writers in the field frequently refer to the impossibility of expecting particularly sweeping changes. That does not mean that firms have to 'muddle through' with no clear longer-term strategic vision. The suggestion is rather that 'adaptive and opportunistic' strategies emerge by a process of 'logical incrementalism' (Kay, 1993, p.4, Quinn, 1991, pp.97-8). Firms build on ideas and experiences from within the existing organisation rather than attempting a complete rupture from the past.

This process is reflected in the visible structures of large companies today. They typically have undertaken some degree of diversification, but most frequently into fields that are closely related to their initial activities. That is consistent with past behaviour based on a gradual process of learning from acquired experience. A firm's history creates possibilities for future development but also sets constraints, ruling out changes that would be too dramatic. The implication for enterprises in the Czech Republic would seem to be very clear. They can be expected to make changes, but ones that will amount to an adaptation from what they have done in the past. Moreover, as the next section indicates, the policy framework has itself created some further constraints that have influenced the ways in which enterprises can respond to the new market environment.

THE SHOCK OF 1991

The 'shock' of 1991, in which the drop in demand from the CMEA and the restrictive macro-economic policies at home led to a 11.5 per cent drop in GDP, was not conducive to long-term strategic thinking. On the contrary, the only possible 'strategy' for many enterprises centred on finding the best means to survive in the face of impending catastrophe. Many Czech firms felt they were threatened with extinction and some even claimed to be receiving clear hints that they were on a government hit list. Thus the pressure for 'reactive' restructuring was felt very strongly across much of the enterprise sector. Ownership was not an important differentiating factor – almost all firms of any size had yet to be privatised – but there were differences between sectors. There certainly was not a universal imposition of harder financial conditions.

Table 7.1 shows the extent of the fall in output across sectors of manufacturing inviting a categorisation into three vaguely defined groups. In one there was either growth in output or demand did not fall by very much and the slump in output was relatively small. This applies particularly to parts of the food, drink and tobacco sectors. It is also true of water, gas and electricity generation which saw a 5.7 per cent drop between 1990 and 1992 and a 1.7 per cent drop from 1992 to 1996. The freedom to set prices enabled many of these enterprises to make substantial profits but they have typically not shown rapid growth in the following years: these are sectors that face stable rather than growing demand. In the second group, including much of engineering and the production of semi-manufactures, the fall in demand was very dramatic, but the following years saw a move from a 'survival' into a 'recovery' phase. In the third group, including textiles, footwear and parts of engineering, there has been continuing decline.

These trends in output are reflected in the extent of financial difficulties. Governments have yielded only partially to appeals from the enterprise sector for writing-off debts passed on to enterprises from before 1989 and have been reluctant to reduce the burden of taxation on companies: this was equivalent to 4.1 per cent of GDP in 1996. These burdens contributed to a loss of 0.58 per cent of turnover in manufacturing in 1996 (*Hospodářské noviny* 30 June 1997). Broadly speaking, there were small profits in those sectors that had enjoyed stable demand levels, or a comfortable basis for rapid recovery. Losses were greatest in leather, printing, machinery and transport equipment other than road vehicles, sectors that suffered continuing deterioration after 1992. These also tended to suffer from the greatest burden of overdue payments.

Table 7.1 Percentage changes in output in Czech manufacturing industry 1990–96

	1990–2	1992–6
manufacturing	−37.1	4.3
food	−27.9	−4.3
drink	9.5	25.4
tobacco	77.0	..
textiles	−43.5	−18.1
garments	−50.9	−29.4
leather	−54.2	−32.7
footwear	−37.5	−11.5
wood, excluding furniture	−40.7	−11.6
non-metal furniture	−35.5	14.1
paper	−21.4	2.9
printing	−28.6	15.8
industrial chemicals	−36.4	2.8
other chemicals	−40.6	18.6
oil refining	−9.7	14.2
rubber	−36.8	30.3
plastic products	−21.7	10.3
ceramics	−31.9	13.9
glass	−25.4	−2.9
other non-metal materials	−37.9	4.8
iron and steel	−36.7	4.4
other metals	−66.8	−10.7
metal products	−41.6	6.5
machinery	−49.0	−10.8
electrical engineering	−56.7	38.1
transport equipment	−47.7	29.8
instruments	−57.8	8.3
other manufacturing	−33.9	−11.1

Source: Czech Statistical Office.

THE DOWNSIDES OF PRIVATISATION

The effects of the 'shock' were sometimes ameliorated and sometimes exacerbated by privatisation, the second main string of the Czech transformation strategy. As indicated in Chapter 4, its actual impact was both complex and varied. Enterprise adaptation requires more than a structure for controlling and disciplining managers. It also requires, at a minimum, a framework within which they can raise the finance for investment plus an environment conducive to the formulation of a long-term strategy. Privatisation could be the key to this where it involved partial or full foreign ownership. This brought an almost instantaneous transition from the 'survival' to the 'recovery' phase. Both voucher privatisation and direct sales to domestic owners brought with them a range of negative features that need to be set against the benefits of greater enterprise independence.

The first negative feature was simply the time and effort that managements devoted to formulating and arguing and haggling over plans. The point has been made several times by Stanislav Kazecký, the director of the ventilation equipment manufacturer ZVVZ of Milevsko who was awarded the title 'manager of the year' in 1995 in recognition of his firm's good results. He attributed successes to an emphasis on a longer-term orientation (Šlapák, 1993, p.39) and to a decision to 'avoid the chaos' of the first privatisation wave in which 'projects were changed at the last minute, costing time and energy for the managers'. Instead, the firm had concentrated on 'restructuring, negotiating with customers, shifting the orientation of foreign trade and the like' (*Rudé právo* 7 November 1994). Privatisation was left to the second voucher wave by which time the enterprise had overcome the worst effects of the 'shock' and pressure for splitting up the company was easily resisted.

The second negative feature of Czech privatisation was precisely this tendency towards fragmentation of the organisational structure of the economy. Reform attempts under central planning had frequently embodied deep suspicion towards large combines that were seen as bureaucratic monopolies able to manipulate higher levels in the planning hierarchy to their own advantage. Fears that this power would still frustrate genuine market reform led to a verbal commitment to 'demonopolisation' during privatisation. In practice, however, much of the organisational fragmentation amounted only to some parts of an enterprise or combine being privatised separately while the core of the enterprise was kept as a single unit. Thus there were 995 state-owned industrial enterprises in 1990. By June 1997 privatisation decisions had been taken creating 910 joint-stock companies, representing 88 per cent of the value of all industrial property set for privatisation (*Statistická ročenka České republiky*, 1997, p.512). The remainder was transferred into private ownership in 3,358 enterprises by means of auctions, free transfer, competitive tenders or direct sales. Alongside this were 503 state-owned enter-prises and 17,885 new, generally much smaller firms.

In many cases, however, privatisation encouraged the severing of important links. The harm was greatest where it led to the separation of important activities, such as research, from production. Before privatisation there had been 120 units undertaking applied research within, or for, industrial enterprises and 109 were privatised as separate entities that generally found new roles producing specialised products, trading or undertaking contract work for foreign organisations. Only the biggest enterprises fought to prevent this effective destruction of most applied re-search while others were more concerned with short-term problems of survival (Adámková, 1997).

In light industry the separation of activities meant the loss – sometimes to for-eign owners interested only in selling imported goods – of links with sales and distribution outlets that had previously been part of a single combine or had worked closely exclusively with the manufacturers. Even where fragmentation appeared closest to demonopolisation, it could still have clearly negative conse-quences. This applied particularly in parts of the food industry where the emer-gence of large numbers of newly independent but essentially similar firms created serious obstacles to a rationalisation of production which, it soon became clear, was an essential precondition for long-term prosperity.

The third problem stemming from Czech privatisation is the form of ownership that has emerged. As already indicated, this has gained an almost mythical status as the root of the Czech economy's difficulties. However, the dominant problem with the ownership structure is neither continuity with the past nor a simple failure to establish clearly-defined owners. Of the 100 'most important' quoted companies at the end of 1996 quoted in a guide to the Czech stock market *(ASPEKT Průvodce českým trhem s cennými papíry*, 1997, No.2), 43 had one clear owner with a share of 30 per cent or more, 31 had no single owner with such a large share while in 26 the state had a dominant share, although these were mostly in the energy and communication sectors. Thus there generally were clearly defined owners that could impose the incentive for profit maximisation on managements.

The real problem, however, was that their aims frequently conflicted with the long-term prosperity of firms they controlled. Their focus on short-term financial gain restricted enterprises' scope for investment (Myant *et al.*, 1996) or could even culminate in 'tunnelling'. Rapid turnover of shares also meant that the identity of the owner could change very quickly, leaving many managements in continual fear of hostile takeover.

The background to this ownership concentration and volatility has been a strong urge to sell shares from several levels of the notional pyramid (cf Mertlík, 1996). The National Property Fund, the state's holding body for shares on the way to privatisation, has rarely made any effort to influence enterprise strategies and has been interested primarily in finding buyers whenever possible. Many of the investment funds have been just as desperate to sell to any buyer. They have suffered from the low levels of enterprise profitability that have limited scope for dividend payments. Particularly smaller funds have faced severe financial difficulties, with investment funds as a whole recording pre-tax losses equivalent to 13 per cent and 10 per cent of turnover in 1995 and 1996 respectively. Corruption may also have played a role here with fund managements concerned only to maximise short-term revenue so as to boost their personal incomes, or even as a prelude to 'tunnelling' the wealth abroad.

Individual shareholders were also quick to see the opportunities of increasing their spending power by selling shares, often to mysteriously anonymous buyers. In view of the confused state of the Czech capital market referred to in Chapter 4, accurate figures are not available but it has been estimated that one third of shares held by individuals were sold shortly after their distribution. The proceeds were spent on immediate consumption or converted into bank deposits and other forms of savings that appeared to offer a more secure and often also a higher return.

The purchasers of these shares are not always easy to identify. Some were rapidly growing Czech financial bodies, often with rather unclear sources of initial finance. Many shares found their way abroad with net inward portfolio investment over the 1993–6 period equivalent to 27 per cent of the original book value of shares exchanged for vouchers. The main purchasers were institutional investors in the UK. The Czech banks were also major purchasers.

An optimistic view would see this as the basis for the 'third' wave of privatisation in which rationalisation and beneficial mergers could proceed across industry. Cases are taken up below that could fit with that, but the overall picture is confused. Property changes can be associated with takeovers by financial groupings with little understanding of the needs for rationalisation in production or with diversification by large industrial enterprises into activities that they might be better advised to leave alone. There are also many cases of managements diverting their energies into gaining control of their companies as a protection against the possibility of hostile takeover.

RESTRUCTURING IN ENTERPRISES

This section examines the extent to which the key elements of the Czech transformation – the 'shock' and privatisation – have stimulated enterprise restructuring and laid the basis for future success. 'Success' is impossible to define around a simple quantitative indicator – profits, for example, may be negative both in firms that are investing and growing and in firms facing terminal decline – but it is possible to identify firms that do appear to be building themselves a bright future. Although there are very substantial differences between sectors, it is possible to point to three broad generalisations.

The first is that, contrary to frequent claims, enterprises have undergone substantial changes and managements have been active in seeking alternatives. They have, however, faced severe financial constraints and a lack of expertise that together often ruled out an 'ideal' option. Far from leading to inactivity, this has stimulated a search for strategic alternatives that can use the existing technological level. The distinction between 'reactive' and 'deep' restructuring therefore misses an important part of the change that has taken place. Enterprises have very often found an 'active' form of restructuring that does not fit into the 'deep' category.

The second generalisation is that the low level of management experience and ability has often led to unimaginative strategies and outright mistakes. The forms of privatisation have accentuated these problems, but themselves reflect a failure to recognise the need for a longer-term vision which would have implied, for example, leaving scope for rationalisation across sectors or for the coordination of research with production. The weakness is most visible for those Czech enterprises that have been able to undertake significant levels of investment, but frequently seem to have misused their financial strength.

The third is that discussions of the most desirable forms of ownership structure under the specific conditions of Czech privatisation are of only limited value. The success of an enterprise depends ultimately on its sphere of activities and past heritage and on the ability and desire of management to formulate a satisfactory and appropriate long-term strategy. Every form of ownership can be associated with both success and failure. Moreover, the form of ownership is often as much a consequence as a cause of a firm's potential.

Thus management control in many enterprises has given managers the security to formulate and implement a long-term strategy. They frequently boast of a commitment to the firm in which they have built their careers and of feeling responsible for the fate of the workforce and the local community. However, management control is also associated with cases of abuse of power by some managers and with some absolute catastrophes in which the government dumped a problem enterprise onto an individual. Control by banks can be associated with success, although often because banks have the means and the desire to buy up shares as an investment and have therefore targeted more successful enterprises. However, a high share of bank ownership is also found in some problem companies as the banks have been persuaded to help them survive.

Dispersed ownership by funds or individuals is more likely in less successful enterprises, but often because nobody else wants to buy them. More concentrated ownership by funds may bring stability for management, especially with those controlled by big banks more likely to take a longer-term view. Other funds, however, may drain a firm of financial resources in their search for quick returns. State ownership is often associated with problem cases that cannot be sold, but the example of the Budvar brewery referred to below demonstrates the possibilities for success.

Light industry

The figures in Table 7.1 show the effects of the 'shock' of 1991 on the light consumer goods sectors of textiles, garments, leather and footwear. It meant a collapse of both domestic and export markets and there was no hope of help from the government for these sectors. They had never been favoured in the past and had no powerful political voice. The later years saw continuing decline. Employment fell from 278,000 in 1989 to 125,000 in 1996.

In 1989 the sectors produced standardised, unexciting but solid products. Exports, mostly to the Soviet Union, accounted for 28 per cent of total output. Output decline was caused by the collapse of traditional markets in the East, a limited success in finding new export markets and penetration of the domestic market by both high-quality western European goods and low-priced goods from Asia. Thus the representative body for the textile industry estimated for 1996 that only 30 per cent of the Czech market was covered from domestic production, 30 per cent from illegal imports allowed in by lax customs controls and the rest from legal imports.

There has, however, been a massive reorientation with two thirds of production going for export, albeit often into highly volatile markets. There were small overall trade surpluses in garments and fabrics. The footwear industry underwent a similar transformation (Myant, 1997) leaving light industry as a whole still in the midst of a struggle for survival.

The fates of different parts of light industry varied slightly. Manufacturers of thread and materials had no option but to undertake very vigorous 'reactive' restructuring, reducing labour forces and closing down parts of their production, although they were also able to find some new markets in western Europe. The more successful enterprises in the garment and footwear sectors were able to survive more comfortably by a very active search for contract work for western firms, most of which was outward processing trade. This meant producing to precise specifications, using materials provided by the western company and returning all the output for export. Despite the apparent radicalism of this change, it still fits with an 'incremental' approach to adaptation. In fact, it was the ideal option for managements with little skill in market-oriented activities. It was also a logical response to the break-down of relations between domestic firms that came both with privatisation and with the financial difficulties of 1991: contract work for western companies was not particularly profitable, but it brought speedy and guaranteed payment. This was not true of work for Czech companies.

Contract work alone has been associated with some positive reorganisation of work, with an emphasis on smaller units and greater flexibility, but it does not develop into more permanent links nor does it involve significant transfer of technology. It is rightly seen by Czech companies purely as a stop-gap measure. Czech-owned firms have pursued a variety of imaginative, but highly risky, strategies to return to the more profitable work of producing under their own brand names, despite the lack of resources for investment in modernisation. This has involved largely unsuccessful investment in the former Soviet Union and in reestablishing domestic sales outlets. The most successful firms – such as OP of Prostějov which was privatised into effective management control and has retained a 6,000-strong workforce level – pursued a simpler strategy of investment in new technology. That, however, was only possible for those that were at a high enough level and well enough connected in the West to earn handsomely from contract work and other exports. These together have accounted for 70 per cent of the firm's output.

There are a relatively small number of foreign-owned firms in light industry, but they can serve to indicate the 'ideal' strategies that Czech-owned enterprises might like to pursue. Investors have typically picked on relatively small Czech companies – they leave the bigger ones to struggle on alone – and have achieved rapid growth in output and often also in employment. They sometimes target the domestic and sometimes specific export markets. The key has been high levels of investment bringing new technology and also modern methods of motivating and stabilising the labour force. Some of the claims sound like propaganda – 'the whole factory was reconstructed from top to bottom' (K. Haselwander of Schoeller Křešice, *Právo*, 2 July 1998) – but the figures show investment at between 5 and 30 per cent of turnover. The lower figure can be matched by only a few Czech-owned companies.

The 'third wave' could provide the beginnings of a solution for Czech-owned firms. With profitability low shares have typically not been snapped up by predatory financial groupings and there has been little interest from abroad in established Czech companies. This has made it possible for firms active in the industry to lead the process of concentration.

The biggest group emerged around Centrotex, the foreign-trade company inherited from central planning that was itself largely owned by textile firms. Its management claimed to be aiming to bring together a number of textile and garment firms, ending the cut-throat price competition between them, stabilising their ownership structures and encouraging banks to take the plunge of financing investment. By the end of 1997 it controlled 6 companies and claimed to be integrating activities between them. This, however, was at best a small and belated beginning for the sector as a whole. Moreover, the acquisitions had been financed by bank loans and, by 1998, repayments were overdue. Centrotex faced financial disaster amid rumours of possible 'tunnelling' from the firms it controlled.

Engineering and transport equipment

The engineering industry had accounted for 29 per cent of industrial employment in 1989, covering an enormous range of products, including heavy capital equipment, motor vehicles and lighter consumer goods. As indicated in Table 7.1, it was hit very hard by the 'shock' of 1991. The situation was worst for those enterprises oriented towards the Soviet market, but subsequent recovery depended on the strategies adopted by managements which in turn depended to a great extent on the enterprise's past history and current potential. These strategies were much more varied than in other sectors, but three broad possibilities can be identified, with scope for finding a combination between them, especially in the larger and more diversified engineering combines.

The first was to remain under Czech ownership and stick with the same finished product. With a very few exceptions, this has been disastrous. The reasons for this choice were partly objective. Thus firms with modern equipment dedicated to a particular finished product were faced with greater problems of adaptation. Nevertheless, subjective factors were always important. A no-change strategy was particularly likely for enterprises with an internationally-known finished product and a proud tradition often stretching back to long before the Communist period. It is not unique to engineering, but far more common there than in other parts of the economy, reflecting the past favoured status of the sector and its continuing strength in gaining access to credit. Very occasionally, it probably was the basis for the best available strategy. Usually, however, there was at least one alternative available, even if it might not have been very inviting.

The second option was to remain under Czech ownership while allowing a shift towards less sophisticated products for export to the West. There is some analogy here to the search for contract work in light industry, but there have been three important differences. The first is that it tends to be more profitable, thereby laying the basis for investment and expansion for the Czech firm. The second is that, as domestic materials are used, there is more possibility of recreating or strengthening links between domestic firms. The third is that there is more scope for autonomous product development from these simpler products. There is therefore a possibility of climbing back up the scale towards more sophisticated products. This may mean sale of finished products, often with some technologically advanced parts provided by a western partner, although more usually it means progressive improvement of the essentially simpler product. More ambitious attempts to break out into completely new fields by investing abroad or by broad diversification appear to have been very risky.

The third option was to link up with a foreign firm. In engineering this may involve integration into a wider production structure, but the foreign firm is not usually attracted unless there is significant potential on the Czech market: not much inward investment has been directed towards immediate export alone. The Czech brand name may be submerged, but the foreign firm can typically bring investment and employment.

These different possibilities can be illustrated starting with one of the best-known examples of a firm that has failed to adapt, although it had a number of clear alternatives at different periods. The Tatra lorry manufacturer, with an output in 1989 of 14,824 of its tough vehicles, ideal for construction projects in extreme conditions, could have gone into partnership with three other Czech vehicle producers. This would have been in line with an assessment by government researchers before 1989 and of a government report in 1990 that the companies had no serious chance if they remained isolated (Myant, 1989, pp.236–7, and Myant, 1993, p.250). It could have pursued a deal on offer in 1992 to assemble lorries for Iveco. Instead, its management persuaded the government to support privatisation as an independent company with 96 per cent of the shares exchanged for vouchers.

In this case, then, dispersed ownership was a result of a management's determination to pursue a mistaken strategy. There have, however, been active interventions by the owners, and even a takeover by Škoda-Plzeň in February 1996. None has fundamentally altered the strategy which left Tatra still with half its original workforce while running at derisory levels of output – the lowest point was 422 vehicles in 1995 – and building up debts by 1997 equivalent to 0.33 per cent of total annual GDP. The key factor explaining the extent of this catastrophe was an exaggerated pride in the end product that prevented successive managements from seeing the need to retreat to less prestigious forms of production. This, it should be added, was encouraged by the government which may well have been actively involved in encouraging banks to continue extending credit. In some cases the state has been more open in helping to bail out prestigious enterprises.

Tatra is not typical of engineering enterprises, but neither is it an isolated example. There are even firms so tied to their past that they have tried to resurrect production programmes that had been abandoned years before. There is the stubborn motorcycle producer Jawa that stuck rigidly to faith in its product despite doubts from within the government before 1989 and a fall in output from 106,000 vehicles in 1988 to 7,000 in 1994. Finally in 1996, with debts of Kč 500 million, it was sold off to another Czech engineering firm that was prepared to carry the debt and even to finance new investment, albeit in old technology, while remaining absolutely determined to maintain the production of motorcycles.

The form taken by the second option varies widely between enterprises and there have been failures as well as successes. The former has generally been associated with over-ambitious diversification or investment abroad, with China appearing both particularly attractive and dangerous to Czech companies. It is, of course, impossible to judge whether a different strategy would have brought better results, but the greatest successes have tended to come from strategies more solidly based on past experience.

The most impressive of all has been ZPS, a machine-tool firm based in Zlín. This was a well-established and proud company that could trace its origins back to 1903. It had sold to Third World and advanced market economies but by the late 1980s 70 per cent of output was going to the Soviet Union. By 1997 it was exporting 70 per cent of output, but to the USA, western Europe and some developing countries. The greatest success began in 1992 when efforts led to an agreement to sell machine tools in the USA. A still more lucrative deal was signed in 1995 with the US branch of the Japanese Okuma company, again for selling specialised machine tools in the USA, a market that was taking 20 per cent of the firm's total output. It is thereby keeping in touch with the peak levels of technology, but it relies on Japanese or US electronics for its machine tools and this accounts for about 60 per cent of the value of its products. Moreover, it has deliberately maintained a degree of product diversity and sells simpler machine tools in Third World markets while earning substantial revenue from exporting castings to western machine-tool manufacturers.

This then was a strategy built on past capabilities. It did not require particularly high levels of investment in new technology – investment has reached around 5 per cent of turnover – and the problem of finding markets was solved by foreign partnerships. Nor was finance needed to cover sales on credit as, unlike some other branches of engineering, machine-tool purchasers tend to pay up quickly. The Czech company can compete successfully thanks to the skills of its own workforce and increased its turnover fivefold between 1992 and 1997 to contribute 0.6 per cent of total Czech exports.

The 'third wave' did not bring threats of takeover. ZPS has been under dispersed ownership by solid financial institutions. It did, however, create opportunities to expand capacity by buying up other small engineering firms that had been unable to find recovery strategies. Ultimately, however, expansion has proved beyond the firm's financial capabilities. Its expansion has been based on building up an exceptionally high level of debts to banks which, at 95 per cent of sales in 1995, was surpassed only by Tatra among major engineering companies. Thus even its degree of success does not mean freedom from constraints and ZPS started looking in 1998 for a possible foreign partner to take a share in ownership and to provide finance for a further major expansion.

A somewhat less successful case illustrating a more diversified strategy is provided by the giant Škoda-Plzeň heavy engineering combine. Its restructuring story includes ad hoc government help, fragmentation of production programmes, foreign ownership, the search for new export markets and even involvement in takeovers to establish an ever more diversified conglomerate. Before 1989 it had over 38,000 employees and a product range spanning railway locomotives, trolley-buses and power generating equipment, with a major share in eastern Europe's nuclear power programme. It suffered an initial fall in output in line with engineering as a whole. This, plus non-payment of bills by customers including even the state-owned railways, forced the combine into 'reactive' restructuring with closures of some plant and reductions in the labour force. This had fallen to 17,000 by the end of 1997.

The first search for a solution led in two directions. On the one hand the firm moved to simpler products, including railway wagons for Siemens instead of locomotives to the Soviet Union, and forgings and castings for export to various western firms. Profits were low, but payment was rapid and guaranteed. On the other hand Škoda sought a permanent solution by linking with a foreign partner and by 1992 that was clearly going to be Siemens. Ultimately, however, the management was not prepared to accept terms that did not ensure the survival of the whole combine.

With the combine in deep financial crisis, the government was persuaded to sponsor a rescue package, also involving banks, under which 20 per cent of the shares were sold to the new General Director Lubomír Soudek. It is not clear how he raised the necessary financial resources. Amid rhetoric about the prowess of Czech engineering skills, full foreign ownership was ruled out but subsidiaries of the combine were able to link up with individual foreign partners. Complete organisational fragmentation was also ruled out with the government accepting that it would have been an impossibly complex task to sort out the financial implications.

This reasonable stability in ownership enabled the firm to develop a highly diversified strategy that could take it beyond the 'survival' stage. The crucial constraint was that it could not hope to compete with the best in the world. Productivity was well below the western European level. It had retained a research facility, with about 200 employees and accounting for about 1 per cent of turnover, but that is negligible when compared with the spending of major engineering companies elsewhere. It is equivalent to about 0.3 per cent of the total spent by Siemens.

Investment has reached about 5 per cent of sales which is a low figure by international standards and not all of it has been wisely spent. The common feature to much of the firm's strategy has remained the low requirement for investment and expensive technology. Some activities are a continuation from the firm's past. In 1998 it renewed sales of railway locomotives to Russia, after 2,500 had been supplied to former USSR in previous decades. It has developed from its switch towards simpler 'heavy' products and components for western firms with a Kč 800 million investment, financed partly by the European Bank for Reconstruction and Development, to gain dominance in European markets for the production of the biggest crank shafts for electricity generation and large ships. It has developed its strength as the world's second largest producer of trolleybuses by investing in assembly facilities abroad, most notably in a joint venture in the USA.

Although Soudek's claims to be a major force in world engineering seem exaggerated, as do some of his predictions of future growth, the combine has been successful in Czech terms. It has moved beyond a struggle for pure survival, although it was profitable only briefly in 1994 before rigorous accounting practices were introduced. By 1997 it had reached three times the level of 1992 output and contributed 2.4 per cent of total Czech exports.

The 'third wave' brought both threats and new opportunities. There were rumours of a possible takeover attempt in mid 1998 with 29 per cent of the shares held abroad: both Siemens and the Košice steel manufacturer were seen as potential bidders. Škoda, however, has been unable to resist the opportunity to become an even broader conglomerate, betraying a familiar emotional attachment to failed end-products. Thus it bought controlling shares in the two crisis lorry manufacturers Liaz and Tatra. In both cases the Škoda management greatly exaggerated their potential and seems to have been attracted by the thought of having its name back on a vehicle, implicitly challenging the status of the Škoda car manufacturer of Mladá Boleslav which was a completely separate company. The Škoda-Plzeň management may also have been encouraged by hints that the government would arrange to write-off the lorry manufacturers' debts. In practice, Škoda devoted a significant share of its R&D resources to new product development in motor vehicles and has been rewarded only with the prospect of continuing losses. By 1998 it was seeking to sell the two companies.

Diversification was a major factor contributing to losses calculated as Kč 1.1 billion in 1996, equivalent to almost 10 per cent of turnover. This was partly the result of the need to allow for past unpaid debts, but major contributors were Tatra, Liaz, joint ventures in China and the USA and an east German company bought in 1994 from the east German privatisation agency the Treuhandanstalt for DM 1, but with a commitment to maintain 900 employees. The only completely new venture, a plant for mass-producing aluminium cans, also proved to be a failure and was put up for sale in 1998. Škoda, however, was still on the look-out for more possible acquisitions across the financially-troubled Czech engineering industry.

While parts of the Škoda story can be repeated across Czech engineering, completely different possibilities are opened up to firms by foreign ownership. As in light industry, it provides an immediate solution to financial difficulties, problems of strategy formulation and ownership stability. Thus there is no need to endure the fragmentation of production processes when the old finished product can be improved with new investment or sold through an established sales network.

There have been a few failures when the inward investor has not been interested in modernising the Czech operation. There have also been many cases of potential investors ultimately failing to agree on terms largely because, as in the case of Škoda-Plzeň and Tatra, they have not been intending to maintain employment levels and previous production programmes. Foreign ownership has therefore been associated mostly with enterprises that already have considerable potential and that generally do not need the reductions in labour force that have hit most Czech-owned firms. Thus the firms' strategies are generally very much simpler than that of a Czech-owned counterpart and may appear to be much closer to continuity with the past, albeit with levels of investment that sometimes exceed 30 per cent of turnover.

The most important case of incorporation into a foreign company has been the purchase of the Škoda car manufacturer by Volkswagen enabling dramatic success by the modernisation of production and development from existing models. It has amounted to the transformation of a whole sector bringing similar improvements across a range of existing component manufacturers alongside new inward investment from others (Myant, 1997). In other branches of engineering, inward investment has meant the modernisation of a single enterprise only, although in such cases the good payment discipline is beneficial for cooperation across the Czech economy. Very often the first interest has been in the domestic market, although with the possibility of gradual integration into an international production process.

Milk processing

While light industry and much of engineering have suffered from severe financial constraints, parts of the food and drink sector can stand as a warning against the dangers of easy financial conditions when managements lack the ability and imagination to use their advantages wisely. The clearest example is the milk-processing industry. Before 1989 it had been based on a large number of small plants serving local markets but organisationally incorporated into multi-plant combines. Technology is fairly easily transferable with available modern equipment and therefore need not involve foreign ownership. However, the scale of production required points to clear advantages in expanding beyond the previous local markets.

The 'shock' of 1991 actually gave milk-processing firms a period of temporary prosperity as farmers were unable to cut milk output and the price of the industry's input therefore fell dramatically. The resulting profits were used rather mechanically to finance indiscriminate investment and modernisation across the sector. In the following years, however, farms were able to adapt to the lower level of demand – the number of cows in 1997 was half the 1989 level – and it was the milk processors who were left with excess capacity and severe financial difficulties while the remaining farmers began to enjoy a 'golden age'.

Lack of coordination was accentuated by privatisation which enabled individual managements to pursue their own parochial ambitions by seeking independence. As the enterprises seemed to be reasonably successful in short-term financial terms the government, with no other conception for the development of the sector, had no objection. The milk-producing combines were split up, leading to a plethora of small, independent producers, estimated at 130 in mid 1996. In many cases, firms with almost identical production profiles were competing with each other, while capacity utilisation was estimated at 60–70 per cent over the industry as a whole (*Hospodářské noviny* 23 April 1998).

The key to success has been demonstrated by the South Bohemian Dairies (Jihočeské mlékárny, JčM). It did not have the best or most modern equipment. Its advantage was a management that could stand out against fragmentation and ensure privatisation of the old combine as a whole. The management immediately set about its plan of cutting the number of plants from 15 to 6, with specialisation and modernisation of those that remained. It was a hard battle to win acceptance for this plan, but employment fell only by 8 per cent between 1991 and 1995 at which time the firm was ranked as the biggest Czech-owned company in the food industry. With about 20 per cent of the country's milk production, it had five times the turnover of the next biggest milk-processing firm.

It still faced many of the familiar problems of Czech-owned companies. Poor payment discipline of customers made cooperation in production very difficult and threatened the security of sales. The solution was to gain control over outlets and to this end resources were diverted to buying shares in two big wholesalers in September 1996. JčM was thereby able to increase output after a low point in 1994 while the sector as a whole was in gradual, but continual, decline. It was therefore slightly better placed to face the renewed problems in 1997 when domestic demand was squeezed again by the government's macroeconomic measures.

The 'third wave' brought both new threats and a glimmer of hope for the sector. There have been many voices from within the industry complaining that greater pressure from international competition is imminent, especially with accession to the EU, and that survival may depend on fusions and the reduction of excess capacity. There have been some attempts by firms to come together, but they have appeared rather half-hearted and had not by 1998 involved rationalisation of production. This only becomes a realistic possibility where an owner can impose its authority.

JčM lacks the financial resources to undertake any such task, even if it had the inclination. In fact, as a successful company privatised largely by voucher into dispersed ownership, it has been worried about the possibility of takeover. The threat was clear during 1996 and 1997 as shares changed hands several times ending, it appeared, with a framework that will eventually enable the management to gain majority control. However, it is unclear how this will be financed.

The most active in acquisitions in this sector is Kovopetrol of Plzeň, a conglomerate that emerged in October 1993 out of a company involved in risky international trade deals. It developed its own investment funds and share dealing businesses alongside firms in the milk, oil and wood industries. By early 1998 it controlled 7 milk-processing firms with a capacity equivalent to almost 10 per cent of total Czech output. Its management claimed to be aiming to restructure and specialise production, to stabilise links with suppliers and distributors and to create conditions for investment and modernisation. Its promises were greeted with some scepticism – JčM appeared to be nervous of a possible takeover by Kovopetrol – but rationalisation across at least some of its firms appeared to be under way in 1998. However, the process is very slow and many other firms have been left facing possible bankruptcy and the even more immediate wrath of farmers to whom bills have not been paid.

Brewing

The brewing industry was one of the most favourably placed of all, weathering the 'shock' of 1991 with nothing approaching the catastrophic drops in output experienced elsewhere. It recorded profits of Kč 3 billion in 1992. Small annual changes in demand and output have reflected weather conditions as much as longer-term trends. Moreover, despite complaints about out-dated equipment, productivity in terms of physical output per production worker was estimated at about 80 per cent of the German level, a figure similar to that accepted by Bass when it took over the Prague brewery. The domestic market has proved totally secure, with imports never exceeding a negligible level. Exports reached 9 per cent of output in 1995 and potential has always seemed good, based on the industry's long-standing international reputation and a few well-known brand names.

This comfortable situation might have been expected to encourage compla-
cency but, if anything, the exact opposite was the case. Privatisation again
cemented a fragmented structure with 70 breweries organised into 45 firms. Some
of the key firms in the industry responded to fears of over-capacity and stagnating
demand by strategies of vigorous expansion. Investment passed 20 per cent of
sales in a number of cases – a quite exceptional figure for Czech-owned firms –and
the biggest ones have continued to be highly profitable. The same strategy was
copied across all size ranges but bigger firms have clear advantages in their ability
to advertise successfully, to develop distribution facilities and to control restaurants
and other outlets. Inevitably, a number of firms have run into severe financial difficulties as the loans they required to finance investment have come up for
repayment. Thus, as in milk-processing, allowing fragmentation of the industry has
contributed to difficulties in a sector that seemed to have survived the 'shock' of
1991 largely unscathed.

Foreign brewers have been eager to acquire Czech companies but, in contrast
to the engineering industry, inward investment was never encouraged by the
government. In some cases it was actively blocked around the refusal to sell the
'family silver', meaning especially Budvar and Plzeňský Prazdroj, to foreigners.
Budvar is a somewhat exceptional case as it controls the Budweiser label in much
of the world and is therefore of enormous value to the US giant Anheuser-Busch
which uses the same brand name wherever it can. There is a fear that any private
owner of Budvar could be tempted to sell up to the US firm and it has remained
under state ownership. It could, however, more than double its output between
1989 and 1995 proving that both private and foreign ownership are unnecessary
when a management has a clear strategy, adequate financial resources and a strong
product.

Plzeňský Prazdroj, claiming to produce the genuine Pilsner beer, was privatised largely by voucher and therefore could, and at one point nearly did, fall under
foreign ownership. It has pursued a strategy of vigorous expansion increasing its
share in the Czech market from 16 per cent in 1992 to 25 per cent in 1997. It has
also taken an initiative in expanding abroad with exports to western and eastern
Europe and investment and joint production in parts of the former Soviet Union.

The first successful move by a foreign company was made by the UK firm
Bass which bought into the Prague brewery, with 11 per cent of the Czech market,
in November 1993. It later gained a full majority share. Bass brought investment,
but did not change the product or the basic technology. It brought no gains in the
domestic market, although it did open up export markets to take 17 per cent of
output by 1996. Fears that it would use the firm as a base from which to sell imported beer were soon allayed with Czech customers showing little interest. In fact,
much of Bass's activities have focused on further acquisitions.

The 'third wave' has brought some help to smaller breweries when they have been bought by one of the Czech giants. A few efforts by smaller Czech brewers to join together on their own have proven unsuccessful. Several, however, have found a road to survival in face of financial difficulties by inviting in a foreign owner purely as a means to cover for their high levels of investment. This may, in effect, be delaying rationalisation across the sector.

The threat of foreign takeover plus the potential for expansion abroad has also stimulated the biggest Czech companies to try to unite forces. Radegast, the successful brewery in North Moravia with a 14 per cent share of the market in 1997, fought off a takeover attempt by Bass in mid 1997. It then attempted a merger with Plzeňský Prazdroj which would have created a giant company controlling about 40 per cent of the Czech market. This was blocked by the Czech anti-monopoly agency, but with the possibility during 1998 that it would still be allowed.

As is so often the case, this proposed merger raised complex issues. It was presented as a step towards creating a powerful and prestigious Czech firm that could expand exports and raise finance for further investment. It was effectively sponsored by the UK branch of the Japanese investment bank Nomura which had become the ultimate dominant owner of both brewing firms and that had also bought a chain of UK pubs. The merger, however, would probably also crush smaller Czech breweries leading to a still greater dominance of the domestic market. They led the objections along with Bass which, of course, could also be worried about competition in the UK.

However, dominance by one firm is not unusual in smaller market economies and rationalisation around an internationally-known company could be the best outcome for the Czech economy as a whole. In brewing more than any other sector there is the potential for Czech firms to claim a place on the world stage in their own right. As the discussion of other sectors has indicated, the more usual picture is of a struggle against severe constraints even among firms that can claim to be the most successful.

Note: The research reported above was derived from case studies of over 100 enterprises in light industry, engineering and transport equipment, brewing and milk processing. Information was derived from material published by the companies and in *Hospodářské noviny, Ekonom, Lidové noviny, Mladá fronta dnes, Rudé právo, Práce* and *Právo* over the period 1989 to 1998.

REFERENCES

ASPEKT Průvodce českým trhem s cennými papíry, quarterly, Prague: ASPEKT Kilcullen.

Adámková, A. (1997), 'Mít či nemít', Ekonom, No.13.

Aghion, P. and W. Carlin, 'Restructuring outcomes and the evolution of ownership patterns in Central and Eastern Europe', in Zecchini, 1997.

Carlin, W., J. van Reenen, T. Wolfe (1994*), Enterprise Restructuring in the Transition: An Analytical Survey of the Case Study Evidence for Central and Eastern Europe*, EBRD Working Paper No.14.

Coffee, J.C. Jr. (1996), 'Institutional investors in transitional economies: Lessons from the Czech experience', in Frydman, Gray and Rapaczynski, Vol.1.

EIU (Economist Intelligence Unit) (1998), *Country Report. The Czech Republic*, First Quarter.

Frydman, R., C. Gray and A. Rapaczynski (1996) (eds)*, Corporate Governance in Central Europe and Russia*, 2 vols, Budapest: Central European University Press.

Frydman, R. and A. Rapaczynski (1997), 'Corporate governance and the political effects of privatisation', in Zecchini, 1997.

Kay, J. (1993), *Foundations of Corporate Success: How Business Strategies Add Value*, Oxford: Oxford University Press.

Kornai, J. (1980), *The Economics of Shortage*, 2 vols, Amsterdam: North Holland.

Mertlík, P. (1996), 'Privatizace po česku: pět let putování od veřejného vlastnictiví k veřejnému vlastnictví?' *Politická ekonomie*, **44**, 499–514.

Mlčoch, L. (1995), 'Restrukturalizace vlastnických vztahů očima institucionálního ekonoma', *Politická ekonomie*, **43**, 297–306.

Myant, M. (1989), *The Czechoslovak Economy 1948–1988: The Battle for Economic Reform*, Cambridge: Cambridge University Press.

Myant, M. (1993), *Transforming Socialist Economies: The Case of Poland and Czechoslovakia*, Aldershot, UK and Brookfield, US: Edward Elgar.

Myant, M., F. Fleischer, K. Hornschild, R. Vintrová, K. Zeman and Z. Souček (1996), *Successful Transformations? The Creation of Market Economies in Eastern Germany and the Czech Republic*, Cheltenham, UK and Lyme, US: Edward Elgar.

Myant, M. (1997), 'Enterprise restructuring and policies for competitiveness in the Czech Republic', *Ekonomický časopis*, **45**, 546–67.

OECD (1996), *Economic Surveys, The Czech Republic*, Paris.

Quinn, J. (1991), `Strategic change: logical incrementalism', in H. Mintzberg and J. Quinn, *The Strategy Process: Concepts, Contexts, Cases*, 2nd edn, Prentice-Hall.

Šlapák, M. (1993), 'Platební neschopnost znají z vyprávění', *Ekonom*, No.33.

Statistická ročenka České republiky, Prague: Czech Statistical Office.

Wallace, C. (1996), 'The pirates of Prague', *Fortune*, 23 December.

Zecchini, S. (1997) (ed.), *Lessons from the Economic Transition: Central and Eastern Europe in the 1990s*, Dordrecht: Kluwer Academic Publishers.

8. Innovation and the East German Transformation

Frank Fleischer and Kurt Hornschild

Despite very substantial differences in the transformation processes in eastern Germany and the countries of east-central Europe, a number of key common features stand out. Thus despite radically different macroeconomic regimes and privatisation processes, there is a common weakness in the development of the most modern branches of manufacturing industry. In eastern Germany rapid reunification and the chosen form of privatisation led to the elimination of much of the old structure of industry and to an unprecedented decline in industrial output and employment. The transformations in the CEECs were eased by sharp devaluations, supporting the export of relatively simple products, and by the possibility of protectionist measures. Privatisation was associated to a considerable extent with the same enterprises continuing in business and the extent of the fall in industrial production was kept within limits.

Nevertheless, the long-term problems should be seen as essentially similar. The road to economic prosperity depends on a kind of structural transformation that has as yet taken place neither in eastern Germany nor in any country of east-central Europe. Rising living standards ultimately depend on overcoming the present low-wage and cheap-product status. That in turn depends on a shift towards the most modern and research-intensive sectors. A considerable body of theory, as well as experience in a number of countries, now points to the crucial role of research and its efficient application in developing the competitiveness of industrial enterprises. This is an area of very serious weakness both in eastern Germany and in CEECs.

There are differences between countries and it would be inaccurate to equate the situation in eastern Germany with that across the CEECs. As will be argued, there has been a clear policy orientation in the former case towards maintaining an R&D base and there are some high-tech activities. Nevertheless, it is perhaps fair to suggest that the most important difference is that the weakness is shown even more starkly in the east Germany case, thanks to the absence of the factors cushioning the transition process in the other countries. This, however, has also led to a greater commitment to policy measures that might provide a solution and this experience could therefore be instructive for the CEECs, although the conditions obviously are not identical and a precise copy need not be appropriate. This argument is developed first with a brief description of the current stage of changes in the east German economy. This is followed by discussion of policy measures adopted, of their effect on the state of Research and Development in enterprises and then by ideas on how those policies could be developed and improved in the future.

BACKGROUND

The broad outlines of the 'recovery' phase of the east German transformation are indicated in Table 8.1. The 'shock' of reunification led to a fall in industrial output and employment such that by 1991 per capita GDP stood at 31.3 per cent of the west German level. By 1996 it had climbed to 57.0 per cent of the west German level. Growth was particularly rapid in 1993 and 1994.

Table 8.1 Annual percentage growth rates in components of east German GDP in 1991 prices

	1992	1993	1994	1995	1996
GDP	7.8	9.3	9.6	5.3	2.0
by production					
Productive sectors	9.3	12.2	15.7	5.8	2.1
Transport and trade	8.3	13.4	8.3	6.3	3.3
Other private services	18.6	9.7	8.7	7.8	4.7
State services	−3.3	−2.6	−1.1	0.3	−1.0
by expenditure					
Investment	28.8	16.1	18.1	3.6	0.0
of which housing	37.3	29.5	40.7	16.0	6.5

Source: BMWi, 1997, p.4.

The table includes figures for construction investment, taken from GDP measured by form of expenditure, and this shows the extent to which the driving force appeared to be construction, including housing construction. The ending of this construction boom by 1996 was associated with a general slowdown in growth and boasts of the most rapid growth rate in Europe disappeared.

The slowdown is even clearer from figures on GDP per employee, as shown in Table 8.2. The very rapid growth in this indicator in 1992 and 1993 largely reflected a fall in employment which, as the contrast between figures in Table 8.1 and Table 8.2 indicates, has slowed substantially in subsequent years. Nevertheless, it is still a significant factor. It has been accompanied by the rise in unemployment to a figure consistently above the western German level. It was 15.7 per cent in 1996 in the East against 10.4 per cent in the West. However, employment as a percentage of the population in the 15 to 65 age range remains higher in the East, at 76.4 per cent in 1996 against 70.2 per cent in the West. This aspect of the heritage of the past continues at least in part, as in the CEECs.

Table 8.2 Annual percentage increase in real GDP per employed person

	1992	1993	1994	1995	1996	1997
Eastern Germany	23.6	12.3	7.7	4.1	3.8	4.5
Western Germany	0.8	−0.5	3.3	2.1	2.4	3.5

Note: 1997 figures are from the Statistical Office's forecast of 29 October 1997.
Source: BMWi, 1997, p.7.

The dependence of east German growth on investment is illustrated in Tables 8.3 and 8.4, showing investment per inhabitant both for the economy as a whole and in various sectors. The comparison with western Germany shows a steady growth in investment, subsequently flattening off after 1994, taking the per capita level well past that of the West. The differences are particularly large in trade, transport and communications, in housing construction and in state and other organisations. In manufacturing industry, the East has pulled up from well behind to a slightly higher level of per capita investment than the West. This, however, was as much the result of a fall in investment in western Germany as of an increase in the East. In fact, manufacturing investment had peaked in eastern Germany in 1993 after which successive years saw small declines. Thus the dominant feature of the east German post-transformation recovery remains the dependence on investment in the economic infrastructure and housing. Investment in the infrastructure is also important in much of east-central Europe, but the emphasis on housing is clearly a difference. Figures show east German housing completions rising steadily, from 16,430 in 1991 to 143,376 in 1996.

Table 8.3 Investment per inhabitant in eastern Germany in Deutschmarks

	1991	1992	1993	1994	1995	1996
Total	5,693	8,063	9,803	11,931	12,625	12,630
Agriculture	77	79	66	65	77	84
Productive sectors of which	1,833	2,510	2,722	2,842	2,809	2,685
manufacturing	1,137	1,493	1,612	1,598	1,584	1,507
construction	199	242	257	262	183	157
Trade, transport, communication	1,251	1,702	1,913	2,144	1,963	1.907
Housing	976	1,463	1,984	2,881	3,498	3,754
Other market services	588	784	1,374	1,924	2,312	2,299
State and other organisations	967	1,524	1,734	2,076	1,966	1,901

Source: BMWi, 1997, p.23.

Table 8.4 Investment per inhabitant in western Germany in Deutschmarks

	1991	1992	1993	1994	1995	1996
Total	8,981	9,164	8,394	8,401	8,458	8,278
Agriculture	205	195	165	160	166	164
Productive sectors	2,301	2,268	1,853	1,765	1,738	1,797
of which manufacturing	1,806	1,694	1,302	1,180	1,284	1,314
construction	140	159	153	148	156	151
Trade, transport, communication	710	671	633	537	466	474
Housing	2,152	2,374	2,432	2,610	2,646	2.594
Other market services	2,009	1,940	1,733	1,821	1,991	2,008
State and other organisations	1,028	1,091	1,038	976	949	881

Source: BMWi, 1997, p.23.

The sectoral structure resulting from this transformation is shown in Table 8.5 in comparison with west Germany. The striking feature is the extraordinarily low share of manufacturing alongside the very high share for construction. That again appears as the key characteristic of the east German transformation and one that marks it out very clearly from the CEECs. There is also a rather high share for public services alongside a low share for private services, although the total shares of the service sector, including transport and communications, are very similar.

Not only has the manufacturing sector declined from the scale typical under central planning. The important point is the nature of that decline which has taken place by the effective elimination of the large-firm sector and of those branches associated with export or R&D-intensive production (cf Myant *et al.* 1996). One consequence of this is that what remains of east German manufacturing is strongly orientated towards the domestic market. The share of exports in the output of manufacturing and construction firms with 20 or more employees has fallen from 13.9 per cent in 1992 to 12.2 per cent in 1996, compared with a growth from 26.8 per cent to 30.9 per cent in western Germany over the same period.

Table 8.5 Gross value added by sector, 1996, per cent of total GDP

	Eastern Germany	Western Germany
Productive sectors	35.8	34.8
of which	15.2	27.0
manufacturing		
construction	16.8	5.2
other productive	3.8	2.6
Trade, transport and communications	13.8	15.2
Private services	31.6	39.3
Public services	20.8	14.0
Total	102.0	103.3

Source: BMWi, 1997, p. 3 and 8.

The weak representation of modern sectors is illustrated in Table 8.6. There is a much higher share of mining and extractive industries in eastern than in western Germany. There is also a higher share of consumption goods and a lower share of investment goods. The share in industrial output of the R&D-intensive branches is significantly lower in the East than the West. Even this measure can be deceptive as there are plenty of less sophisticated activities even within these branches. Thus, for example, the high share of east German industrial output coming from railway vehicles need not represent particularly modern technology. The figures for non-R&D-intensive branches complete the picture with east German strength in food, drink and tobacco, branches that can serve very local markets and have little prospect of rapid growth, and in glass and ceramics. Although there is some high-tech production here, including Zeiss of Jena and Hermsdorf ceramics, these branches also include less sophisticated production.

Table 8.6 Percentage shares in turnover of sectors of German industry in 1996

	Western Germany	Eastern Germany
Mining and manufacturing	100.00	100.00
of which		
intermediate products	45.3	47.1
investment goods	31.7	24.8
consumer durables	4.3	3.5
consumption goods	18.8	24.7
total manufacturing	98.8	95.3
Selected R&D-intensive sectors		
Chemicals	10.6	6.6
Rubber and plastics	4.2	3.9
Machinery	12.7	8.9
Computers and electronics	1.3	0.9
Communications	1.9	1.4
Medical and optical equipment	2.4	2.1
Road vehicles	14.1	6.0
Shipbuilding	0.3	1.4
Railway vehicles	0.2	1.5
Total	48.7	33.0
Selected non-R&D-intensive sectors		
Food, drink and tobacco	11.6	20.3
Textiles and garments	2.6	2.1
Printing and publishing	3.4	3.3
Glass and ceramics	3.0	8.5
Total	20.7	34.2

Source: DIW, 1997, p.680.

Table 8.7 indicates the east German share in total German production for some of the R&D-intensive sectors of industry. The total east German shares in population, employment and GDP are respectively 18.8 per cent, 18.6 per cent and 11.2 per cent. In only one of the sectors included below does the east German level clearly pass the region's shares in total population and employment and that is the relatively unimportant case of railway equipment. In only one other, man-made fibres, does the figure pass the region's share in industrial output.

Table 8.7 Share of R&D-intensive branches in east German industry in 1996

	Employment	Turnover	Exports
Chemicals	6.1	4.0	2.3
of which			
plastics in primary form	8.2	4.6	1.3
paints, printing inks and putty	4.1	3.5	2.5
pharmaceuticals	5.8	3.8	2.8
man-made fibres	14.1	8.8	7.0
Rubber and plastics	6.8	5.9	2.1
Machinery	7.2	4.5	2.2
Office machines and electronics	7.5	5.1	2.5
Radio and communications equipment	8.0	4.7	3.3
of which electronic components	10.3	7.7	9.0
Medical and optical equipment	6.8	5.4	3.4
of which optical and photographic			
appliances	10.8	9.3	10.2
Road vehicles	7.2	3.8	1.4
Railway vehicles	44.2	36.1	34.7
Aerospace	2.2	1.7	0.7
All industry	9.0	6.3	2.6

Source: DIW, 1997, p.679.

Two other points stand out. The share in turnover is invariably lower than the share in employment. Although the difference is small in a few cases, this points to the generally lower productivity level in eastern Germany. Other indicators also point to a low level of efficiency, or at least to higher costs per unit of output. This applies to costs of energy, materials, depreciation, services and interest payments. The second point is the very low share in all-German exports. Thus even when there is a presence in high-tech export oriented sectors, it is more likely to be in lower value-added activities with an orientation towards the domestic market.

The important exceptions are railway equipment, electronic components and optical and photographic appliances. The strength in railway equipment stems from continued production in an enterprise inherited from the old east Germany. In the other cases success has been associated primarily with new enterprises, albeit ones that have used an existing base of skilled labour. Thus production of electronic components includes both old and new activities, but with an important role for inward investment, for example from Siemens and AMD in Dresden where the industry was already established. The old optical equipment sector, based around Zeiss in Jena, has largely disappeared, but some parts, such as special glass production, have survived. The photographic industry has reemerged in Dresden around a new enterprise using an old tradition in human capital and benefiting from investment from the USA.

In general, however, east German production is biased towards less sophisticated products that bring smaller returns. This may be a result of a division of labour between western enterprises and their eastern acquisitions with the latter playing the role of an 'extended work bench'. It should, however, be noted again that these figures apply only to enterprises with 20 or more employees. Smaller firms are estimated to account for 30 per cent of employment, but no detailed information is available on their results.

This weak representation for modern sectors is at least as severe across east-central Europe. The difference there, however, is the continued existence and export success of sectors producing simpler products on the basis of low wage costs. That can no longer play a significant role in eastern Germany with wage costs in the economy as a whole 72.8 per cent of the western level in 1996, compared with 46.8 per cent in 1991, and productivity 59.3 per cent of the western level, against 31.0 per cent in 1991. In manufacturing the gap was even smaller with eastern German wage costs 67.2 per cent of western levels while productivity was 64.1 per cent of the western level. Thus wage levels were not quite low enough to compensate for lower productivity.

It should be added that this lower productivity does not necessarily represent an inability to produce efficiently. Most east German firms are now well-equipped in terms of modern technology and have achieved high levels of organisation of production. Indeed, their productivity levels in terms of value added are now clearly above the level of any CEEC. Their main weaknesses continue to stem from poor integration into the international division of labour which means that they cannot fully utilise existing capacity or penetrate the most lucrative markets.

Nevertheless, in the absence of support from less sophisticated sectors that can compete on the basis of low wages, the east German economy can appear viable thanks only to very substantial subsidies from the West. These come in a variety of different forms, but the net level has not varied very much since 1992. At that time it was equivalent to 58 per cent of east German GDP. By 1996 it was equivalent to 40 per cent of a somewhat larger volume of GDP.

Thus the argument here is that the east German transformation has followed a substantially different course from that in the CEECs in terms of the fate of traditional sectors of industry. While these have often disappeared, it has experienced rapid growth around a construction boom and dependence on subsidies from the West. Despite these differences, however, there remains a fundamental similarity in the poor representation for modern industrial activities. In the long term that is probably the decisive factor in determining the growth prospects of an economy. In this sense, then, the similarities between the transformation processes may come to be more significant than the differences.

EAST GERMAN RESEARCH AND DEVELOPMENT

The international success of industries depends on innovation, which in turn depends on efficient industrial research. This applies in particular to industries in high-wage economies such as Germany whose competitive edge is based more on high-quality products than on prices (DIW, 1996). During the transformation phase, industrial research in eastern Germany was in danger of total collapse. Before privatisation enterprises typically lacked the financial strength to fund research and the loss of previous markets also made it very uncertain what direction research should take. Most enterprises were privatised without R&D departments, which were frequently split off by management buy-outs to become 'external' R&D. Thus the link between production and research was often severed with the Treuhandanstalt making little effort to privatise industrial research facilities along with the enterprises. Most west German or foreign enterprises which bought east German firms were already well-equipped with R&D facilities.

Table 8.8 R&D personnel in the German economy

	Germany	Eastern Germany	East German share
1991	321,756	34,922	10.9
1992	306,925	22,439	7.3
1993	293,774	22,032	7.5
1994	284,380	21,400	7.5
1995	283,315	23,740	8.4
1996	276,794	23,194	8.4

Source: SV-Wissenschaftsstatistik, 1998.

The resulting decline in R&D personnel in shown in Table 8.8. The overall fall in eastern Germany, as estimated by the Forschungsagentur Berlin (FAB, 1997), was from 86,000 in 1990 to 16,000 in 1995, with a fall in industry from 75,000 to 13,000. Table 8.9 shows slightly different estimates from SV-Wissenschaftsstatistik. The share in total German R&D personnel remains below the east German share in population and employment. Over the same period, however, total German R&D staff have also declined, so that by 1994 the level was below that of the old federal Republic from before 1989. Figures for 1996 will probably reveal a slight growth with some renewed investment in research.

Table 8.9 East German R&D staff in enterprises classified by employment

Employees	1993	1995	1995/1993
1–19	2,157	3,040	140.9
20–99	4,555	5,280	115.9
100–499	5,885	5,220	88.7
500+	3,888	2,240	57.6

Source: FAB, 1996.

These gross figures reveal only part of the picture. The striking feature about the research in east German enterprises is its concentration into smaller enterprises. This is a largely inevitable consequence of the transformation which led to the disappearance of east German large firms, particularly in research-intensive branches. It is this, rather than the simple quantity of research workers, that represents the greatest and possibly unique weakness of east German R&D. The concentration into smaller enterprises is indicated in Table 8.9. There is a clear majority working in enterprises with under 500 employees and this is also the area where growth has taken place.

The absence of big enterprises leads to a general weakness in east German R&D. Innovative activity is not necessarily the exclusive concern of either large or small enterprises. It often depends on an interrelationship between the two. There is, however, no mixture of big, medium-sized and small enterprises, which have the right connections to industry-related research institutes to manage the transfer of the knowledge from basic research to commercialise or use innovations successfully. Bigger companies are able to bring the benefits of international contacts: they can be an important channel for technology transfer. They can pay for more expensive, longer running R&D projects and offer more possibilities for cooperation with the research in external universities and institutes. They may involve smaller firms with which they have close links, thereby playing an important role in the development of networks of innovative activities in the regions and beyond.

Smaller firms, by way of contrast, are more likely to conduct research with close and rapid market applications. These different in-company research activities complement each other and result in a so-called 'systemic competitiveness' of a national economy. In eastern Germany, however, the absence of the large firms and the situation created by the transformation that has taken place pushes smaller companies towards very limited conceptions of research activity. Their unstable position, the externalisation of R&D facilities, the lack of confidence in export markets and the smaller size of east German firms all exert pressure for innovations that are likely to bring quick results.

It is not clear how this is consistent with official 1996 figures which show R&D personnel as a proportion of total employment at 40 per cent of the west German level while east German spending on R&D per unit of turnover appeared to be 70 per cent of the west German level. Eastern Germany thus accounted for 5 per cent of total German R&D expenditure, a figure that appears remarkably high.

This short description shows the general weakness of east German industrial research. In the manufacturing branches much is invested, per capita of inhabitants more than in west Germany, but with an insufficient level of innovation. In west Germany each DM of investment is connected with an average of 66 per cent of that volume in R&D expenditures; in eastern Germany the associated R&D expenditure is equivalent to only 18 per cent of the investment level.

THE POLICY FRAMEWORK

Had there been no government support, east German research activity could have collapsed completely. Rebuilding from a base of zero would have been extremely difficult. Instead, both federal and state governments pursued deliberate policies aimed at encouraging a new beginning for R&D, at creating a similar R&D infrastructure to that already existing in western Germany and at supporting the formation of new firms. This was a major reason for the stabilisation of research personnel by 1993 and for the growth exhibited in smaller enterprises. A total of DM 4 billion was spent over the 1990 to 1996 period, equivalent to less than 1 per cent of gross transfers from West to East. It came mostly in subsidies for expenditure on R&D personnel, especially in SMEs, and in support for specific projects. There was also public finance for the creation of an R&D infrastructure comparable to that in west Germany.

Arguments for this support can be given both in general and in specific terms. At the general level support can be justified in terms of theories of market failure and the external effects of R&D, which have favourable effects on the whole economy (Brockhoff, 1994). The support can stimulate enterprises to invest more money in R&D, to come to a better or optimal allocation of production factors which would not otherwise be reached, because the enterprises by themselves cannot earn the full return on their investment. The private return is normally lower than the total return to R&D expenditures in the economy. The consequence is a suboptimal level of R&D, if it is based only on private financing. Thus R&D support counteracts 'mistakes' in factor allocation and thereby contributes to creating appropriate conditions for investment, economic growth and the expansion of employment. This is in line with the 'new' growth theory, backed up by a body of German research, which points clearly to the importance of endogenous technical progress in ensuring long-term growth (Romer, 1990, Klodt, 1996, Gries, Wigger & Hentschel, 1994).

More specific arguments relate to east German conditions and the relationship with western Germany. The gap in economic levels has to be a cause of political concern, not least when a commitment to equalisation is contained in the German constitution. As the free market alone has not brought about this equalisation, governments have accepted the need for some specific measures to help in the creation of a basis for self-sustaining growth in the East. One part of this is the economic subsidy. It is not considered a violation of the principles of a market economy as it is conceived as a temporary measure to help in the creation of normal market competition by overcoming specific disadvantages faced by east German enterprises.

It would, however, be unrealistic to expect immediate results. The first step is to make eastern Germany more attractive for sophisticated investment and to help the enterprises to recover from the 'shock' of the economic transformation. Support for R&D can have the ultimate aim of building a body of R&D staff capable of leading the development of a sophisticated industrial structure integrated into the international division of labour. Realistically, however, the first step has to be maintenance of the existing core of R&D staff. There is at the moment no alternative but to make a virtue out of a necessity and to base the development of innovation capacity on the SMEs that do exist. Ultimately, however, an effective innovation system can only develop if larger enterprises also commit themselves to research and to research of an international standard.

Thus the specific programme of east German innovation support is based around seven main objectives. The first, most general and most long-term, is the creation of a basis for sophisticated industrial development as an element of sustainable economic growth. The second, and most immediately pressing, is the retention of the existing base of R&D staff without which there can be little hope of catching up with western German economic levels in the future. The third is maintenance and strengthening of the innovation ability of enterprises. Fourth is the more ambitious aim of helping firms enter the market by innovations, and the expansion of sales and hence to move beyond the struggle for pure survival. Fifth is a more specific aim of compensating firms for their lack of capital, so that they have the financial resources with which to undertake research activities. Sixth is the more general construction of an R&D infrastructure like that found in western Germany. Seventh is support to new firm formation by providing access to new ideas and technologies.

These aims are not subject to serious debate in German political, economic or scientific life. They have not been questioned even during discussions of the application of the Maastricht criteria and hence of the need to limit state spending. The argument remains that the catching-up process appears to have stalled so that public subsidies are still necessary. Constraints mean that every subsidy should be applied as efficiently as possible so as to create the necessary conditions for self-sustaining growth soon. Then the special support can be removed. There is no serious suggestion that it should be removed at once.

This is the background to the subsidies for the economy in general and R&D in particular for eastern Germany. The contributions for R&D personnel costs, special support for R&D projects and the support for new partners for new technology firms – small businesses set up around new technology ideas – are only paid in eastern Germany. Other support for R&D projects and for setting up new technology firms is also paid in west Germany. The support especially rewards research cooperation between East and West and western partnerships in eastern enterprises. The end result is that eastern enterprises can receive more support than western firms.

RESEARCH AND DEVELOPMENT IN ENTERPRISES

The impact of these policy measures has been investigated in a research project undertaken for the Ministry of the Economy by two Berlin institutes, the German Institute for Economic Research (DIW) and the Institute for Socio-Economic Structural Analysis (SÖSTRA), during 1997. The research was based on a survey of east German enterprises of varying sizes. The 1,100 usable responses from 3,800 enterprises approached spanned the important branches of manufacturing and probably gave a representative picture of enterprises that had received R&D support from the federal government. The analysis showed a very heterogeneous picture. There were clear signs of a generally positive trend, but the signals are too weak to suggest that a stable R&D base now exists and certainly too weak to justify reference to a real upswing. This is confirmed by the responses to the five main groups of questions.

The first relates to R&D capacity alone. The average number of R&D personnel per enterprise undertaking innovation activity increased between 1993 and 1996 from 8.6 to 10. This development is almost exclusively the result of the increase in personnel employed to carry out R&D work only on a casual basis. At an average of 13.4 per cent, the proportion of R&D personnel in total employment was relatively high in 1996 in those east German enterprises with R&D departments. Depending on the size of the enterprise, it ranged from 17 per cent in small enterprises with up to 19 employees, to 6 per cent in enterprises with between 200 and 499 employees. Average expenditure on R&D per enterprise increased in the whole period up to 1996. The increase was most marked in the smallest size group, with under 20 employees, in which research spending more than doubled with the share coming from state support rising only slightly, from 8.0 to 10.6 per cent. It appeared that about half the enterprises not carrying out R&D in 1993 had taken it up by 1996.

The second relates to the trends in enterprise earnings. This should give an impression of whether government policies had been adequate to lead to a more general stabilisation. The results showed that the share of enterprises operating at a profit rose between 1994 and 1996 from 27 per cent to 40 per cent, while a further 36 per cent were breaking even. Around 50 per cent of the enterprises surveyed had improved their earnings during this period. However, despite the overall positive development, about one third of enterprises that had started to make a profit slipped back again, and about 16 per cent began running at a loss. This, then, was a mixed picture in which tendencies towards stabilisation are mingled with continuing threats to the existence of many firms.

The third relates to export orientation, which could be a result of successful innovation activity. The export content of turnover in the enterprises surveyed rose on average between 1993 and 1996 from 6.7 per cent to 10.7 per cent. Enterprises with R&D personnel increased their export quota from 8.5 per cent to 13.4 per cent. The total turnover of all enterprises increased by 46 per cent. This suggests some signs of an encouraging trend, but still a strong dependence on domestic markets even for enterprises that were trying to innovate.

The fourth relates to new product ranges. The share of turnover accounted for by new products amounted to between 10 per cent and 32 per cent in the period between 1993 and 1996. Although that rate is reasonably high, enterprises referred to market access and consolidation as problems that were as important as renewal of the product range.

The fifth relates to the specific problems of the external industrial research centres. These include R&D units that split off from bigger firms and were privatised alone, groups from the old GDR Academy of Sciences or from universities that set up private R&D enterprises and some completely new private R&D firms. Around 4,400 people were directly involved in R&D in 1996 in the 240 centres surveyed. The first two kinds received initial subsidies of up to 100 per cent following privatisation. The subsidies had decreased to around 40 per cent by 1996. Many of these research centres have gradually managed to find a market, with 80 per cent of their industrial contracts now coming from the former territory of the Federal Republic. These appear to be the only consistent arena for large-scale R&D projects, but they too suffer from an unstable existence and tend to direct their efforts towards less basic projects promising more rapid market results.

The conclusion must be that, as yet, too few enterprises are reaping the benefits of their R&D efforts. Subsidies have helped them to start catching up and to pave the way for success on the market. Nevertheless, the main results of their innovative activities are yet to be seen, depending on the state of development of the enterprises and innovation cycles. Moreover, despite the extent of government support, and the developments in smaller firms, the fragmentation and disintegration of east German R&D is continuing. This is visible both in enterprises that are failing to find a satisfactory place on the market and in those large enterprises yet to be privatised and currently held by the BVS, the Bundesanstalt für vereinigungsbedingte Sonderaufgaben, the successor to the Treuhandanstalt.

The number of enterprises with R&D departments is still very small in comparison to west Germany and this R&D capacity is likewise not yet firmly established. Nevertheless, many firms have been investing in R&D, and have transformed their product ranges and production processes. Skilled employment has been maintained, thanks to a relatively small amount of public funding supporting in-company training. About 7,000 R&D jobs have been saved through public funding alone. To these should be added indirect employment effects which follow when research results are translated into production and sales.

At one level the outlays appear extremely small. An annual average of only DM 16,000 was provided to co-finance these R&D jobs. This comes nowhere near covering the costs of the jobs to the enterprises. The average rate of subsidisation revealed by the survey was 16 per cent. However, the importance of this is revealed by responses from over 50 per cent of enterprises to the effect that they still had substantial problems with financing R&D and the subsequent phases of the innovation process. 30 per cent claimed that they would be unable to carry out R&D without state support.

Most of the enterprises have not yet developed a complete innovation cycle. They must therefore finance a long-term project without a sound financial base.

Those enterprises that have been on the market for some time already can use profits from previous innovations, but this is not typical in eastern Germany. The specific form of support, emphasising R&D personnel, has favoured a particular kind of innovation. It appears as a corrective against investment funding which favours capital accumulation. However, it has not been sufficient to attract enough medium-sized and large enterprises to undertake activities in eastern Germany.

POLICY OPTIONS

There would appear to be a strong case for continuing long-term state support for innovation in eastern Germany. Broadly two approaches can be distinguished. They should be pursued simultaneously, although their points of departure are two different weaknesses.

The first is the promotion of the economic location. Thus incentives should be provided to attract outside investors to relocate and develop intelligent production and R&D in eastern Germany. That requires a funding system which favours eastern Germany and measures to overcome weaknesses in the regional infra-structure. Localized R&D support might consist, in addition to the investment sub-sidy, of a 20 per cent subsidy towards R&D personnel costs for all enterprises and external research centres in manufacturing industry, regardless of their size. Due to the considerable structural weaknesses in east German industry, localised R&D support should not be planned for too short a term. It needs to cover the duration of one full investment cycle, meaning around ten years.

The second is the promotion of endogenous capacity. Many SMEs still find it extremely difficult to finance their innovation efforts because they have not had the benefits of past innovation successes. There is therefore a case to continue giving them support for a limited time period. The ideal form would appear to be an R&D personnel-cost subsidy totalling 40 per cent for another five years. That would mean an additional 20 per cent on top of the localised R&D support. This 'deficiency' support would expire after five years and the enterprises would sub-sequently receive only the localised R&D support of 20 per cent. These enterprises would still be eligible for other forms of help, such as R&D project support, that are offered by the state and the Länder throughout Germany.

There is also a strong case for support to the external industrial research centres. Many of these institutions have now established the contours of their fields of activity and gained a foothold on the market. However, they will only be able to use the opportunities open to them if they plan for personnel needs over a reasona-bly stable medium term. The need here is for different forms of support, appropriate to the character of institutions seeking contracts for industrial or publicly-funded research. It is up to the government to clarify the extent to which it is willing to provide finance for projects that may be important from the point of view of regional policy, but cannot be financed by contracts alone.

The case for some forms of financial help is overwhelming. It is also clear that it should come in the form of cost subsidies rather than tax relief. This is particularly important for SMEs, because such aid has an immediate financial effect. Tax relief would be little help to firms already constrained by severe financial difficulties which prevent them from financing long-term projects. There would anyway be little gain from tax relief for enterprises that are not making any profit.

In conclusion, however, it must be emphasised that this is only one part of a very slow process of the full transformation of the east German economy into one enjoying self-sustained growth on the basis of modern technology. The main success so far has been to prevent the disappearance of research activity and this has depended on actions from different levels of government. The ultimate success will come when higher support is no longer needed in eastern Germany. That will mark the final success of industrial restructuring.

REFERENCES

BMWi (Bundesministerium für Wirtschaft), (1997), *Wirtschaftsdaten Neue Länder*, Bonn.

Brockhoff, K. (1994), *Forschung und Entwicklung*, Munich and Vienna.

DIW (Deutsches Institut für Wirtschaftsforschung) (1996), *Leistungsfähigkeit der deutschen Wirtschaft im internationalen Vergleich*, DIW-Beiträge zur Strukturforschung, No.165, Berlin.

DIW (Deutsches Institut für Wirtschaftsforschung) (1997), 'Zur Förderung der ostdeutschen Industrieforschung durch das Bundesministerium für Wirtschaft', *DIW Wochenbericht*, No.38.

FAB (Forschungsagentur Berlin) (1996), *Beschäftigungsentwicklung in der wirtschaftsnahen Forschung der neuen Bundesländer 1995*.

FAB (Forschungsagentur Berlin) (1997*), Quantitative Analyse der Entwicklung der Industrieforschung in den neuen Bundesländern im Zeitraum 1990–1995 und 1st-Zustand per 31.12.1996*, Berlin.

Gries, T., B. Wigger and C. Hentschel (1994), 'Endogenous growth and R&D models: A critical appraisal of recent developments', *Jahrbücher für Nationalökonomie und Statistik*, Vol.213.

Klodt, H. (1996), *The German Innovation System: Conceptions, Institutions and Economic Efficiency*, Kiel Working Paper, No.775.

Myant, M., F. Fleischer, K. Hornschild, R. Vintrová, K. Zeman and Z. Souček (1996), *Successful Transformations? The Creation of Market Economies in Eastern Germany and the Czech Republic*, Cheltenham, UK and Brookfield, US: Edward Elgar.

Romer, P.M. (1990), 'Endogenous technological change', *Journal of Political Economy*, **98**, 71–102.
SV-Wissenschaftsstatistik (1998), *Forschung und Entwicklung in der Wirtschaft 1995 bis 1997*, Essen.

9. Are the Transformations Complete?

Martin Myant

'We are in a market mechanism. The basic system changes have been undertaken. We have crossed the Rubicon.' Václav Klaus, Prime Minister of the Czech Republic, speaking to the Union of Industry of the Czech Republic, 5 March 1993.

'The West should distinguish between the states of central Europe much more by the extent to which they have implemented their economic reforms ... The Czech Republic has in economic terms gone the furthest and within two to three years will be fully capable of joining the EC', Vladimír Dlouhý, Minister of Industry and Trade, Czech Republic, 18 November 1993.

These two quotes from leading Czech politicians of the 1990s exemplify the thinking of the early part of the decade. Dlouhý, a minister from the fall of communism until 1997, spoke the then fashionable language of ranking the countries to show which was ahead in its rush to complete the transformation into a fully-fledged market economy. He saw the Czech Republic doing so well that it was effectively ready to claim its place among the advanced market economies of western Europe. Klaus put a similar view in a slightly different way. He was to repeat the same point in front of many audiences over the coming years. The Czech transformation was effectively over and had been a resounding success. The most difficult steps had been taken and the road should lead downhill from there onwards.

This was to prove a popular view outside east-central Europe as well, albeit without quite so much bravado. International agencies and consultancy firms were eager to predict rapid growth in the Czech Republic based largely on faith that privatisation and a western orientation must surely bring economic success. The OECD was a little more cautious than some, but still foresaw acceleration, with growth rates rising and remaining above 5 per cent from the middle of the decade. Forecasts for Slovakia, not seen as a pioneer in market-oriented reform, were less optimistic and frequently below the levels actually achieved (OECD, 1994, 1996a, 1996b).

Behind the views of leading Czech politicians, and many western advisers and commentators, lay a naïve and narrow conception of what the transformation should entail. Klaus and Dlouhý were making their boasts at a time when GDP was barely growing, when enterprises were being privatised into a chaotic and uncontrolled capital market, when R&D in enterprises was dying and receiving no formal government help, when bankruptcy laws that could force the closure of failing enterprises were continually being postponed, when much of manufacturing was struggling to survive by switching towards export of less sophisticated products and when the government had no conception of how to encourage a structural shift towards more modern sectors. Behind the optimism, then, lay an assumption that success required no more than a market economy which was in turn defined in the very simplistic terms of formal private ownership, free prices, trade liberalisation and macroeconomic stability. Everything else, it was implicitly assumed, was either irrelevant or would follow automatically once those basic conditions had been achieved.

The perceived simplicity of the process is reflected in terminology with references to a 'transition' and to 'transitional economies'. These terms have become so ubiquitous that it is practically impossible to avoid using them. However, behind their popularity lies a conception of 'a future that has already been designated' (Stark and Bruszt, 1998, p.5) and that amounts to the advanced market economies of western Europe and North America. There is, then, no need to develop a deeper understanding of the problems of the CEECs as, provided they press ahead with the key policy measures outlined above, they should soon look very much like their western neighbours.

The contributions in this volume point consistently to the need for a broader view of the transformation. The point is not to take issue with claims that market systems have been created. It is rather to emphasise that that does not adequately define the outcome. Rather than a 'transition' to a pre-defined aim, the CEECs are undergoing transformations with more uncertain and varied end results. It can even be argued that the transformations up to the late 1990s have been extremely successful at moving from inefficient and stagnating centrally-planned economies to market economies that, when set against those they would like to emulate, still appear inefficient and backward. With a few exceptions, they cannot compete by innovative and sophisticated products and services and rely heavily on low unit labour costs to find a place in both export and domestic markets. Thus the transformation into modern market economies, similar to the advanced countries of western Europe, has not taken place and is not likely in the foreseeable future.

The weaknesses are likely to become still more apparent with accession to the EU. The European Commission's *Agenda 2000* documents (EC, 1997) generally gave a rather flattering picture suggesting that manufacturing industry in CEECs would be able to stand up in a more competitive environment. It was tempered with some caution, but the assessments of individual countries were surprisingly diverse and did not point to consistent problems across the region. Poland was criticised for the inadequacies of its state-owned banks and for the slow pace of restructuring in state-owned enterprises. Hungary was given a more positive write-up for 'privatisation and restructuring', but warned of the need for advice services for SMEs and of weaknesses in the training and flexibility of its labour market. The Czech Republic received criticism for its financial system and ownership structures while Slovakia was roundly condemned for a slow pace of enterprise restructuring and for a tendency to slip back away from reliance on market mechanisms.

To some extent the European Commission was picking up the fashionable issues in relation to the countries concerned rather than starting from a comprehensive assessment of weaknesses across them all. Thus, for example, labour market issues have attracted more outside attention in relation to Hungary than elsewhere, but they are frequently pinpointed as one of the greatest difficulties for Czech manufacturing firms. The European Commission's approach is consistent with a view that the transformations have largely led to a satisfactory outcome, but for a number of difficulties that are specific to each case. The steps required to put this right frequently amount to a continuation on the road of deregulation and privatisation. There is no suggestion of the need for a more systematic competitiveness policy that would be likely to have common features across the countries concerned.

This is surprising in view of a strong trend both in the EU and the OECD to identify the sources of the competitive strengths and weaknesses of individual countries. Thus in 1997 the OECD produced a report on benchmarking covering the eight areas of the R&D infrastructure, education and the labour force, employment regulations, labour costs, corporate governance environments, corporate taxation, energy costs and telecommunications and infrastructure. The aim was to enable individual countries to identify both strengths and weaknesses in their ability to create an environment likely to encourage and nurture investment and successful businesses (OECD,1997). The notion of benchmarking has also been taken up within the EU, using a slightly different set of criteria (EC, 1996). This, of course, is intended to form the background to 'competitiveness policies' that can be targeted to overcome identified weaknesses.

The case for at least as comprehensive and systematic an approach in CEECs would seem overwhelming. Porter's (1990) notion of 'stages' of competitiveness has been used in several chapters in this volume. Within this framework the CEECs would seem to be basing much of their international competitiveness on products and processes associated with the 'investment-driven' and the 'factor-driven' stages. Competitiveness policy for CEECs should therefore be geared to jumping that difficult hurdle into the 'innovation-driven' stage in which they compete in 'knowledge-intensive' activities. That may be more demanding than the policy framework appropriate to a country already at a substantially higher level.

The discussion in Chapter 1 points to the possibility of learning from other countries that have moved from a 'middle' towards a high level of development. Some elements are clearly not repeatable or appropriate. Thus reliance on the creation of a service-based economy, perhaps along the lines of Hong Kong, is not an option for the foreseeable future. CEECs do not have the hinterland they can service and they also suffer from a poor reputation in crucial areas of financial reliability and macroeconomic stability.

Three other broad strategies, which are not mutually exclusive, could prove important. The first is to focus on attracting inward investment. The second is to follow the Korean road of encouraging the emergence of large domestically-owned firms that can compete on the world stage. The third is to follow the 'third Italy' in which networks of firms in light industry have come together with public sector support to share services and to cooperate in production and sales (Best, 1990). This has enabled Italy to gain and hold a position in sectors such as garments and footwear that have faced annihilation in other western European countries and that could face the same fate in much of east-central Europe.

In various different ways the course of the transformations has created obstacles to each of these possibilities. Attracting inward investment depends on the ability to compete with other possible locations and therefore requires a substantial and sophisticated infrastructure. A common starting point for CEECs was the hope that a foreign partner could be found to rescue troubled enterprises without the need for any further active government role. Czech governments under Václav Klaus were particularly adamant that no 'privileges' would be given to inward investors, which meant that nothing particular would be done to attract them. Moreover, their motives were often regarded with suspicion by the managements of the enterprises they were intended to rescue and, as indicated in Chapter 7, their advances were frequently shunned. The picture varies somewhat across east-central Europe but, at least in comparison with some other parts of the world, inward investment has generally played a limited role in structural transformation, This cannot be expected to change without a considerably more determined policy effort particularly the Czech Republic and Slovakia, the two countries that have pursued the least systematic policies.

The Korean road has also clearly been avoided, although big firms already existed and were inherited ready-made from central planning. The most important Czech example is Škoda-Plzeň. Government policies have enabled it to survive and grow, but not to undertake substantial new investment. The absence even of the 'paternalistic guidance' characteristic of Japanese development is also visible in some of the strange strategic choices and the persistent temptation towards broad diversification into products with no prospects. Škoda seems to be trying to dominate only the rather trivial Czech pond rather than competing on global markets. Slovak privatisation has created some even bigger firms, such as the Košice steel producer, but they too show a strong urge to diversify and to become conglomerate empires on their own rather than competing at the highest level internationally in their core activities. That, of course, is not unusual among big firms in other market economies, but its extent and persistence in CEECs points to the need to find an appropriate policy response.

The 'third Italy' example might seem particularly appropriate as light industry has been so important as an export sector. There are, however, serious obstacles. Following the Italian example would require active government help both in advising firms on strategic decisions and in bringing them together into the appropriate networks. Key elements of the transformation have made this more difficult. As indicated in Chapter 7, financial difficulties make contacts between domestically-owned firms problematic and effectively push them into dependence on western European firms. Privatisation has also been associated with the breaking of important links between production and distribution. Thus the tendency has been towards a fragmentation of networks and towards the creation of obstacles to their regeneration. An active competitiveness policy would have to be aimed at overcoming this heritage of the recent past.

Indeed, any of these strategic orientations is dependent on an active role from government bodies. Thus, for example, both smaller and quite sizeable firms in advanced market economies do receive forms of help towards finding an appropriate strategic orientation. This can include studies and information on market opportunities, on new technology and on the experience of successful firms in a sector. It can even include very detailed discussions and help in identifying a firm's strengths and weaknesses. It is not unusual for government bodies to help bring firms together when they see a potential for cooperation. The account in Chapter 7 indicates that an appreciation of the need for such activities was totally absent in the Czech Republic at least up to 1998.

Thus in their determination to comply with a simplistic notion of how a market economy functions, there has been a strong tendency to ignore the need for forms of government activity that are normal in western Europe. The case for bodies able to advise enterprises on possible strategies would seem much stronger in CEECs than in western Europe, in view of the quality, expertise and experience of managements in the former case. There would also seem a stronger case for an active role in rationalisation across sectors, in view of the structures that were inherited from central planning and the inability of capital markets to ensure rationalisation

on their own. In view of the obsolete technology and financial constraints in domestically-owned firms, it would also seem a government responsibility to find
means to raise levels of productive investment.

These are general problems across all CEECs which could point to essentially
similar policy solutions. There are, however, also differences which have implications for future prospects and hence for the bias of possible competitiveness
policies. They stem from three main factors. The first is the timing of the transformation which was well under away before the collapse of communist power in
Poland and Hungary. This reflected a greater degree of political independence
from the Soviet Union which left them less tied to the CMEA. They had had more
contacts with market economies over a long period of time and pursued economic
policies that had left them heavily in debt to the West and hence compelled to
export more for hard currency. This early start may have brought substantial indirect benefits. Greater contacts with the capitalist world contributed to less naivety
and less willingness to accept that the fastest possible privatisation and the greatest
possible degree of trade liberalisation would bring nothing but benefits. They
therefore have less need to revise past thinking and to undo damage caused, for
example, by over-hasty Czech privatisation.

The second source of differences is the economic structure inherited from the
past and other unalterable characteristics, such as the countries' sizes. All CEECs
had sectors that could find export markets in advanced market economies. The
important question is whether these sectors have the potential for further development. Thus Poland has been able to export raw materials, but these are not the
products with rapidly growing demand. However, as the biggest economy in the
region, it can attract inward investment in assembly plants and has sought to
develop policies to encourage this trend. There is less of a basis for this in Hungary
or in the Czech Republic and Slovakia which chose, with the break-up of the
Czechoslovak federation at the start of 1993, to seek their fortunes as smaller
domestic markets.

The Czech Republic had a greater number of enterprises with a presence
around the world, including several in engineering, glass and related industries and
brewing. Particularly its strength in engineering could provide a basis for future
growth, but only if Czech-owned firms can move back up towards more sophisticated products that do not compete primarily by low wages. Slovakia's strength is
in semi-manufactures, while those sectors associated with the 'innovation-driven'
stage have been very weak. Its growth performance has been very dependent on
the sales of a relatively narrow range of basic products, including steel, heavy
chemicals and paper. Unless it can gain complete dominance in east-central
Europe for these kinds of products, which seems unlikely, it can only expect to
enjoy sustained growth on the basis of a very deep transformation towards com-

pletely new sectors. Hungary has a recent history of exporting agricultural products and a weak position in mineral raw materials. Its growth would also seem heavily dependent on building a new base in more modern sectors, a process in which it appears to have made some progress.

The third source of differences is the policy framework adopted since 1989. Both the central elements, privatisation and macroeconomic stabilisation, followed slightly different courses, as indicated in Chapters 3 and 4. The resulting macro-economic conditions have been more favourable to the export of raw materials and basic products in the Czech Republic and Slovakia than in the other countries and that may have had some impact on the extent of structural changes. The great concern in the Czech Republic with holding down inflation may have limited scope for new private-sector investment, but this is also at a low level in the other countries.

Differences in privatisation may be of more lasting significance. Hungary's early caution was followed by a greater willingness to sell to foreign companies and to encourage inward investment on greenfield sites. That has often been justi-fied around the need to repay debts built up in the past, but it also reflected both a wise reluctance to rush into untried methods and the absence of a pronounced fear of foreign domination. Poland also faced severe debt problems, but its govern-ments, despite several twists and turns, have opted for slower and more complex forms of privatisation. Foreign owners are often regarded with suspicion, but the pure form of voucher privatisation was also rejected on the sensible grounds that it need not create a sound basis for enterprise restructuring.

The Czech voucher method proved very successful at transferring property into private hands. Despite some claims to the contrary, these often were very clearly defined private owners, but ones who contributed little or nothing to over-coming the problems faced by enterprises. Slovak privatisation deviated from the Czech model with the break-up of Czechoslovakia and was subsequently charac-terised by sale on highly favourable terms of large enterprises to the ruling party's 'cronies' (*Business Central Europe*, April 1998). This, however, kept large com-panies intact and ensured that their owners were not burdened with further enor-mous debts. Provided they can find and stick to appropriate strategies, they could have considerable potential.

Other aspects of the policy environment also vary across the region. Govern-ments in the Czech Republic were verbally the least interventionist and lacked any long-term perspective beyond faith in the market. This should not be taken too literally as steps were gradually taken to create elements of an industrial policy with, for example, credits and guarantees to exporters. There was also considerable help behind the scenes to troubled enterprises inherited from the past. Polish governments from 1993 onwards appeared to be the most systematic in their policy making with attempts to identify weaknesses in their economy's potential and to propose remedies (Kołodko, 1994). They had limited resources and policy making was still characterised by a great deal of uncertainty and hesitation. Nevertheless, some steps did bring clear results the measures to attract particular kinds of inward investment and the degree of protection given to domestic markets are elements that contributed immediately to the country's growth performance.

However, none of this alters the central point that the CEECs suffer from a number of very similar weaknesses and problems. If they are to enjoy sustained growth in the future they all need to improve elements of the basic infrastructure of an advanced economy, including in particular their research and education potential. They need to create environments in which firms can invest and cooperate in established networks. They also need to find the means to improve the ability of management to formulate coherent strategies that will enable them to operate in a global environment.

These are not new problems. They have been faced in many other countries before. The important point, however, is that there is no remedy for the CEECs' problems without a recognition that their transformations into modern market economies are far from complete and that they need coherent policies to improve their levels of competitiveness. The philosophy behind the two quotes that opened this chapter, and the conception of a modern market economy that lies behind them, is not adequate to that task.

REFERENCES

Best, M. (1990), *The New Competition: Institutions of Industrial Restructuring*, Cambridge: Polity Press.

EC (European Commission) (1996), *Benchmarking the Competitiveness of European Industry*, Luxembourg: Office for Official Publications of the European Communities.

EC (European Commission) (1997), *Agenda 2000, EU Commission's Opinion on 10 Applications*, Brussels.

Kołodko, G. (1994), *Strategia dla Polski*, Warsaw: Poltext.

OECD (1994), *Economic Surveys, The Czech and Slovak Republics*, Paris.

OECD (1996a), *Economic Surveys, The Czech Republic*, Paris.

OECD (1996b), *Economic Surveys, The Slovak Republic*, Paris.

OECD (1997), *Industrial Competitiveness: Benchmarking Business Environments in the Global Economy*, Paris.

Porter, M. (1990), *The Competitive Advantage of Nations*, London: Macmillan.

Stark, D. and L. Bruszt (1998), *Postsocialist Pathways: Transforming Politics and Property in East Central Europe*, Cambridge: Cambridge University Press.

Index